# FLY ME TO THE MOON

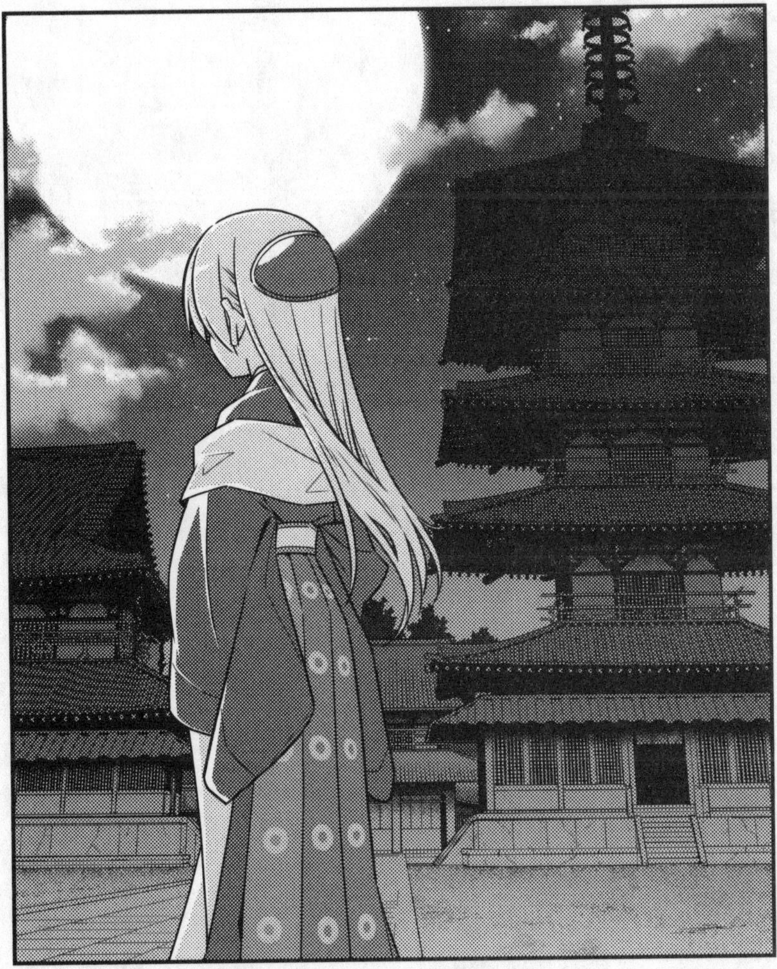

VOLUME 4

**KENJIRO HATA**

# FLY ME TO THE MOON

## Contents

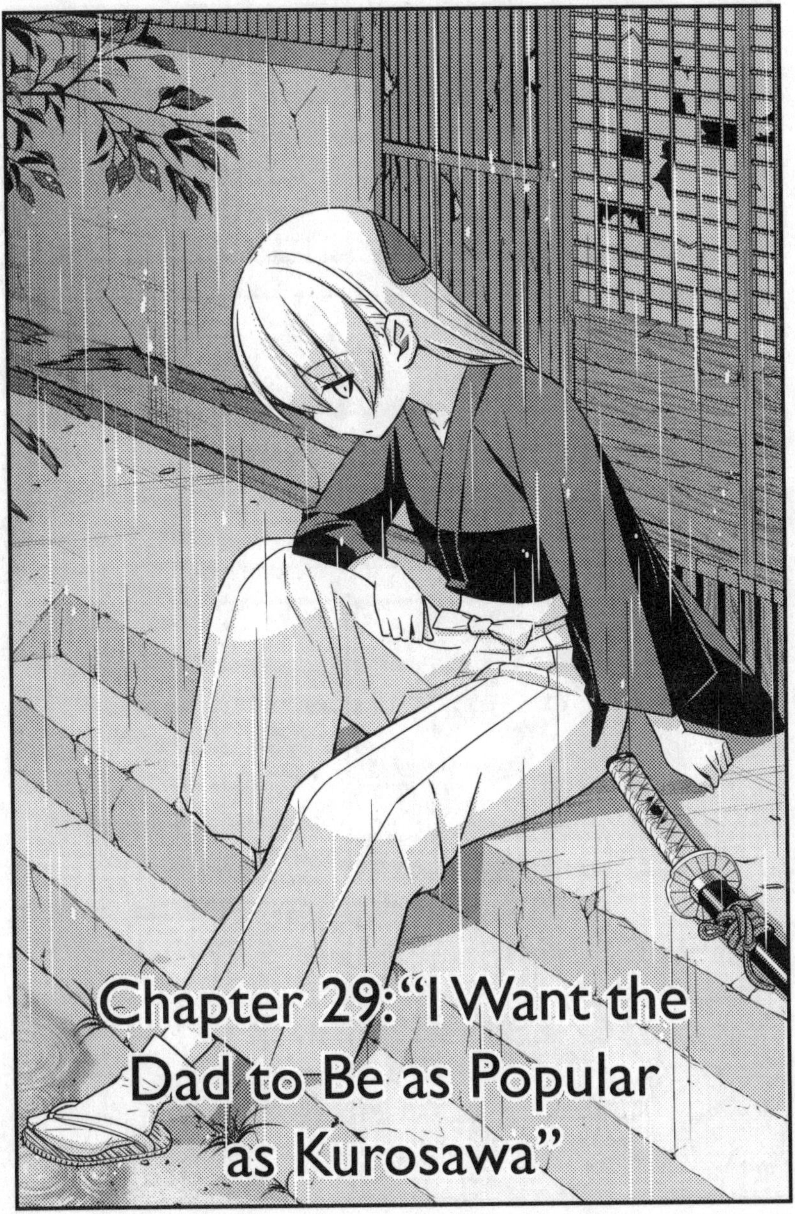

# Chapter 29: "I Want the Dad to Be as Popular as Kurosawa"

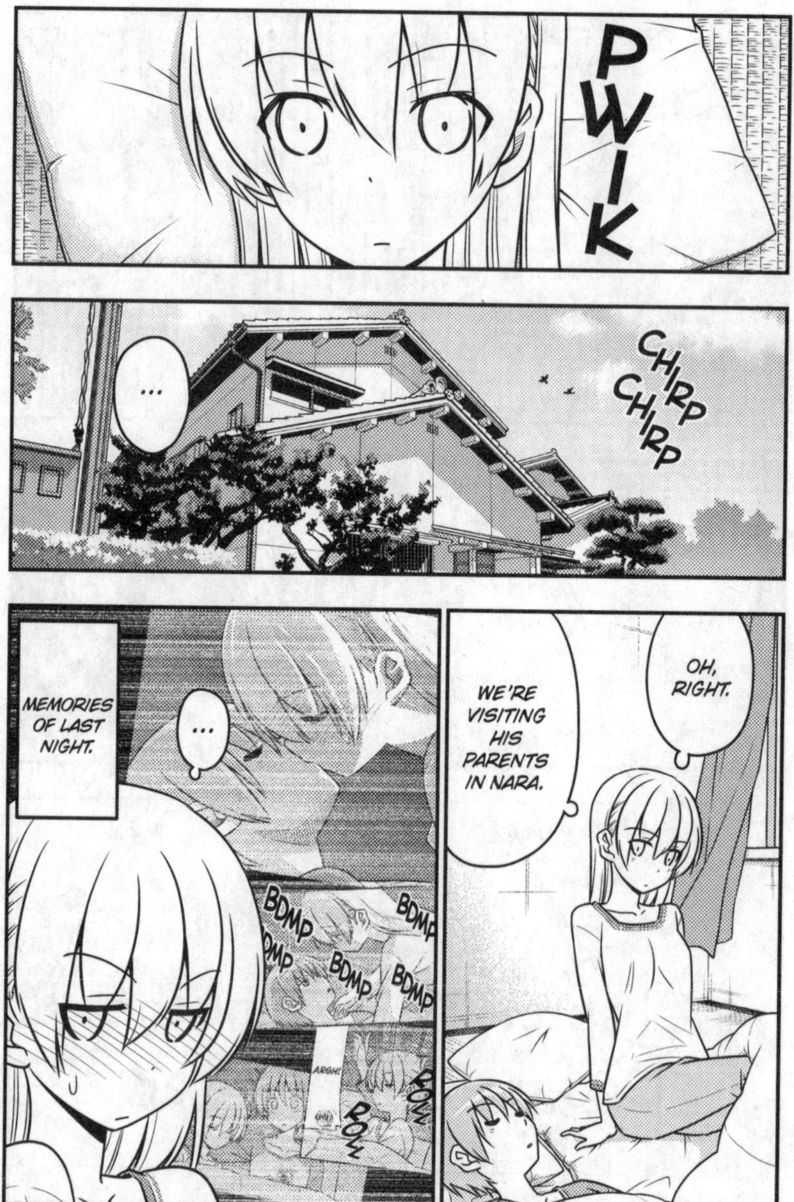
PWIK
CHIRP CHIRP
...
OH, RIGHT.
WE'RE VISITING HIS PARENTS IN NARA.
...
MEMORIES OF LAST NIGHT.
BDMP BDMP BDMP BDMP BDMP
ARGH!
ROLL ROLL

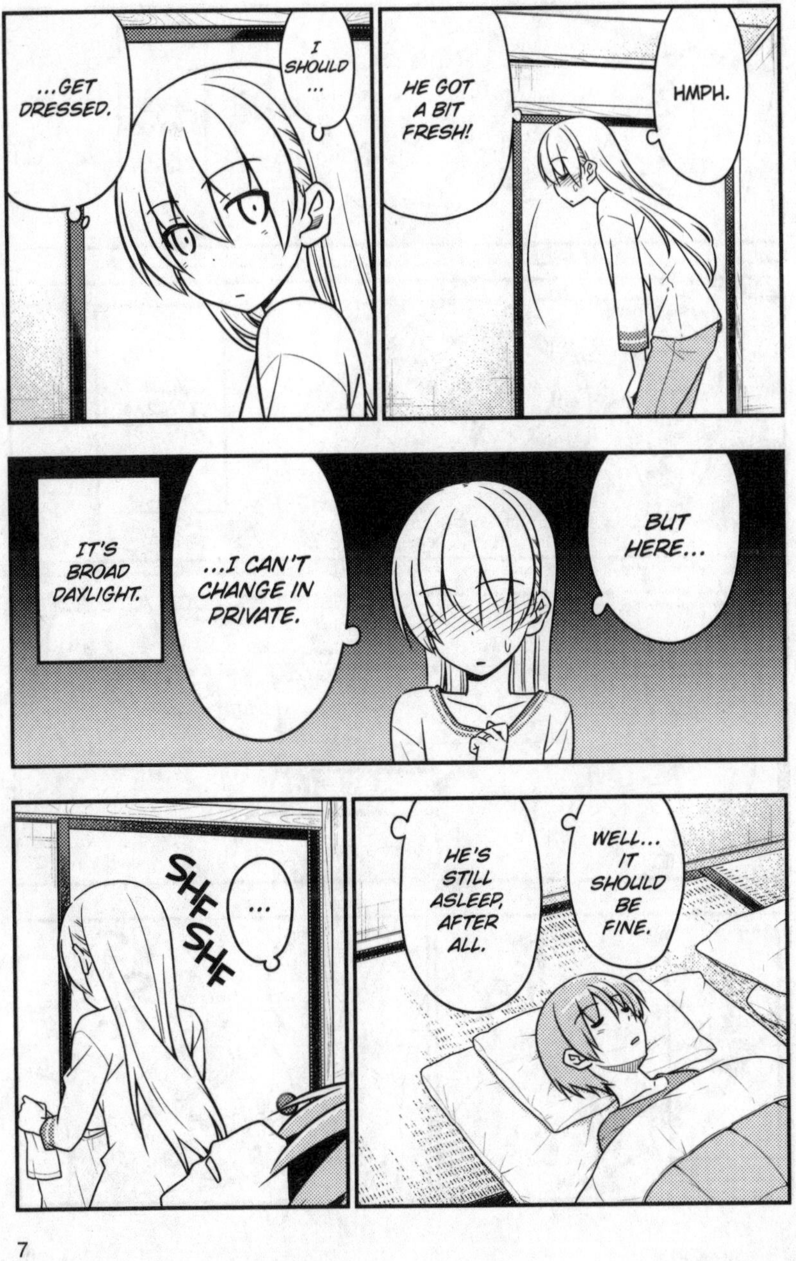
HMPH.
HE GOT A BIT FRESH!
I SHOULD ...
...GET DRESSED.
BUT HERE...
...I CAN'T CHANGE IN PRIVATE.
IT'S BROAD DAYLIGHT.
WELL... IT SHOULD BE FINE.
HE'S STILL ASLEEP, AFTER ALL.
...
SHF SHF

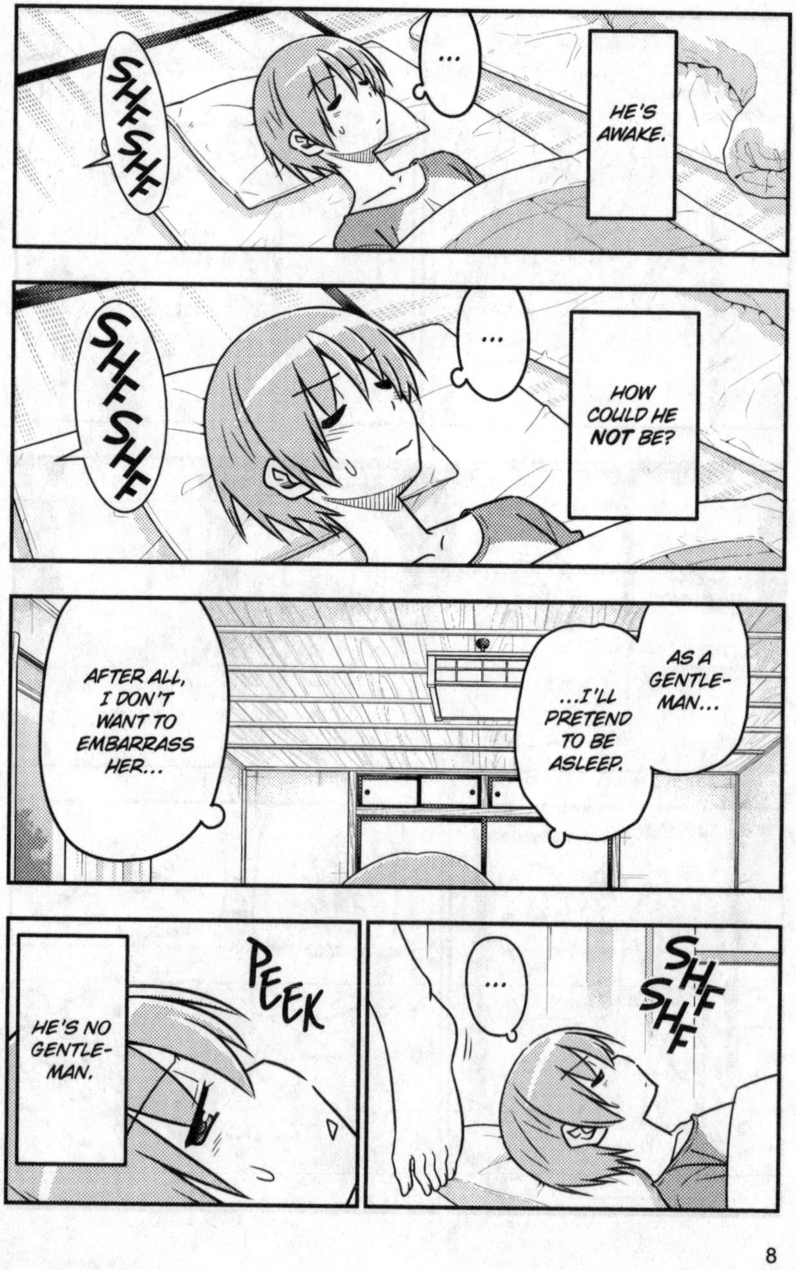
HE'S AWAKE.
...
SHF SHF
HOW COULD HE NOT BE?
...
SHF SHF
AS A GENTLE-MAN...
...I'LL PRETEND TO BE ASLEEP.
AFTER ALL, I DON'T WANT TO EMBARRASS HER...
SHF SHF
...
PEEK
HE'S NO GENTLE-MAN.

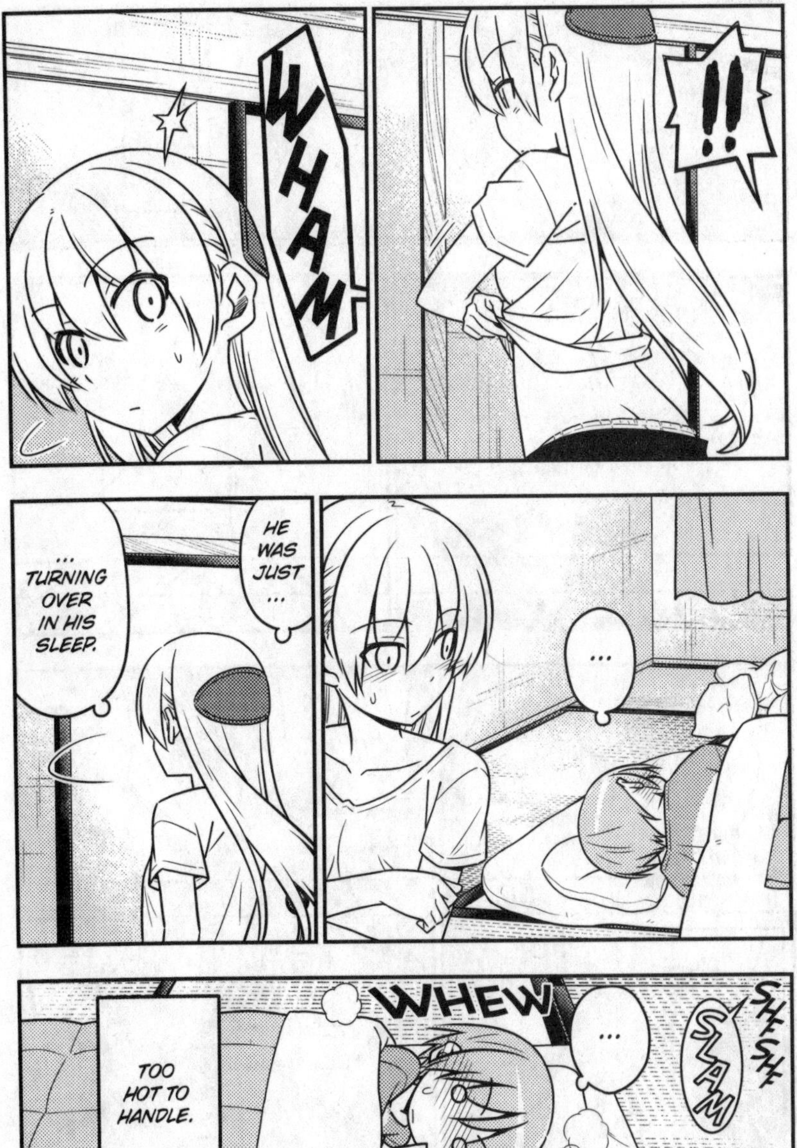
!!
WHAM
...
HE WAS JUST ...
... TURNING OVER IN HIS SLEEP.
SHSH
SLAM
...
WHEW
TOO HOT TO HANDLE.

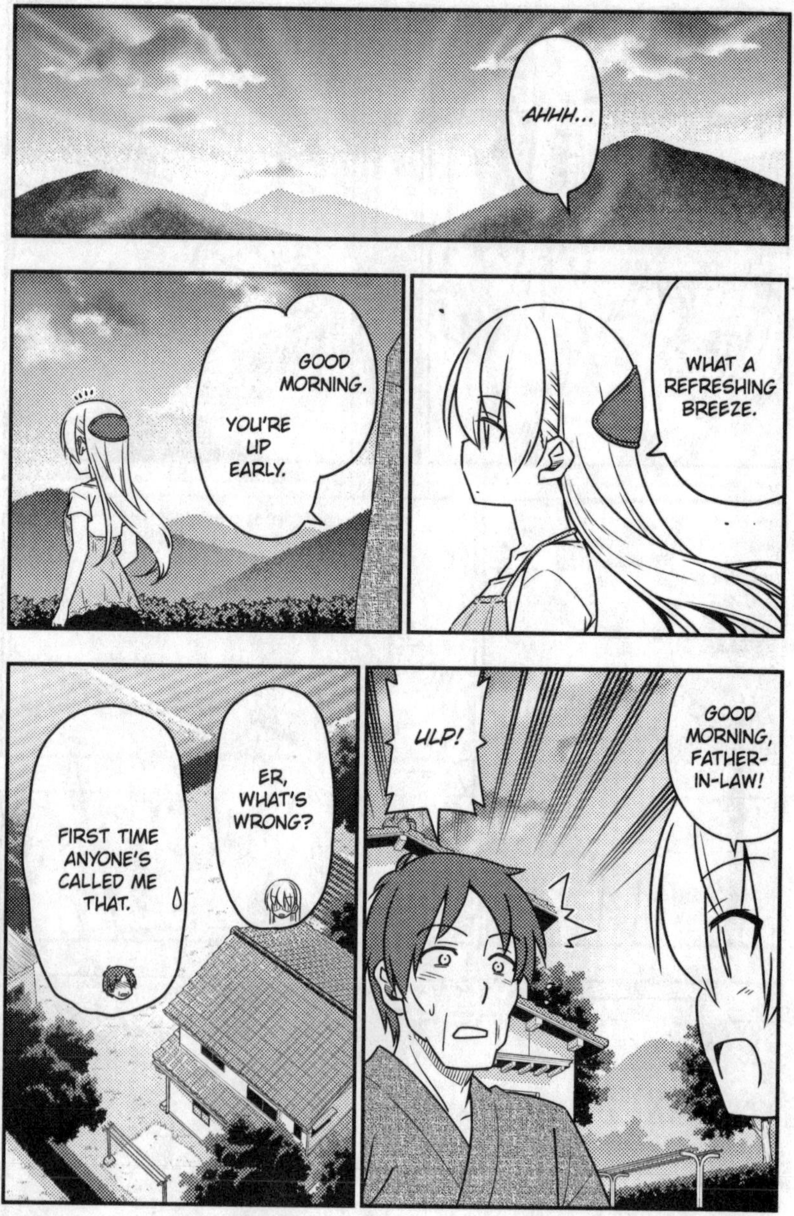
AHHH...
WHAT A REFRESHING BREEZE.
GOOD MORNING.
YOU'RE UP EARLY.
GOOD MORNING, FATHER-IN-LAW!
ULP!
ER, WHAT'S WRONG?
FIRST TIME ANYONE'S CALLED ME THAT.

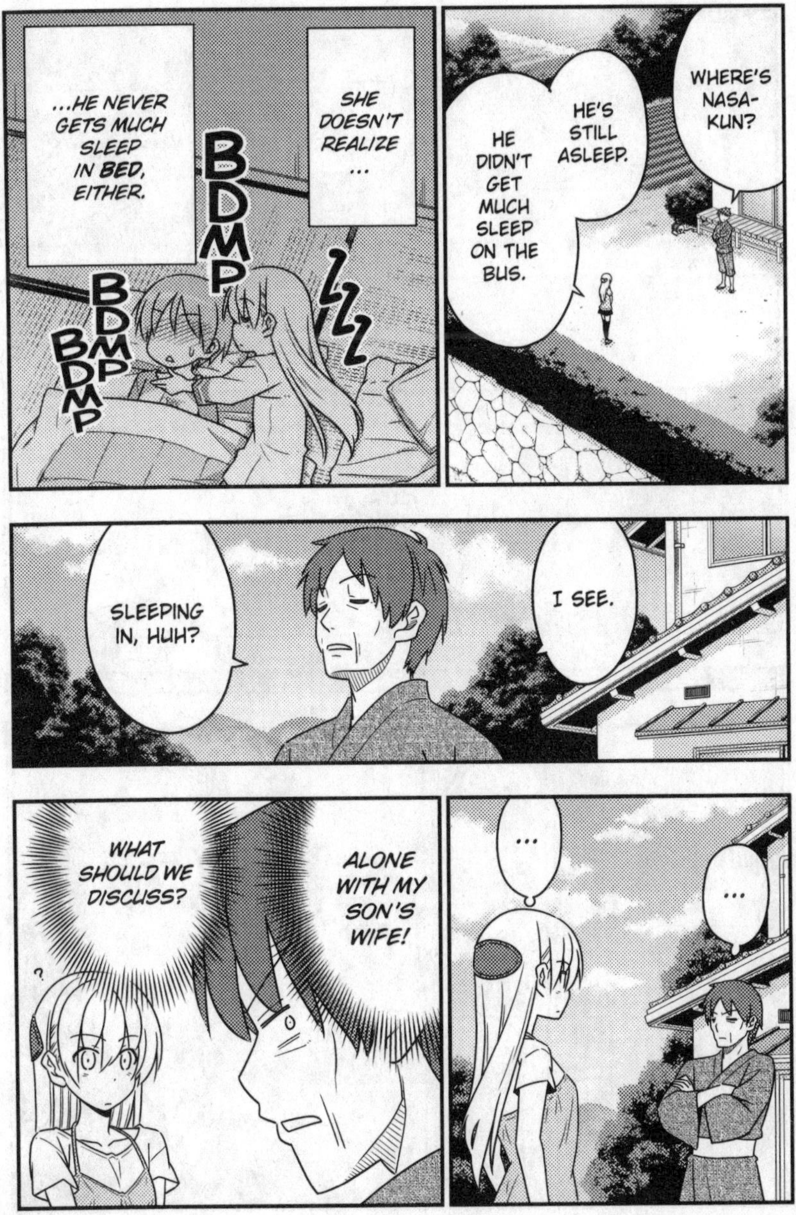
WHERE'S NASA-KUN?
HE'S STILL ASLEEP.
HE DIDN'T GET MUCH SLEEP ON THE BUS.
SHE DOESN'T REALIZE ...
...HE NEVER GETS MUCH SLEEP IN BED, EITHER.
BDMP
BDMP
BDMP
BDMP
ZZZ
I SEE.
SLEEPING IN, HUH?
...
...
ALONE WITH MY SON'S WIFE!
WHAT SHOULD WE DISCUSS?
?

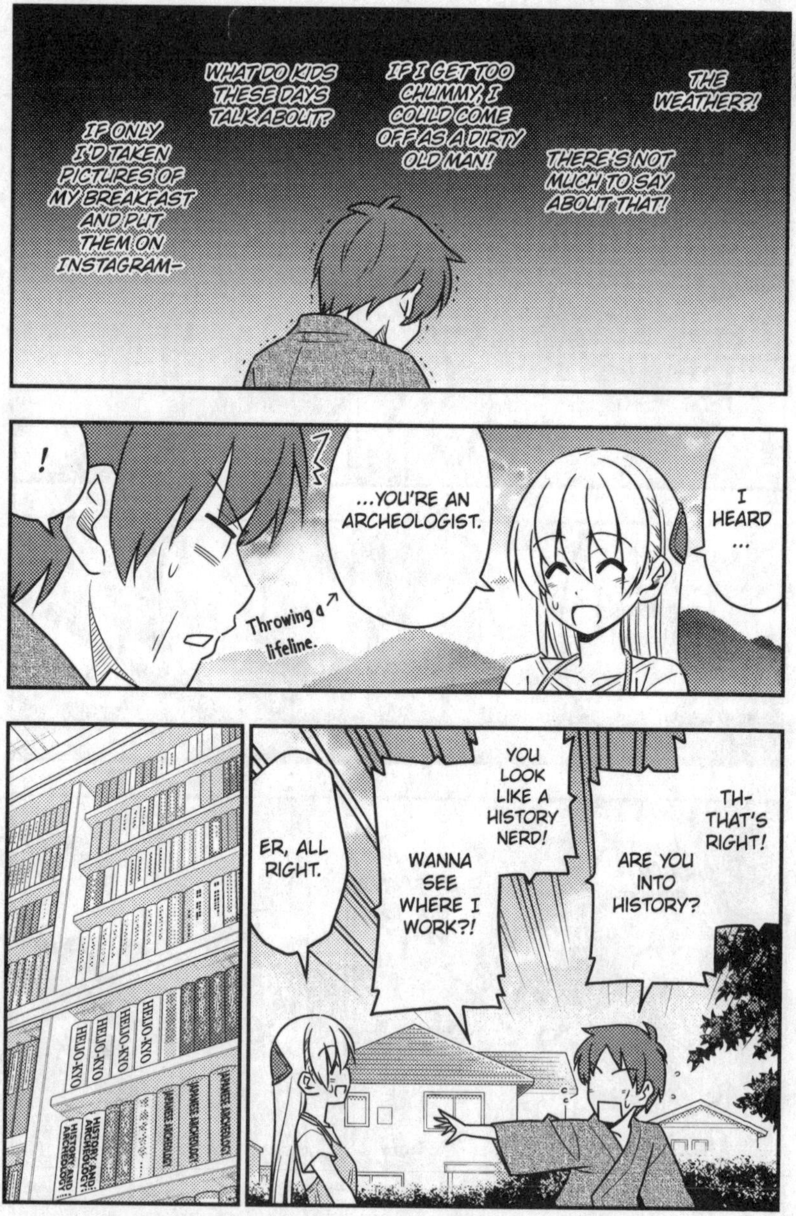
THE WEATHER?!
THERE'S NOT MUCH TO SAY ABOUT THAT!
IF I GET TOO CHUMMY, I COULD COME OFF AS A DIRTY OLD MAN!
WHAT DO KIDS THESE DAYS TALK ABOUT?
IF ONLY I'D TAKEN PICTURES OF MY BREAKFAST AND PUT THEM ON INSTAGRAM-
I HEARD...
...YOU'RE AN ARCHEOLOGIST.
Throwing a lifeline.
!
TH-THAT'S RIGHT!
ARE YOU INTO HISTORY?
YOU LOOK LIKE A HISTORY NERD!
WANNA SEE WHERE I WORK?!
ER, ALL RIGHT.
HELLO-KYO
HELLO-KYO
HELLO-KYO
JAPANESE ARCHEOLOGY
JAPANESE ARCHEOLOGY
JAPANESE ARCHEOLOGY
HISTORY AND ARCHEOLOGY
HISTORY AND ARCHEOLOGY

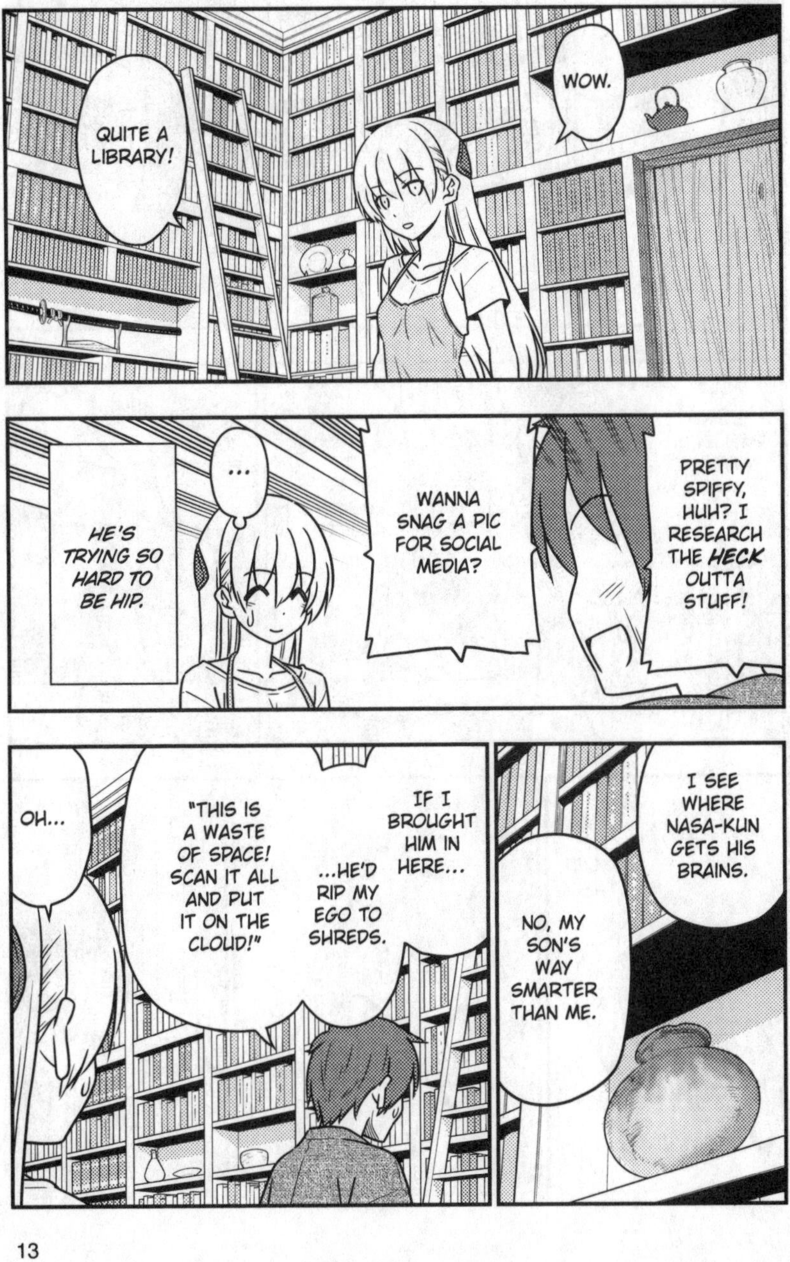
WOW.
QUITE A LIBRARY!
PRETTY SPIFFY, HUH? I RESEARCH THE *HECK* OUTTA STUFF!
WANNA SNAG A PIC FOR SOCIAL MEDIA?
...
*HE'S TRYING SO HARD TO BE HIP.*
I SEE WHERE NASA-KUN GETS HIS BRAINS.
NO, MY SON'S WAY SMARTER THAN ME.
IF I BROUGHT HIM IN HERE...
...HE'D RIP MY EGO TO SHREDS.
"THIS IS A WASTE OF SPACE! SCAN IT ALL AND PUT IT ON THE CLOUD!"
OH...

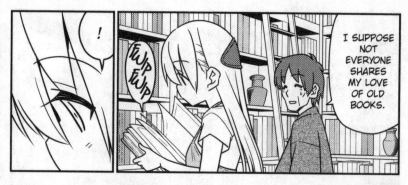

I SUPPOSE NOT EVERYONE SHARES MY LOVE OF OLD BOOKS.
FWIP FWIP
!
HEH ...
IS SOME-THING FUNNY?
HUH?
IT'S JUST ...
...I'D BE SO EMBAR-RASSED ...
...IF SOMEONE COMPILED MY OLD LOVE LETTERS ...
...AND PUBLISHED THEM LIKE THIS.
LOVE LETTERS ?
YOU CAN... *READ* THIS?

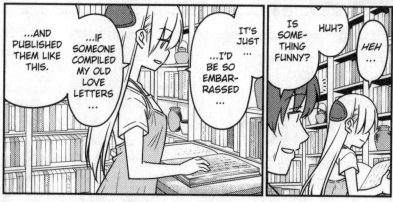

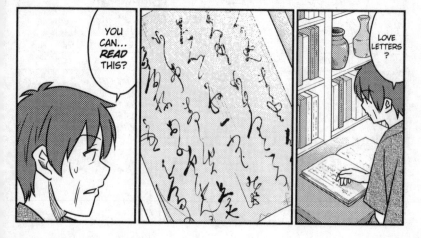

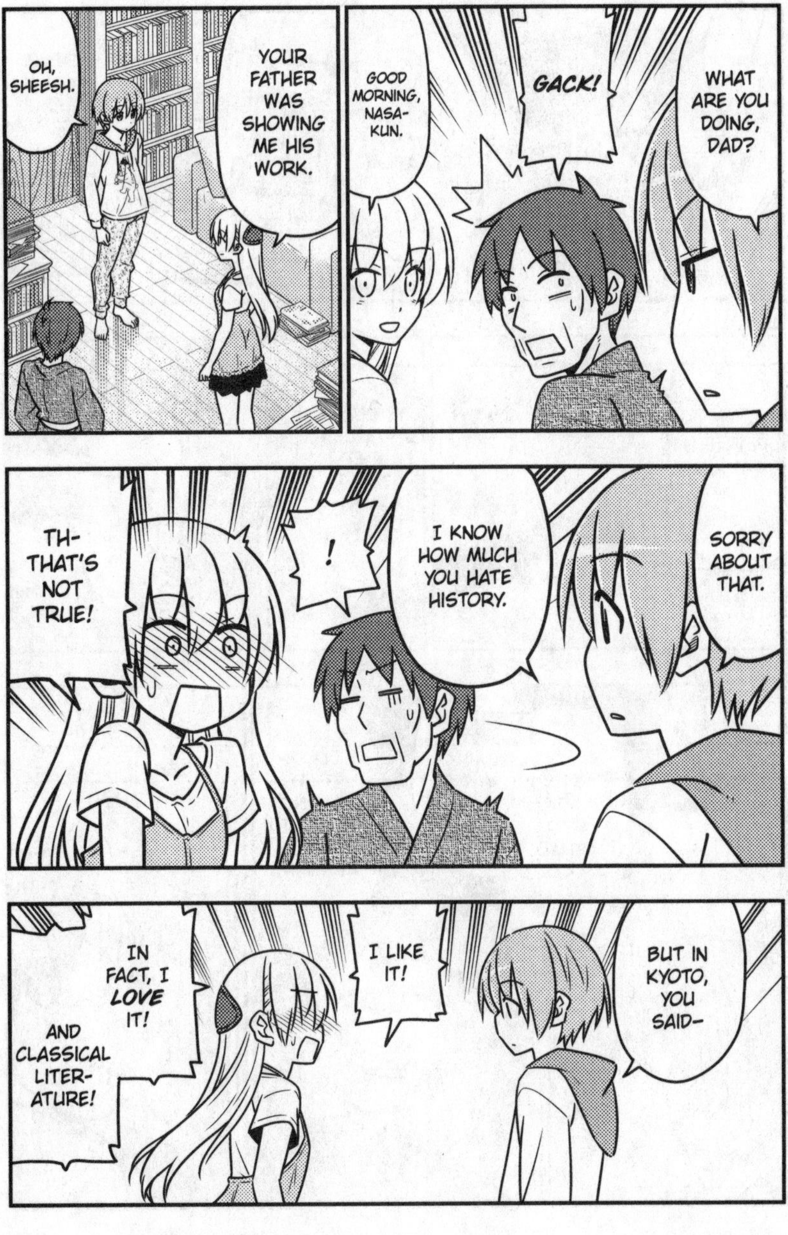
WHAT ARE YOU DOING, DAD?
GACK!
GOOD MORNING, NASA-KUN.
YOUR FATHER WAS SHOWING ME HIS WORK.
OH, SHEESH.
SORRY ABOUT THAT.
I KNOW HOW MUCH YOU HATE HISTORY.
!
TH-THAT'S NOT TRUE!
BUT IN KYOTO, YOU SAID-
I LIKE IT!
IN FACT, I LOVE IT!
AND CLASSICAL LITERATURE!

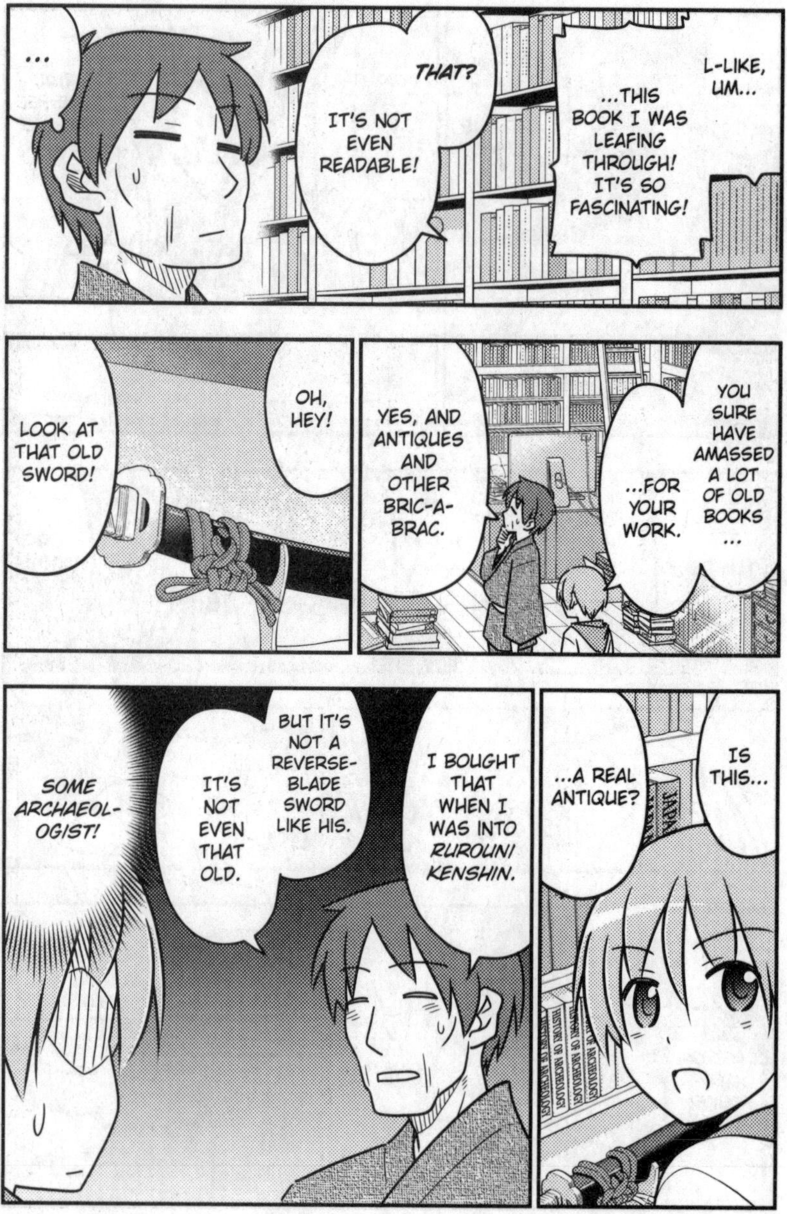
L-LIKE, UM...
...THIS BOOK I WAS LEAFING THROUGH! IT'S SO FASCINATING!
THAT? IT'S NOT EVEN READABLE!
...
YOU SURE HAVE AMASSED A LOT OF OLD BOOKS...
...FOR YOUR WORK.
YES, AND ANTIQUES AND OTHER BRIC-A-BRAC.
OH, HEY!
LOOK AT THAT OLD SWORD!
IS THIS...
...A REAL ANTIQUE?
HISTORY OF ARCHEOLOGY
I BOUGHT THAT WHEN I WAS INTO RUROUNI KENSHIN.
BUT IT'S NOT A REVERSE-BLADE SWORD LIKE HIS.
IT'S NOT EVEN THAT OLD.
SOME ARCHAEOLOGIST!

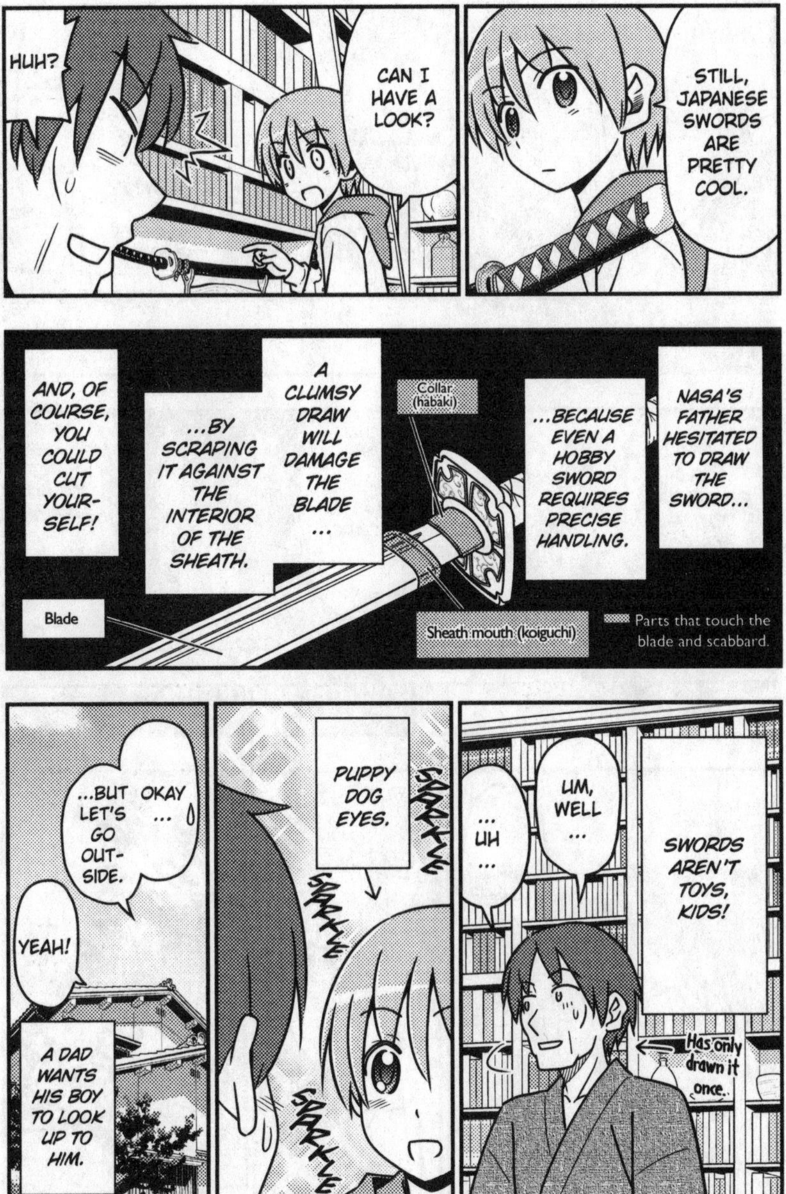
STILL, JAPANESE SWORDS ARE PRETTY COOL.
CAN I HAVE A LOOK?
HUH?
NASA'S FATHER HESITATED TO DRAW THE SWORD...
...BECAUSE EVEN A HOBBY SWORD REQUIRES PRECISE HANDLING.
Collar (habaki)
A CLUMSY DRAW WILL DAMAGE THE BLADE...
...BY SCRAPING IT AGAINST THE INTERIOR OF THE SHEATH.
AND, OF COURSE, YOU COULD CUT YOURSELF!
Parts that touch the blade and scabbard.
Sheath mouth (koiguchi)
Blade
SWORDS AREN'T TOYS, KIDS!
UM, WELL...
...UH...
Has only drawn it once.
SPARKLE
PUPPY DOG EYES.
SPARKLE
SPARKLE
OKAY...
...BUT LET'S GO OUTSIDE.
YEAH!
A DAD WANTS HIS BOY TO LOOK UP TO HIM.

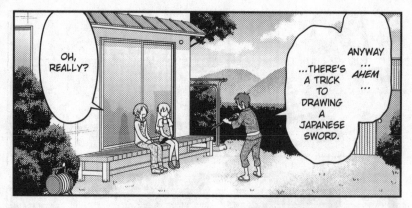

ANYWAY ... AHEM ...
...THERE'S A TRICK TO DRAWING A JAPANESE SWORD.
OH, REALLY?
I'M SO NERVOUS!
THIS IS A REAL BLADE!
CAN I PULL IT OUT SMOOTHLY ...
...AND RESHEATH IT WITH EQUAL GRACE?
...
BRR BRR BRR BRR BRR BRR BRR BRR BRR BRR
MR. YUZAKI?
...!

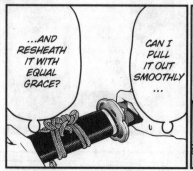

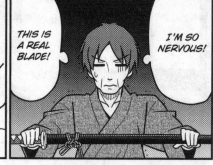

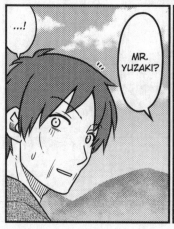

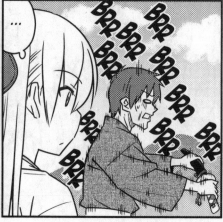

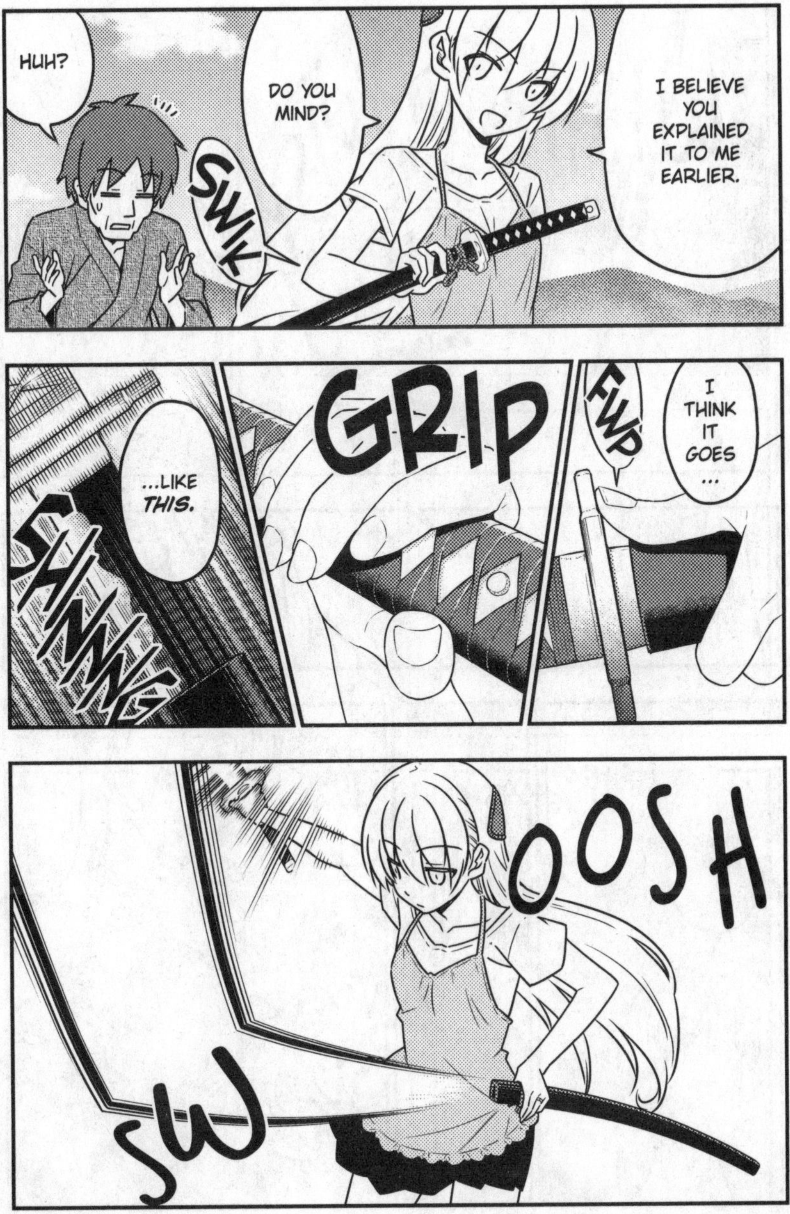
I BELIEVE YOU EXPLAINED IT TO ME EARLIER.
DO YOU MIND?
SWIK
HUH?
I THINK IT GOES ...
FWP
GRIP
...LIKE *THIS.*
SHING
SWOOSH

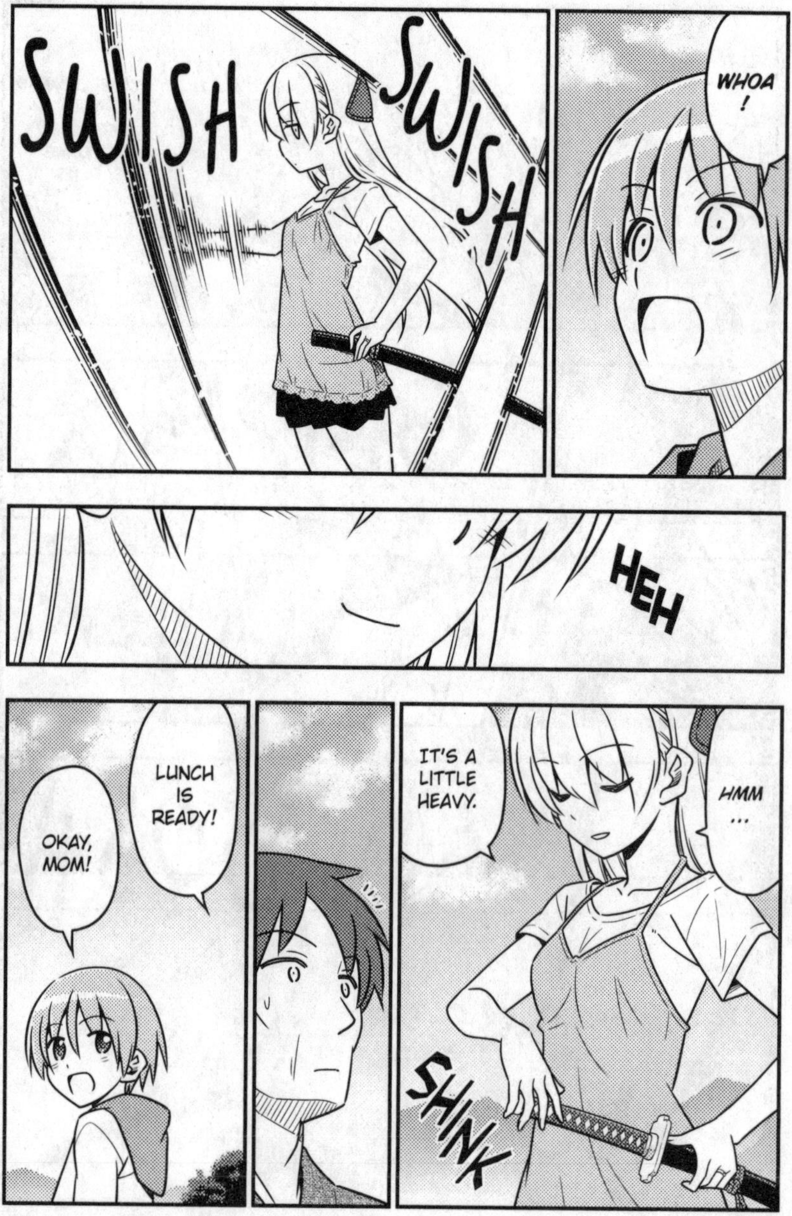
WHOA!
SWISH
SWISH
HEH
HMM...
IT'S A LITTLE HEAVY.
SHINK
LUNCH IS READY!
OKAY, MOM!

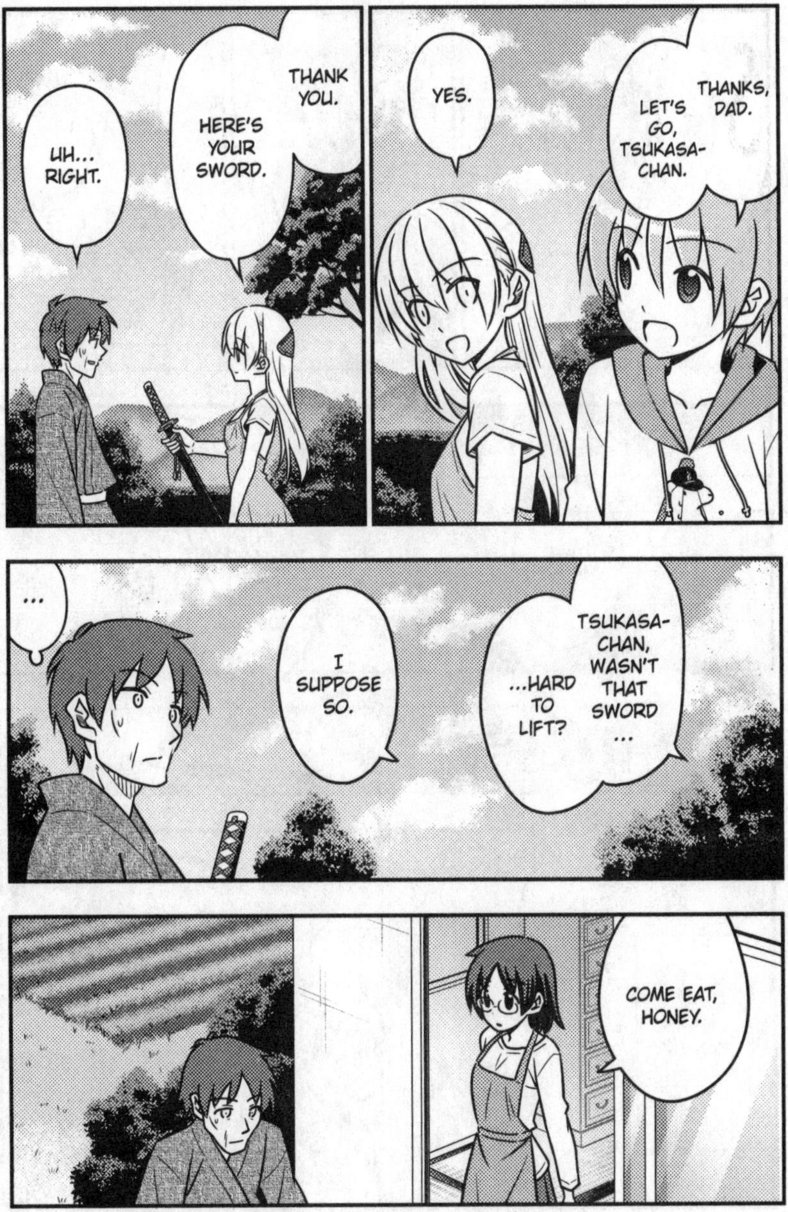
THANKS, DAD.
LET'S GO, TSUKASA-CHAN.
YES.
THANK YOU.
HERE'S YOUR SWORD.
UH... RIGHT.
TSUKASA-CHAN, WASN'T THAT SWORD ...
...HARD TO LIFT?
I SUPPOSE SO.
...
COME EAT, HONEY.

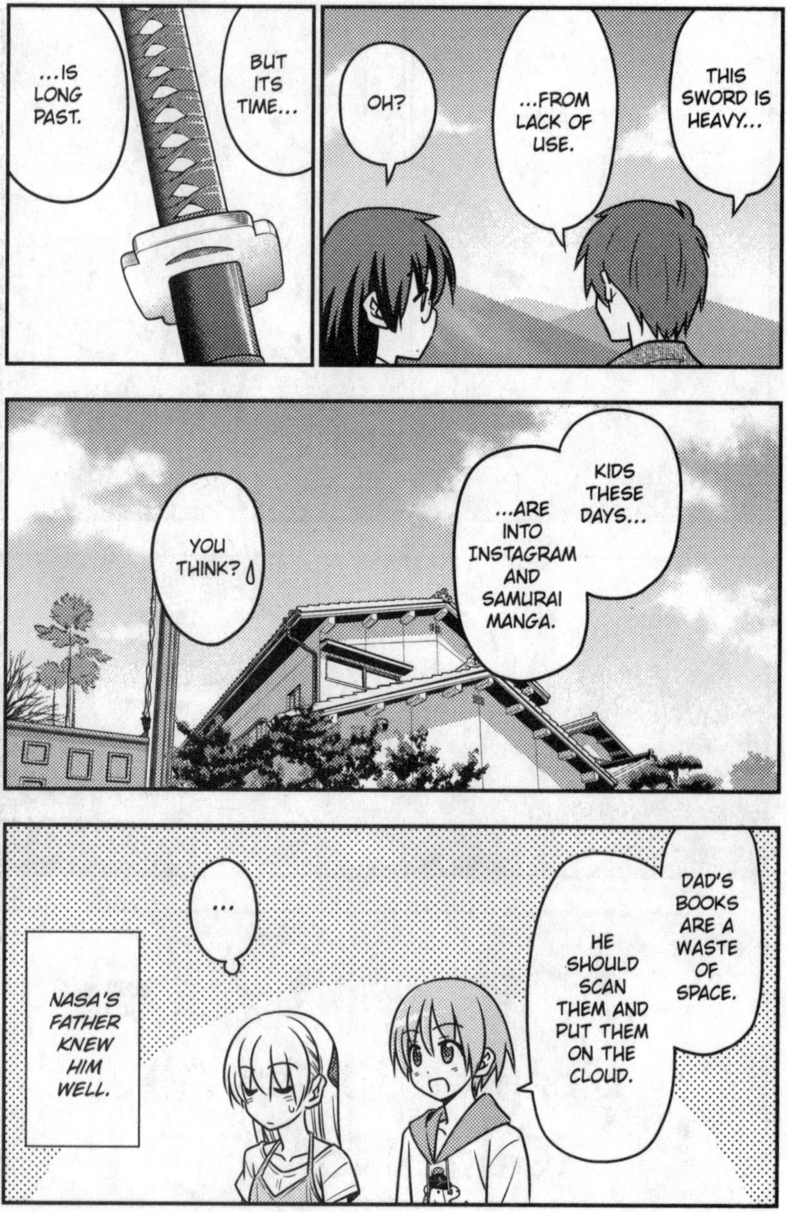
THIS SWORD IS HEAVY...
...FROM LACK OF USE.
OH?
BUT ITS TIME...
...IS LONG PAST.
KIDS THESE DAYS...
...ARE INTO INSTAGRAM AND SAMURAI MANGA.
YOU THINK?
DAD'S BOOKS ARE A WASTE OF SPACE.
HE SHOULD SCAN THEM AND PUT THEM ON THE CLOUD.
...
NASA'S FATHER KNEW HIM WELL.

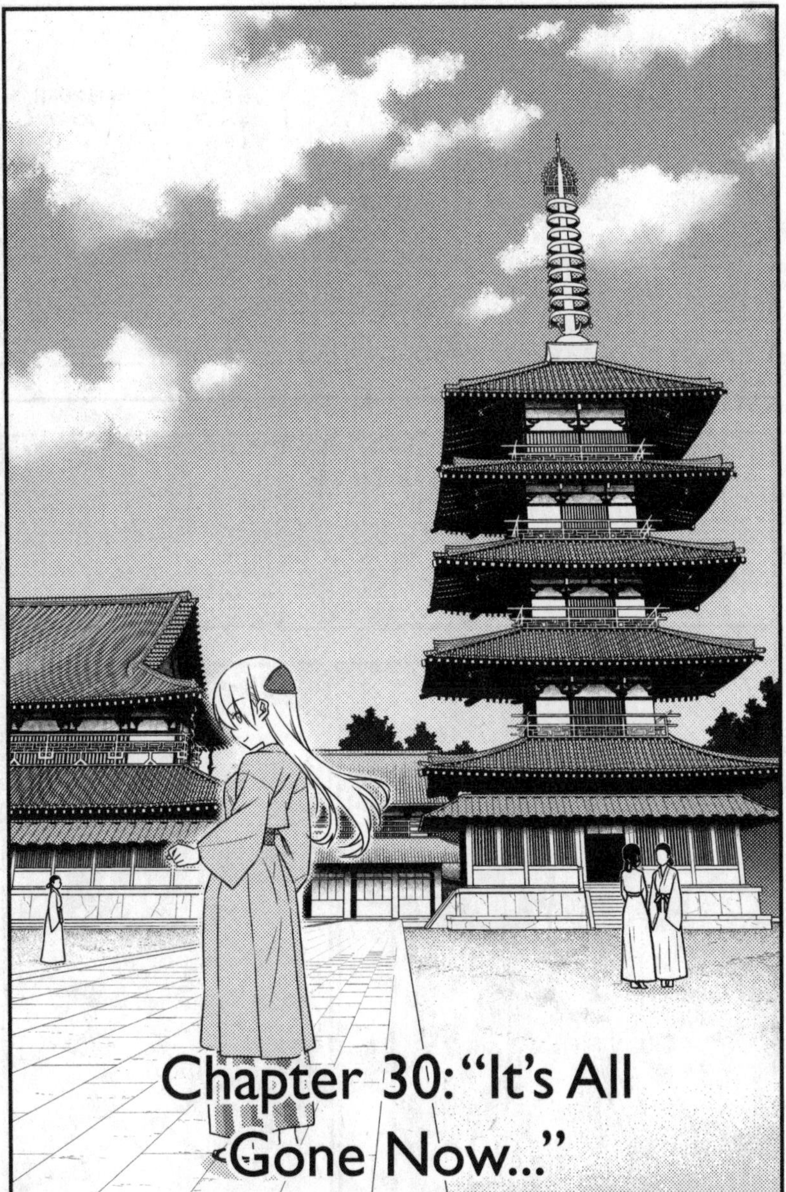
Chapter 30: "It's All Gone Now..."

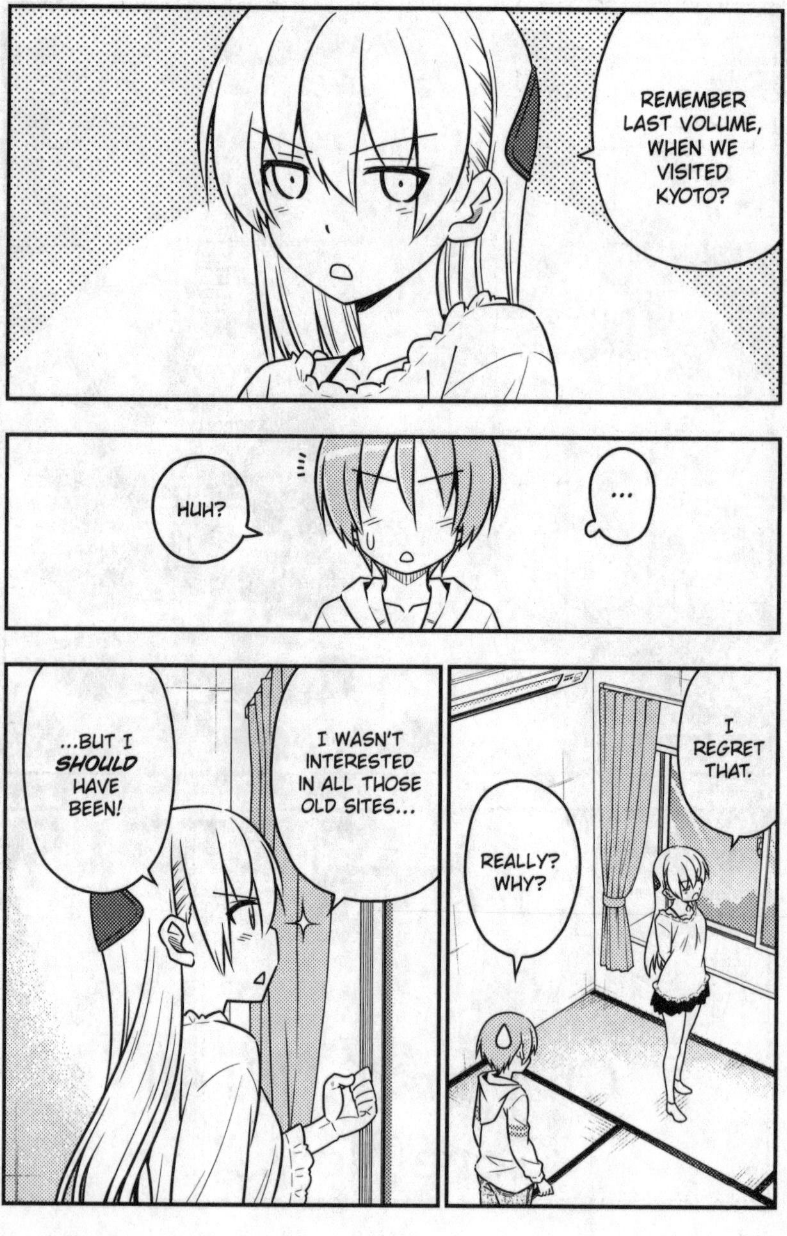
REMEMBER LAST VOLUME, WHEN WE VISITED KYOTO?
...
HUH?
I REGRET THAT.
REALLY? WHY?
I WASN'T INTERESTED IN ALL THOSE OLD SITES...
...BUT I **SHOULD** HAVE BEEN!

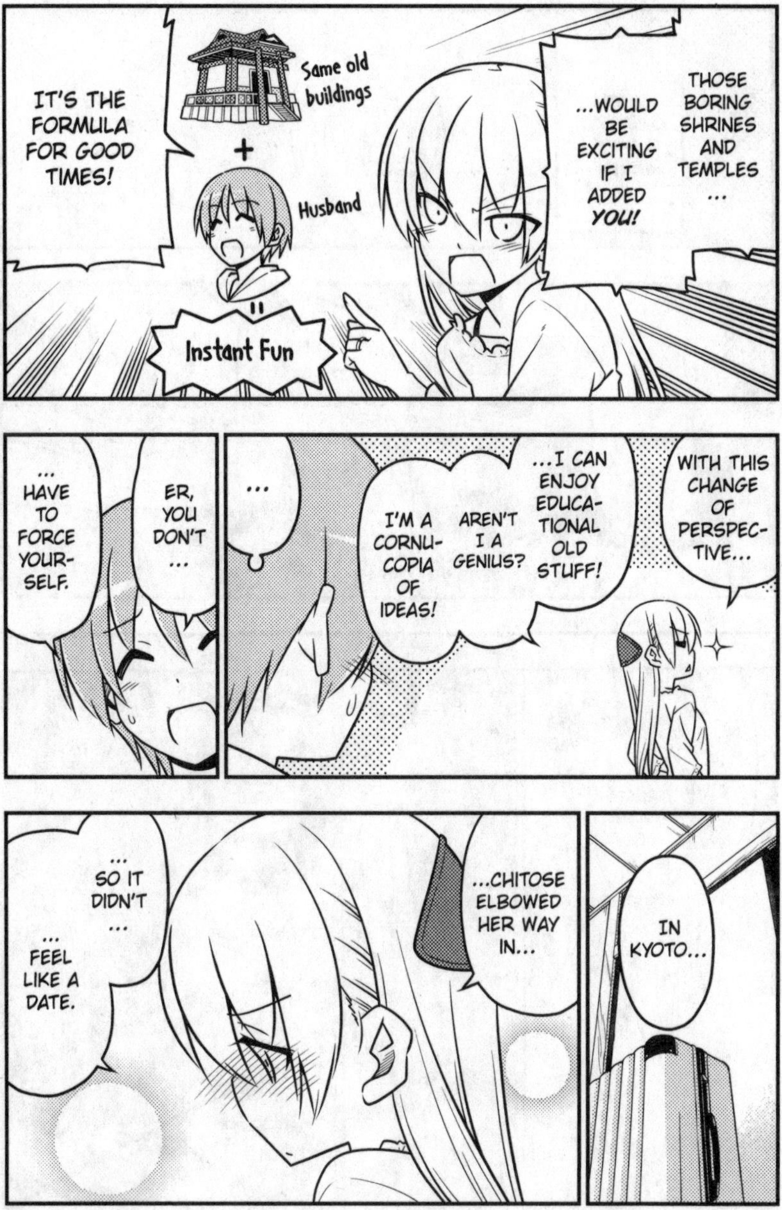
THOSE BORING SHRINES AND TEMPLES...
...WOULD BE EXCITING IF I ADDED *YOU!*
Same old buildings
+
Husband
=
Instant Fun
IT'S THE FORMULA FOR GOOD TIMES!
WITH THIS CHANGE OF PERSPEC-TIVE...
...I CAN ENJOY EDUCA-TIONAL OLD STUFF!
AREN'T I A GENIUS?
I'M A CORNU-COPIA OF IDEAS!
...
ER, YOU DON'T...
...HAVE TO FORCE YOUR-SELF.
IN KYOTO...
...CHITOSE ELBOWED HER WAY IN...
...SO IT DIDN'T...
...FEEL LIKE A DATE.

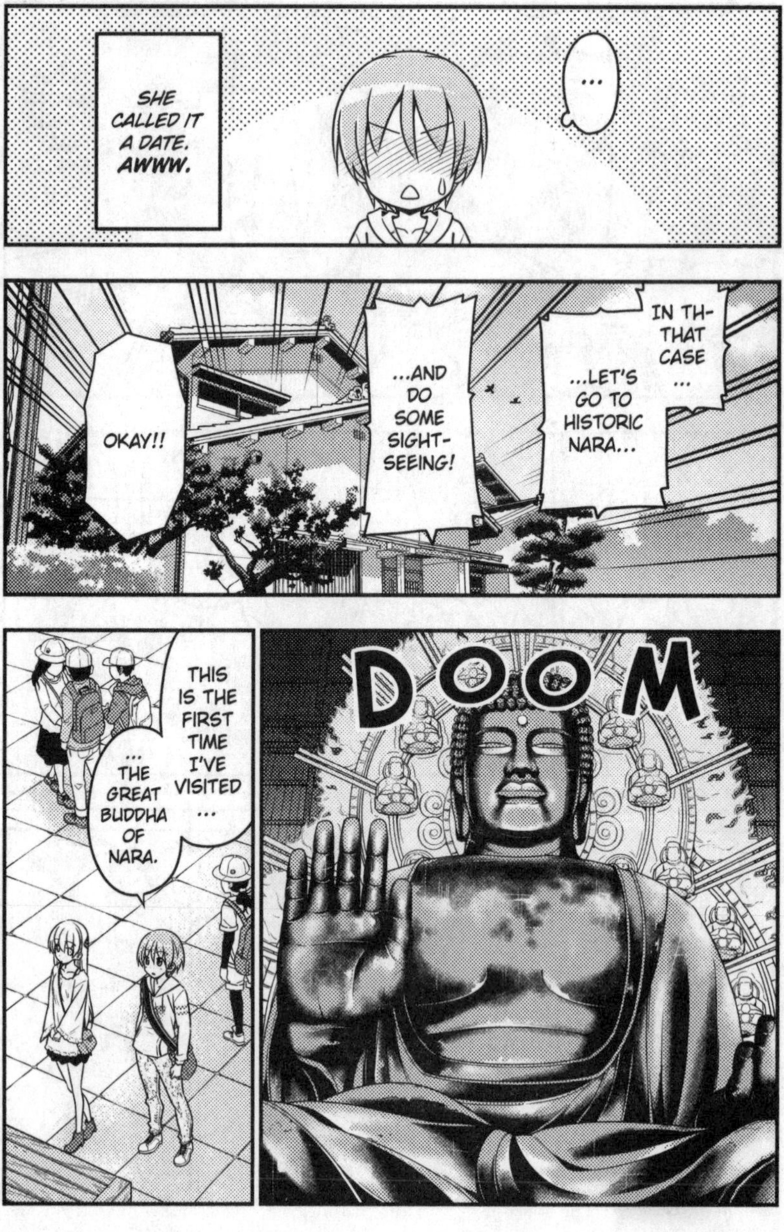
...
SHE CALLED IT A DATE. AWWW.
IN TH-THAT CASE ...
...LET'S GO TO HISTORIC NARA...
...AND DO SOME SIGHT-SEEING!
OKAY!!
DOOM
THIS IS THE FIRST TIME I'VE VISITED ...
... THE GREAT BUDDHA OF NARA.

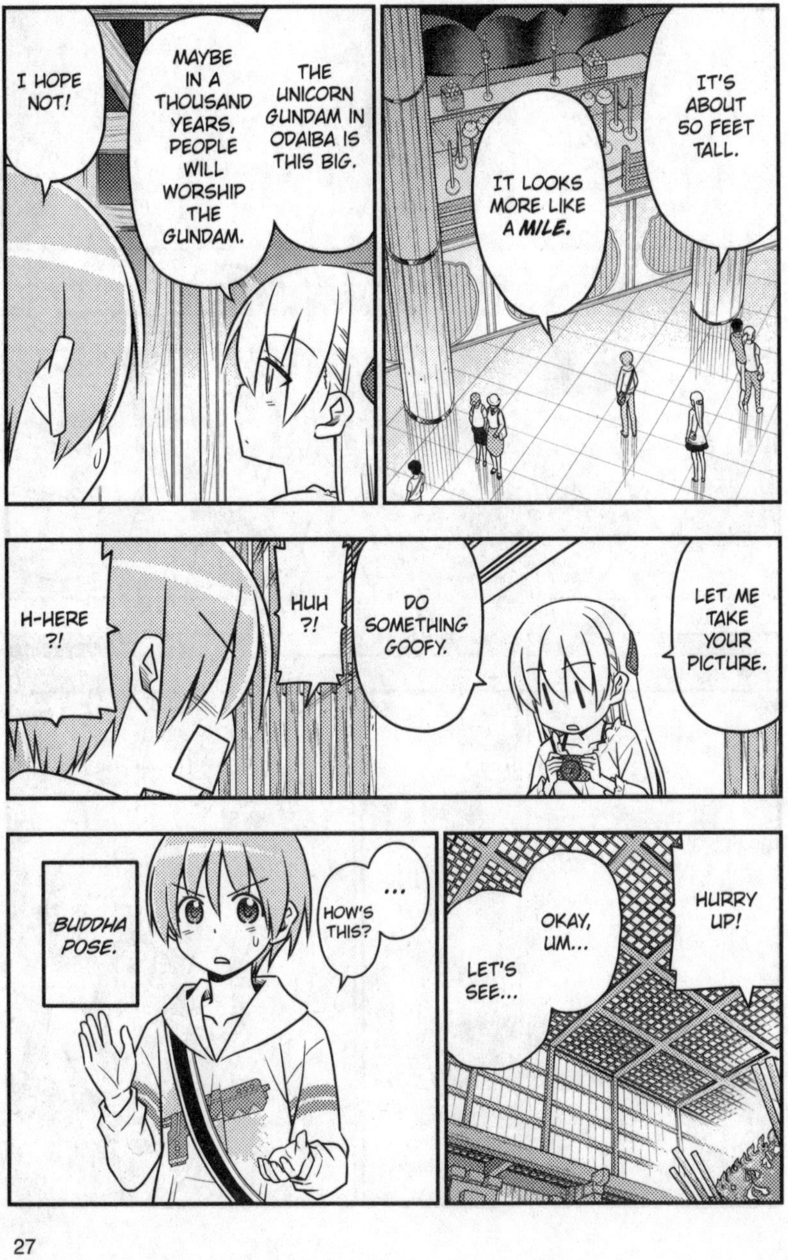
IT'S ABOUT 50 FEET TALL.
IT LOOKS MORE LIKE A *MILE.*
THE UNICORN GUNDAM IN ODAIBA IS THIS BIG.
MAYBE IN A THOUSAND YEARS, PEOPLE WILL WORSHIP THE GUNDAM.
I HOPE NOT!
LET ME TAKE YOUR PICTURE.
DO SOMETHING GOOFY.
HUH ?!
H-HERE ?!
HURRY UP!
OKAY, UM...
LET'S SEE...
...
HOW'S THIS?
*BUDDHA POSE.*

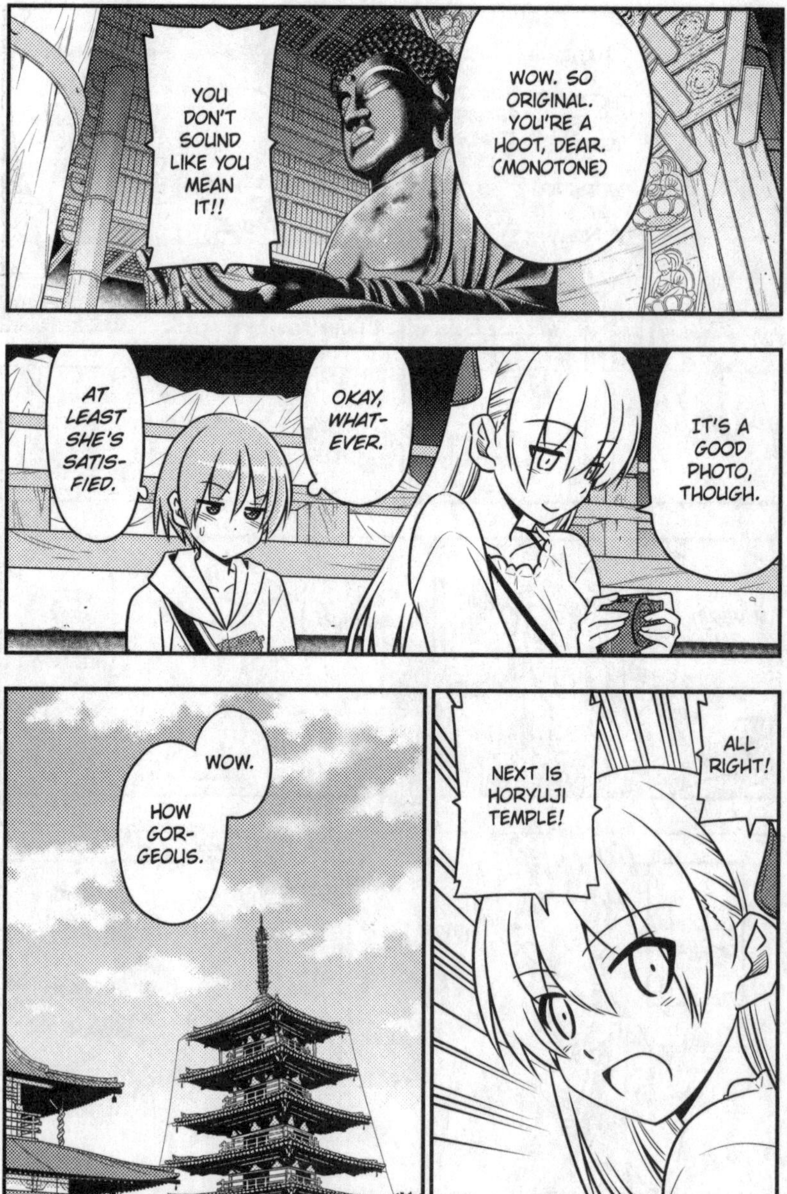
WOW. SO ORIGINAL. YOU'RE A HOOT, DEAR. (MONOTONE)
YOU DON'T SOUND LIKE YOU MEAN IT!!
IT'S A GOOD PHOTO, THOUGH.
OKAY, WHAT-EVER.
AT LEAST SHE'S SATIS-FIED.
ALL RIGHT!
NEXT IS HORYUJI TEMPLE!
WOW.
HOW GOR-GEOUS.

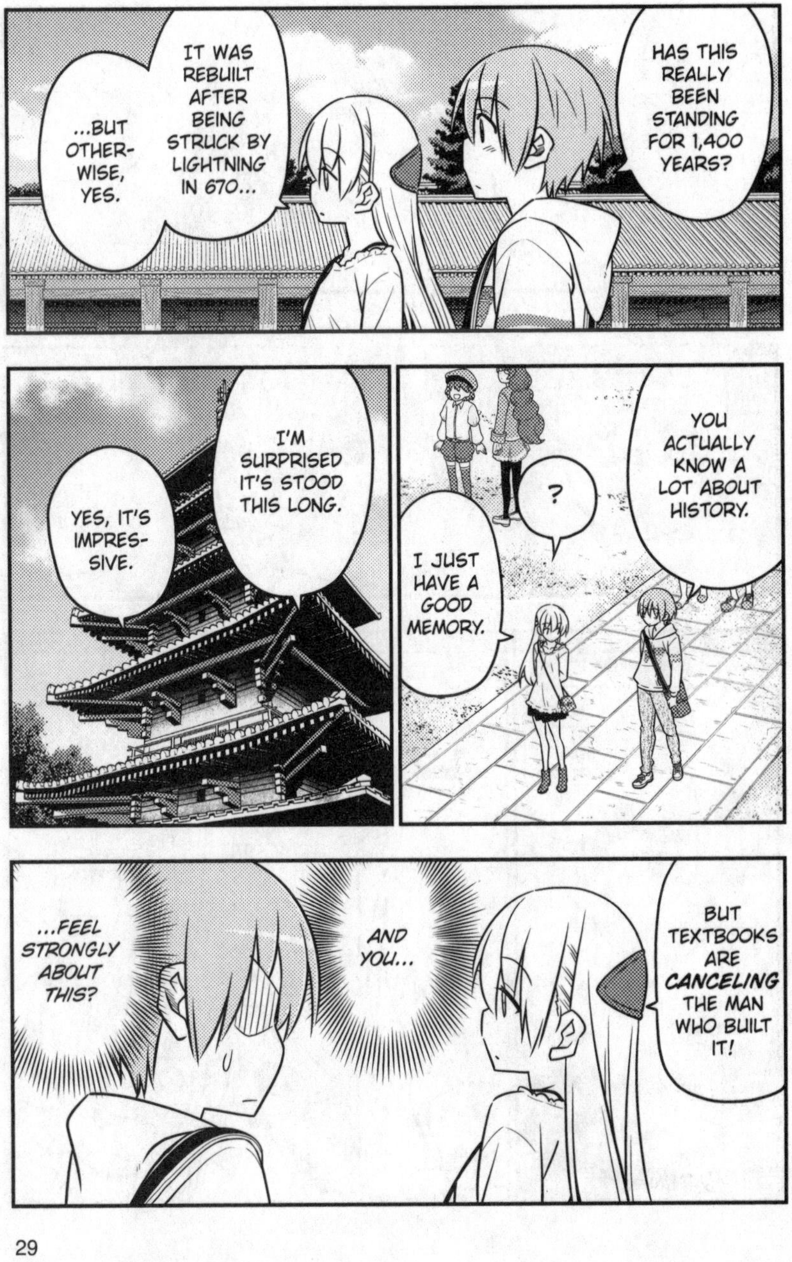
HAS THIS REALLY BEEN STANDING FOR 1,400 YEARS?
IT WAS REBUILT AFTER BEING STRUCK BY LIGHTNING IN 670...
...BUT OTHER-WISE, YES.
YOU ACTUALLY KNOW A LOT ABOUT HISTORY.
?
I JUST HAVE A GOOD MEMORY.
I'M SURPRISED IT'S STOOD THIS LONG.
YES, IT'S IMPRES-SIVE.
BUT TEXTBOOKS ARE *CANCELING* THE MAN WHO BUILT IT!
AND YOU...
...FEEL STRONGLY ABOUT THIS?

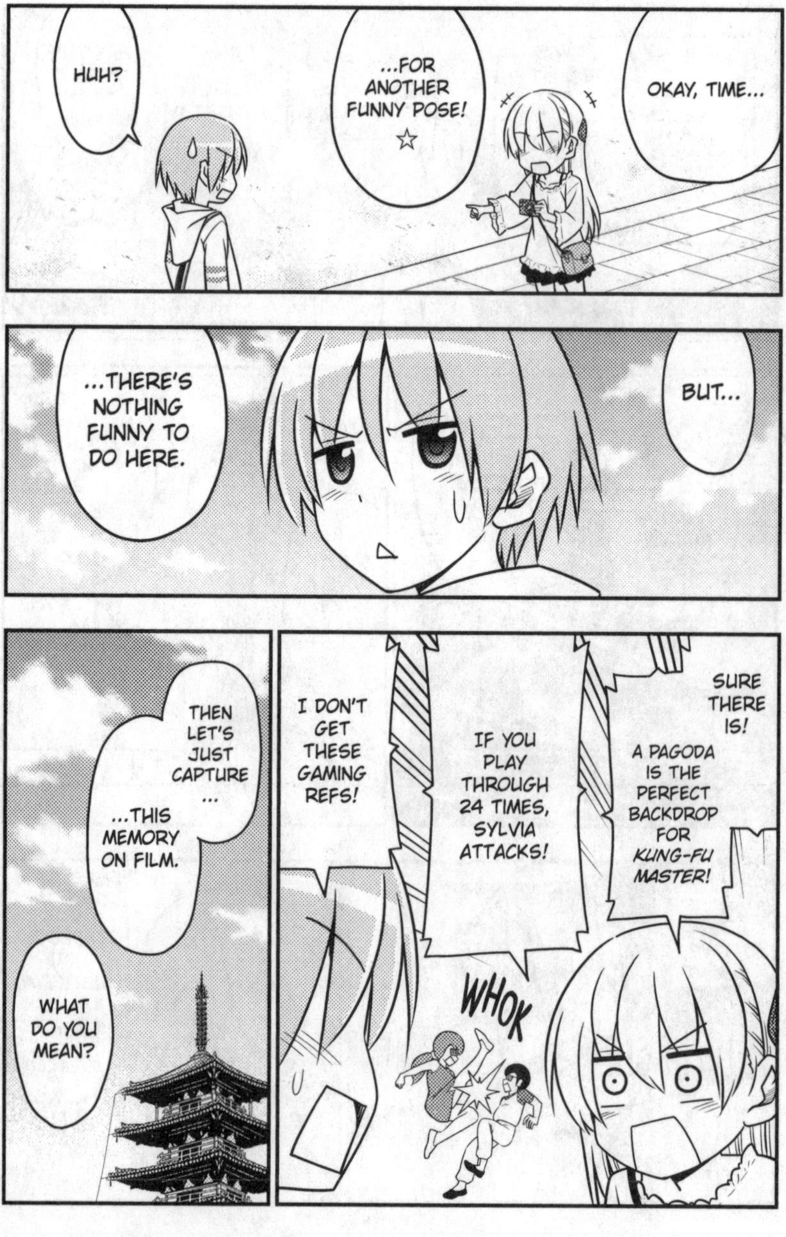
OKAY, TIME...
...FOR ANOTHER FUNNY POSE! ☆
HUH?
BUT...
...THERE'S NOTHING FUNNY TO DO HERE.
SURE THERE IS!
A PAGODA IS THE PERFECT BACKDROP FOR *KUNG-FU MASTER*!
IF YOU PLAY THROUGH 24 TIMES, SYLVIA ATTACKS!
I DON'T GET THESE GAMING REFS!
WHOK
THEN LET'S JUST CAPTURE ...
...THIS MEMORY ON FILM.
WHAT DO YOU MEAN?

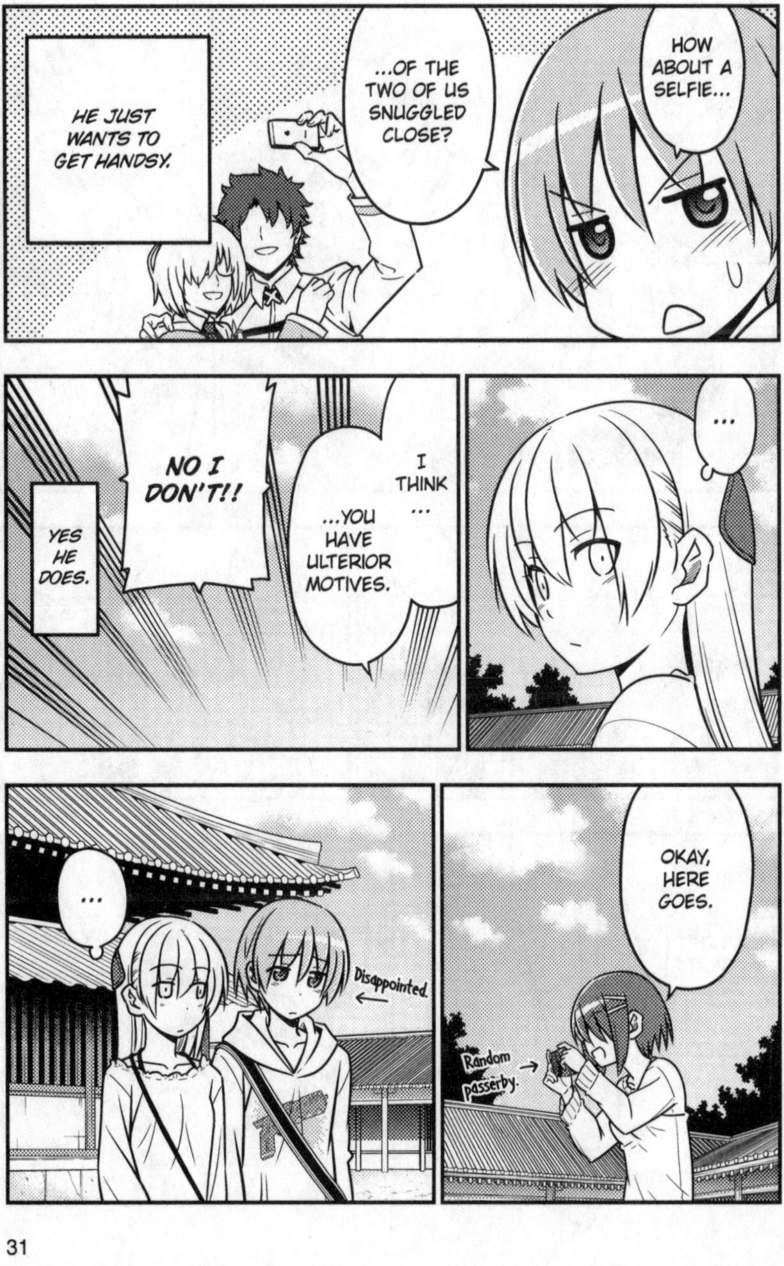
HOW ABOUT A SELFIE...
...OF THE TWO OF US SNUGGLED CLOSE?
HE JUST WANTS TO GET HANDSY.
...
I THINK ...
...YOU HAVE ULTERIOR MOTIVES.
NO I DON'T!!
YES HE DOES.
OKAY, HERE GOES.
Random passerby.
...
Disappointed.

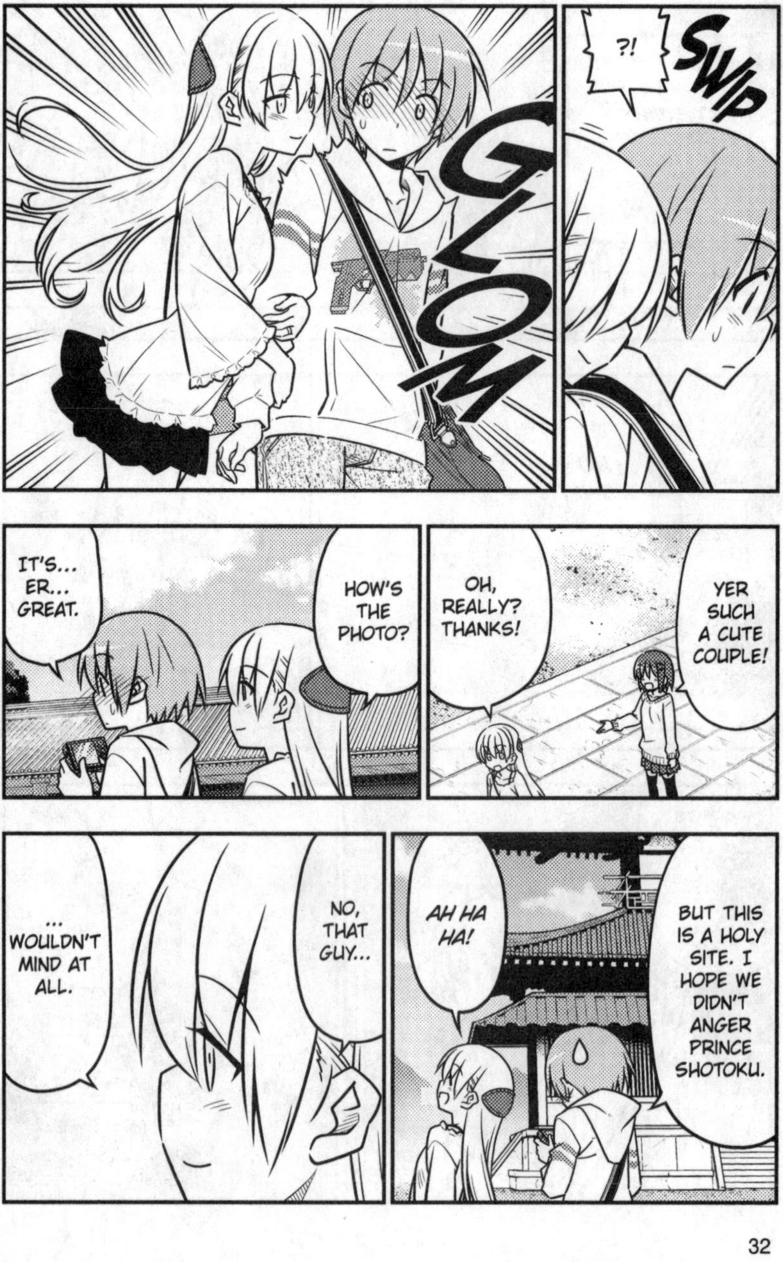
?!
SWIP
GLOM
YER SUCH A CUTE COUPLE!
OH, REALLY? THANKS!
HOW'S THE PHOTO?
IT'S... ER... GREAT.
BUT THIS IS A HOLY SITE. I HOPE WE DIDN'T ANGER PRINCE SHOTOKU.
AH HA HA!
NO, THAT GUY...
... WOULDN'T MIND AT ALL.

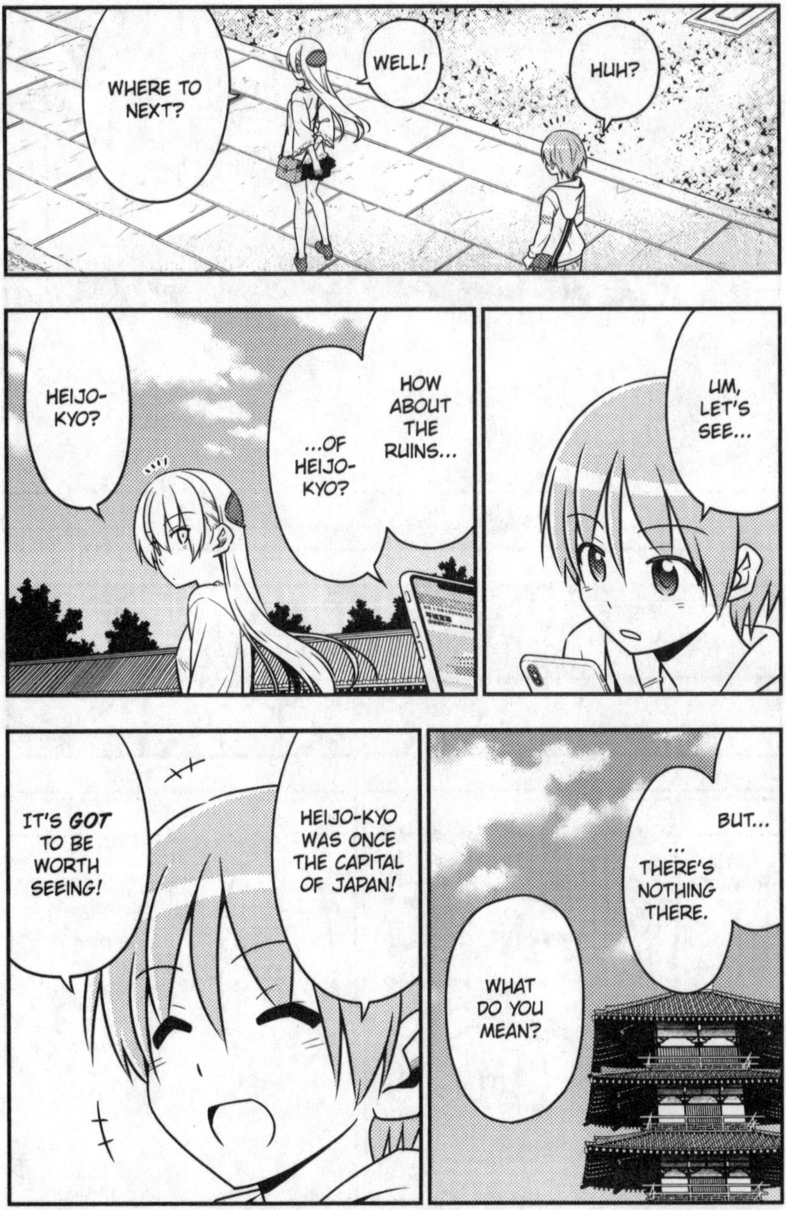
HUH?
WELL!
WHERE TO NEXT?
UM, LET'S SEE...
HOW ABOUT THE RUINS...
...OF HEIJO-KYO?
HEIJO-KYO?
BUT... ...THERE'S NOTHING THERE.
WHAT DO YOU MEAN?
HEIJO-KYO WAS ONCE THE CAPITAL OF JAPAN!
IT'S **GOT** TO BE WORTH SEEING!

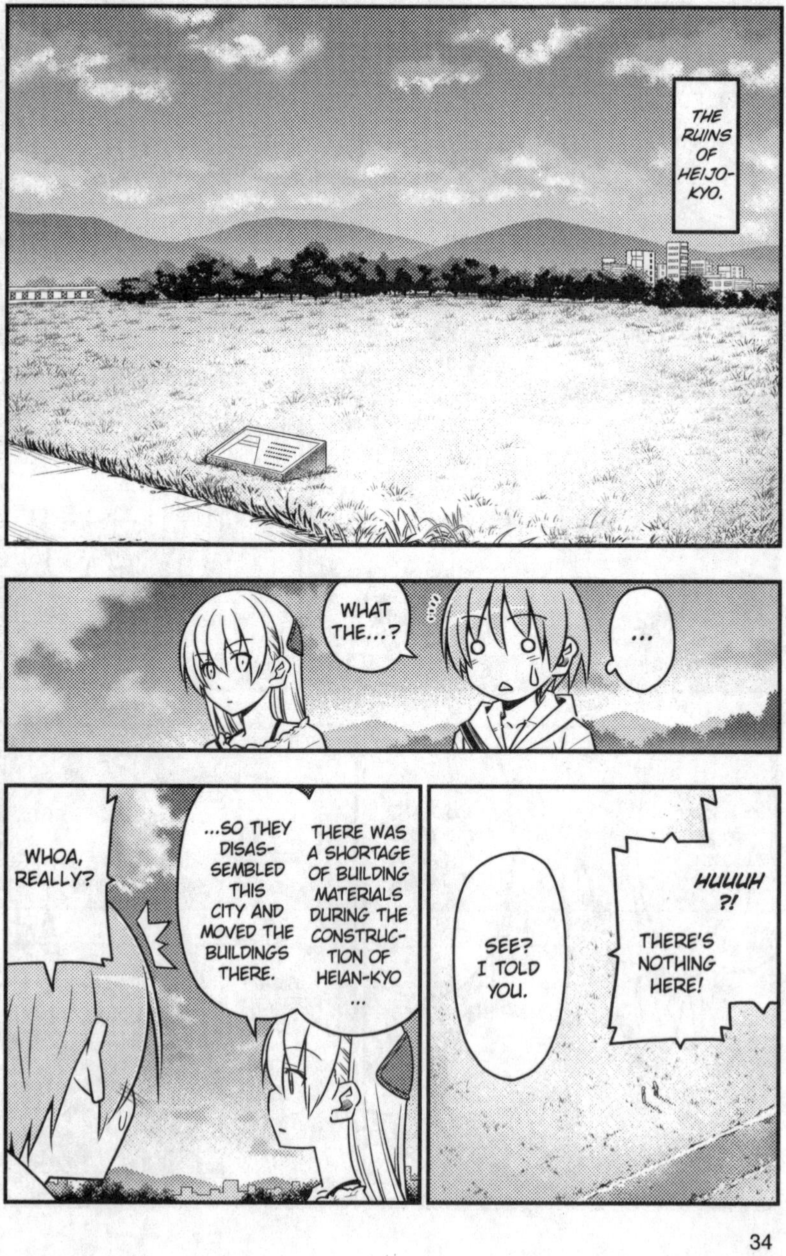
THE RUINS OF HEIJO-KYO.
...
WHAT THE...?
HUUUH?! THERE'S NOTHING HERE!
SEE? I TOLD YOU.
THERE WAS A SHORTAGE OF BUILDING MATERIALS DURING THE CONSTRUCTION OF HEIAN-KYO...
...SO THEY DISASSEMBLED THIS CITY AND MOVED THE BUILDINGS THERE.
WHOA, REALLY?

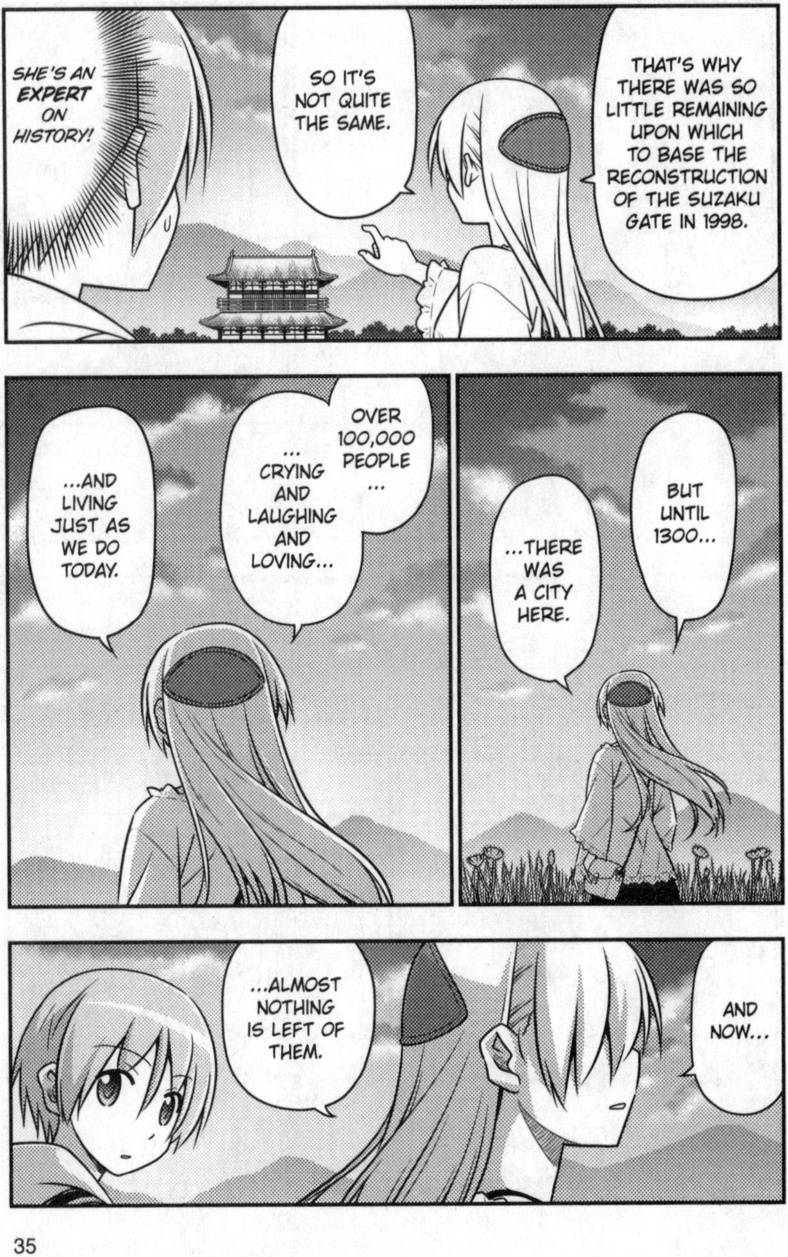
THAT'S WHY THERE WAS SO LITTLE REMAINING UPON WHICH TO BASE THE RECONSTRUCTION OF THE SUZAKU GATE IN 1998.
SO IT'S NOT QUITE THE SAME.
SHE'S AN *EXPERT* ON HISTORY!
BUT UNTIL 1300...
...THERE WAS A CITY HERE.
OVER 100,000 PEOPLE ...
... CRYING AND LAUGHING AND LOVING...
...AND LIVING JUST AS WE DO TODAY.
AND NOW...
...ALMOST NOTHING IS LEFT OF THEM.

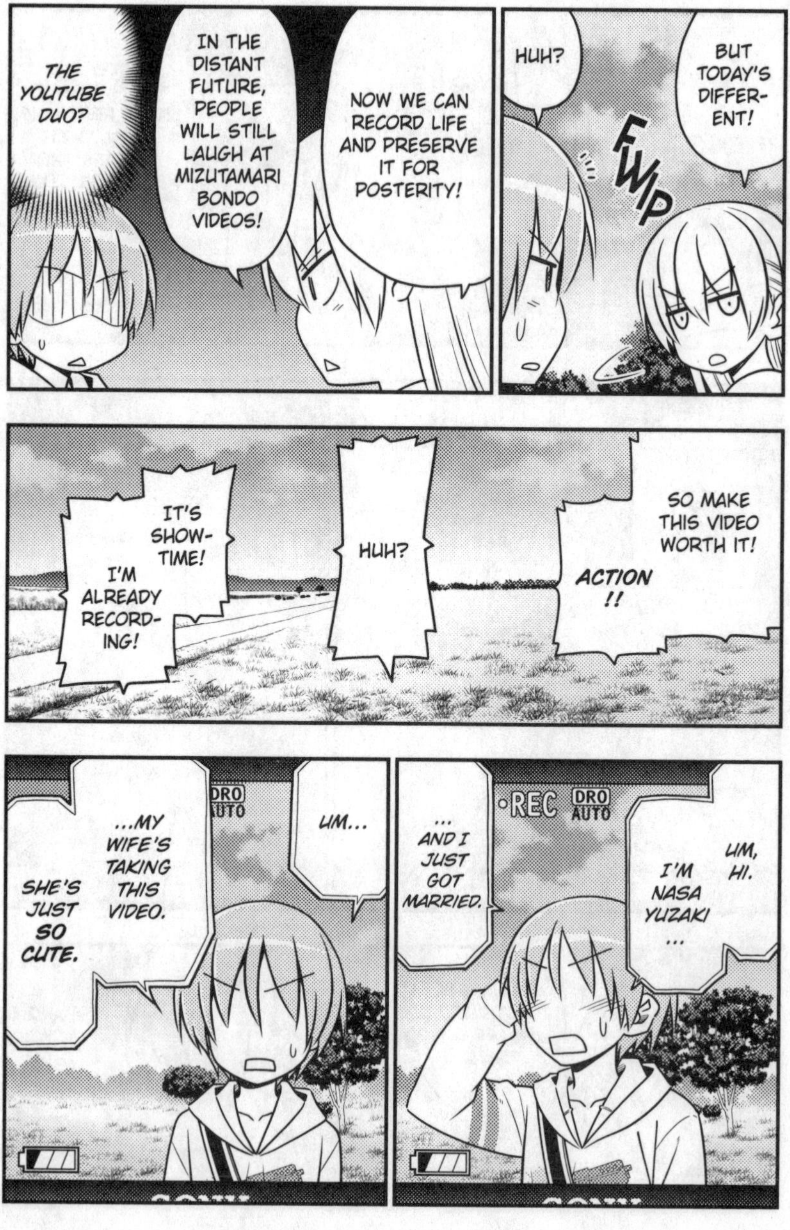
BUT TODAY'S DIFFER-ENT!
HUH?
FWIP
NOW WE CAN RECORD LIFE AND PRESERVE IT FOR POSTERITY!
IN THE DISTANT FUTURE, PEOPLE WILL STILL LAUGH AT MIZUTAMARI BONDO VIDEOS!
THE YOUTUBE DUO?
SO MAKE THIS VIDEO WORTH IT!
ACTION !!
HUH?
IT'S SHOW-TIME!
I'M ALREADY RECORD-ING!
•REC
DRO AUTO
UM, HI.
I'M NASA YUZAKI ...
... AND I JUST GOT MARRIED.
DRO AUTO
UM...
...MY WIFE'S TAKING THIS VIDEO.
SHE'S JUST SO CUTE.

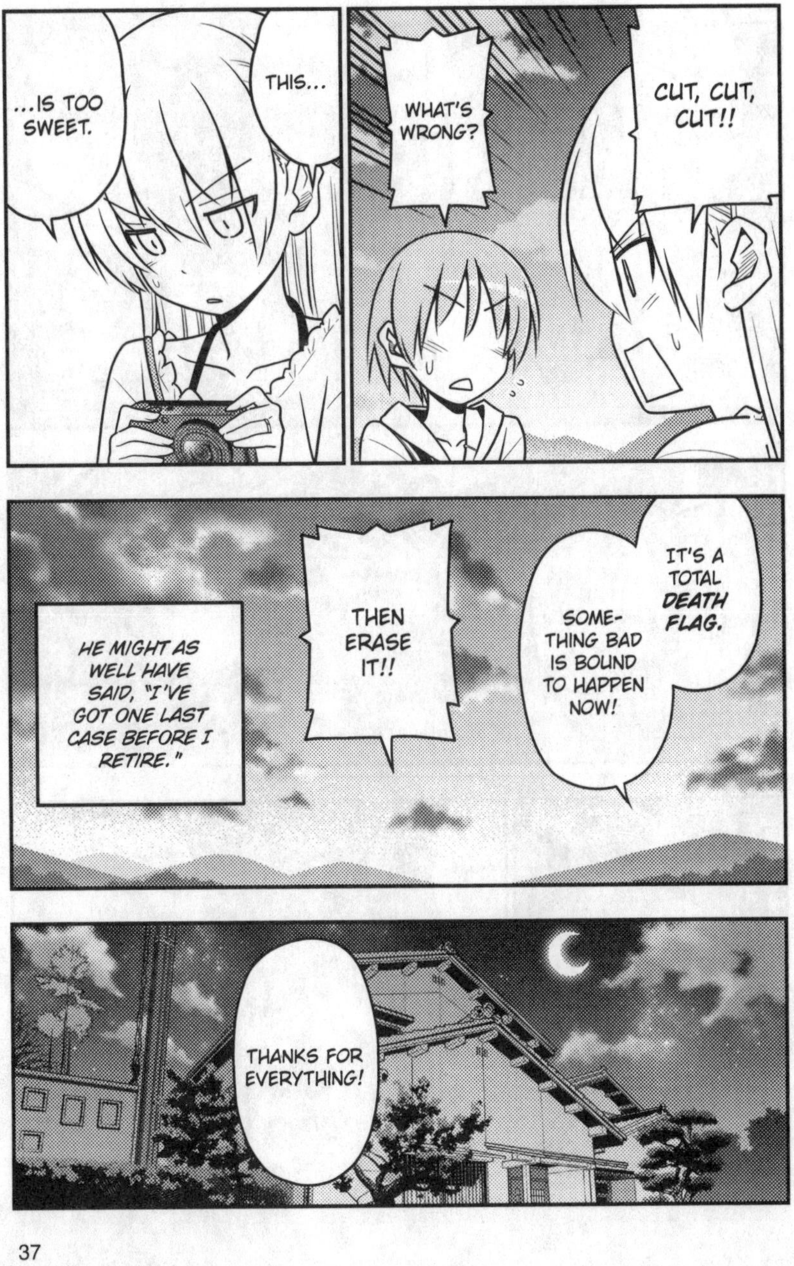
CUT, CUT, CUT!!
WHAT'S WRONG?
THIS...
...IS TOO SWEET.
IT'S A TOTAL **DEATH FLAG.**
SOME-THING BAD IS BOUND TO HAPPEN NOW!
THEN ERASE IT!!
*HE MIGHT AS WELL HAVE SAID, "I'VE GOT ONE LAST CASE BEFORE I RETIRE."*
THANKS FOR EVERYTHING!

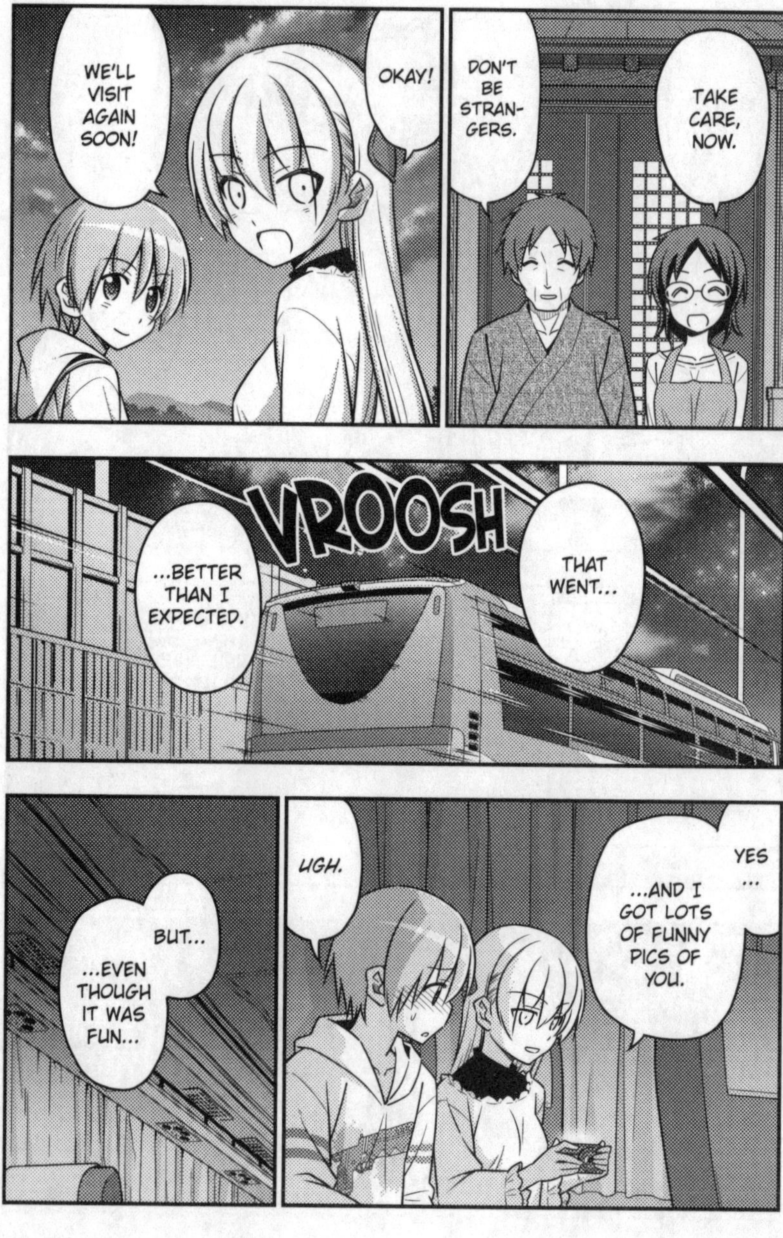
TAKE CARE, NOW.
DON'T BE STRANGERS.
OKAY!
WE'LL VISIT AGAIN SOON!
THAT WENT...
VROOSH
...BETTER THAN I EXPECTED.
YES...
...AND I GOT LOTS OF FUNNY PICS OF YOU.
UGH.
BUT...
...EVEN THOUGH IT WAS FUN...

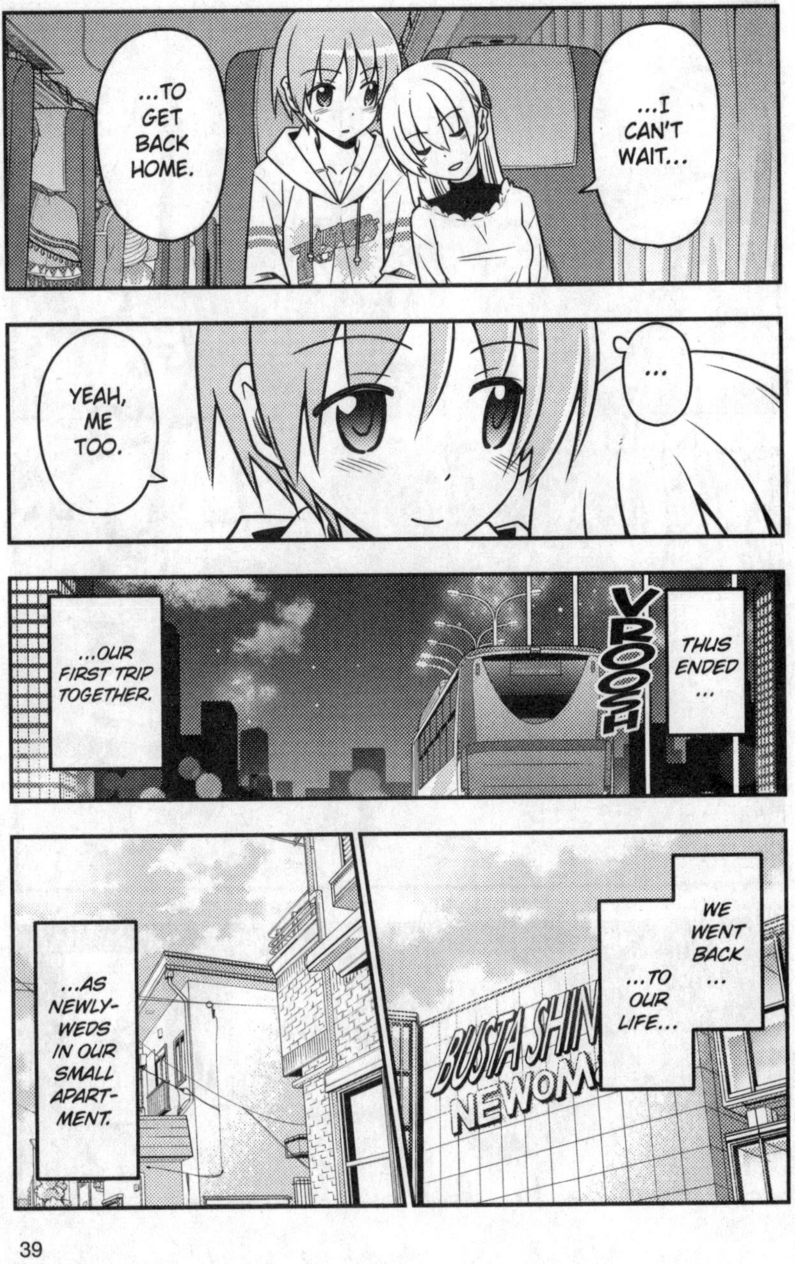
...I CAN'T WAIT...
...TO GET BACK HOME.
...
YEAH, ME TOO.
THUS ENDED ...
VROOSH
...OUR FIRST TRIP TOGETHER.
WE WENT BACK ...
...TO OUR LIFE...
BUSTA SHIN
NEWOM
...AS NEWLY-WEDS IN OUR SMALL APART-MENT.

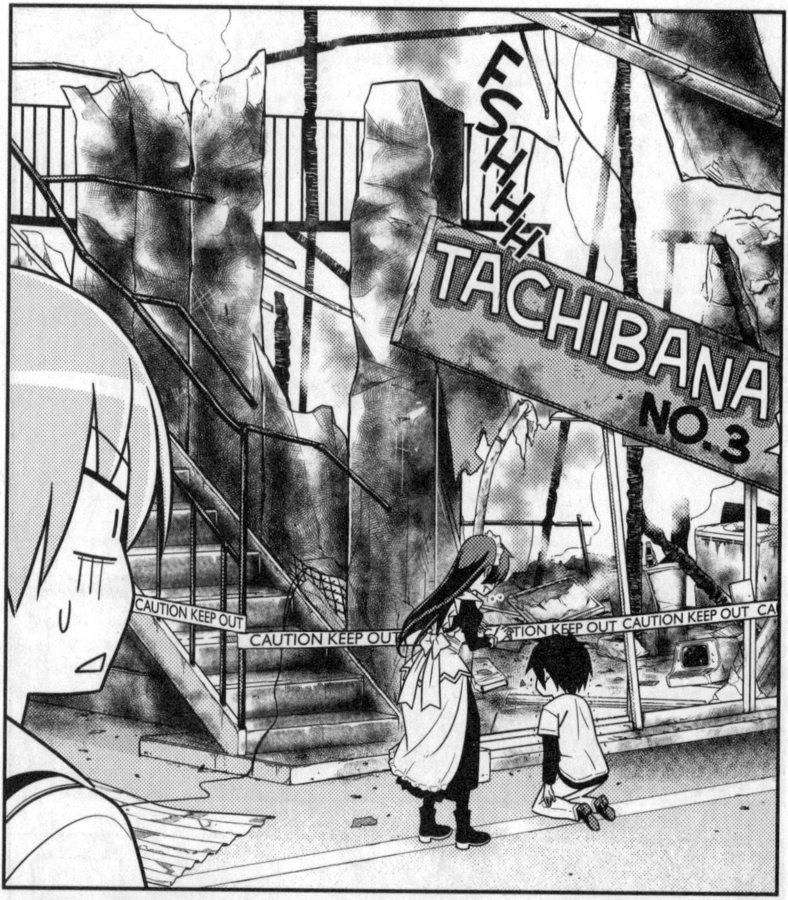
FSHHH
TACHIBANA
NO. 3
CAUTION KEEP OUT
CAUTION KEEP OUT
CAUTION KEEP OUT CAUTION KEEP OUT CA

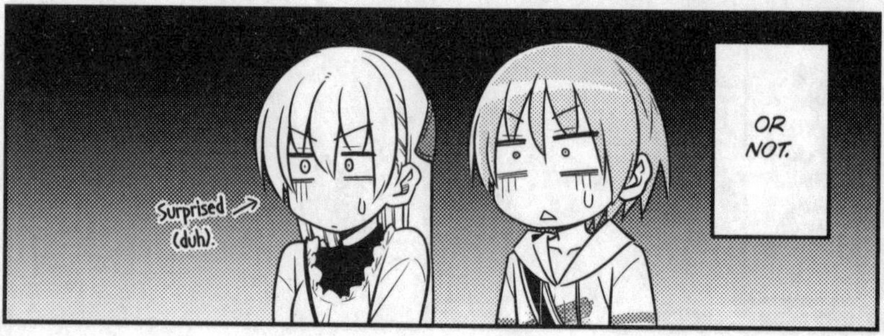
OR NOT.
Surprised (duh).

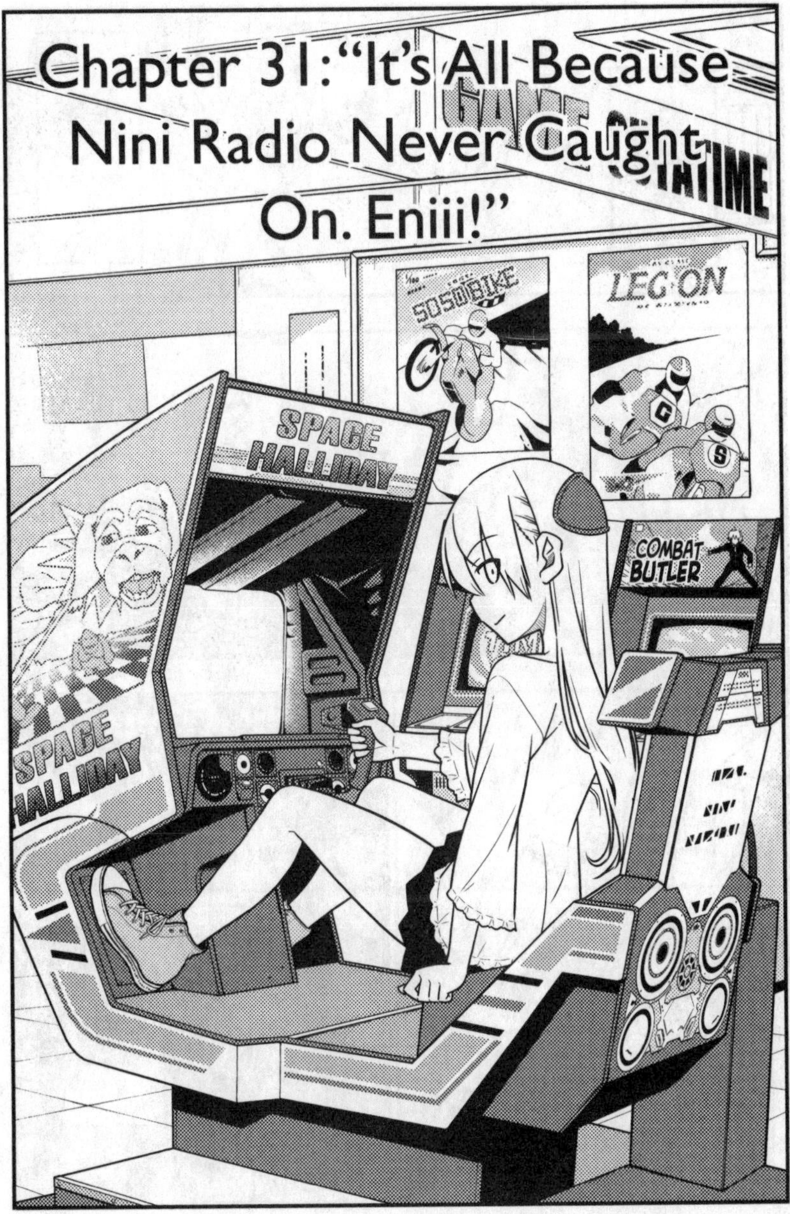
Chapter 31: "It's All Because Nini Radio Never Caught On. Eniii!"
SOSOBIKE
LEG·ON
SPACE HALLIDAY
COMBAT BUTLER
SPACE HALLIDAY

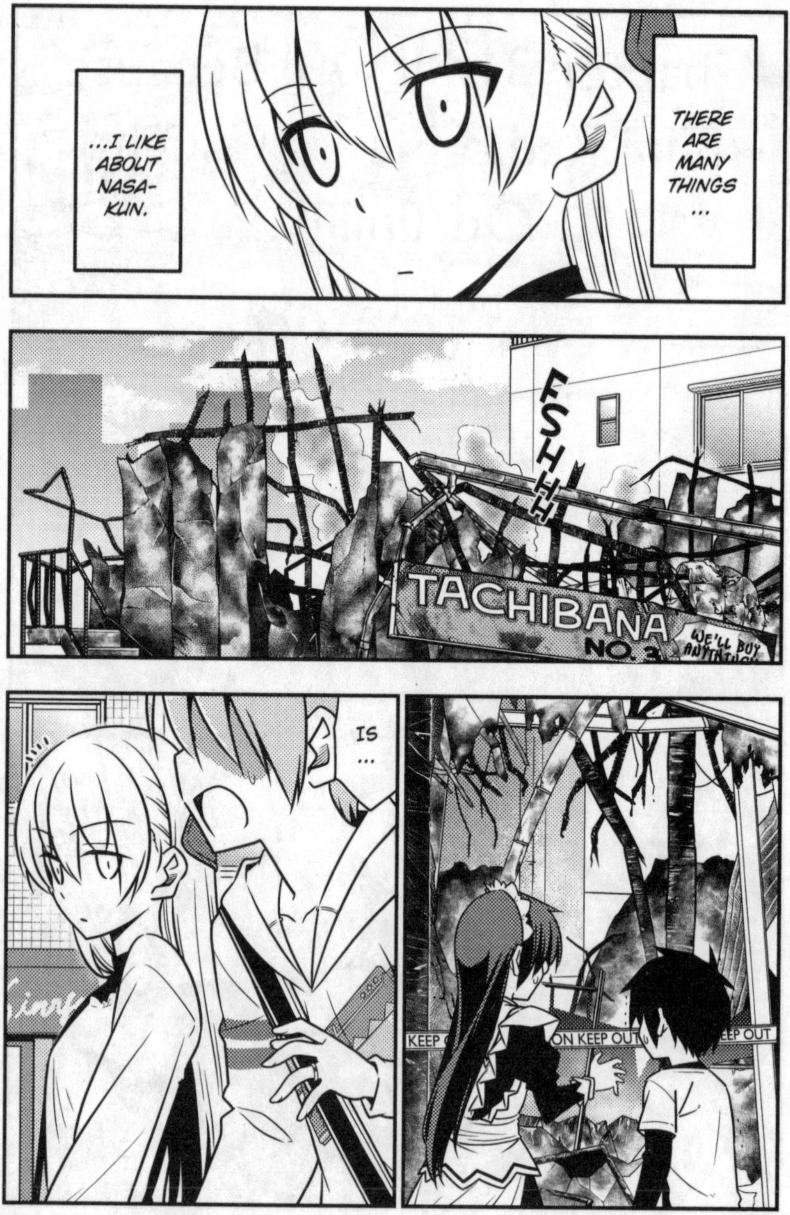
THERE ARE MANY THINGS ...
...I LIKE ABOUT NASA-KUN.
FSHHH
TACHIBANA
NO. 3
WE'LL BUY
KEEP
ON KEEP OUT
IS ...

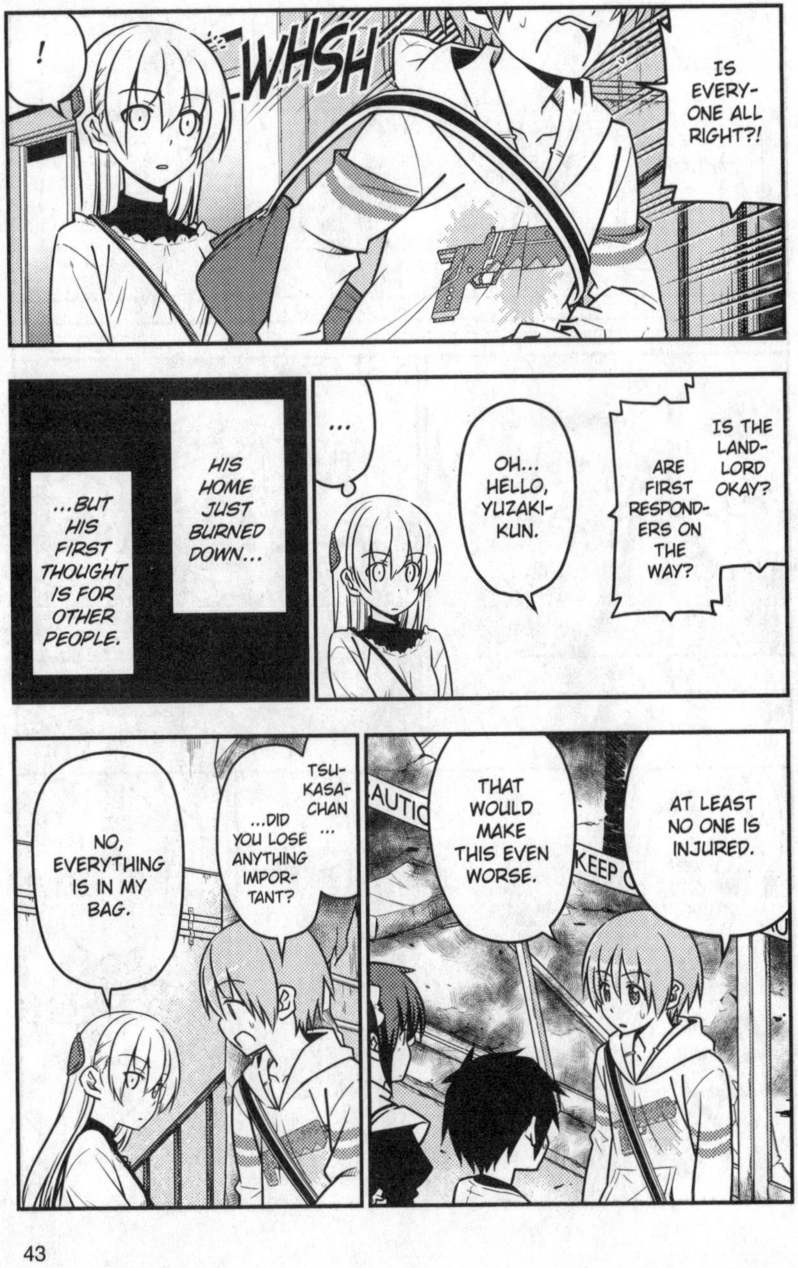
IS EVERYONE ALL RIGHT?!
WHSH
!
IS THE LANDLORD OKAY?
ARE FIRST RESPONDERS ON THE WAY?
OH... HELLO, YUZAKI-KUN.
...
HIS HOME JUST BURNED DOWN...
...BUT HIS FIRST THOUGHT IS FOR OTHER PEOPLE.
AT LEAST NO ONE IS INJURED.
THAT WOULD MAKE THIS EVEN WORSE.
TSUKASA-CHAN...
...DID YOU LOSE ANYTHING IMPORTANT?
NO, EVERYTHING IS IN MY BAG.

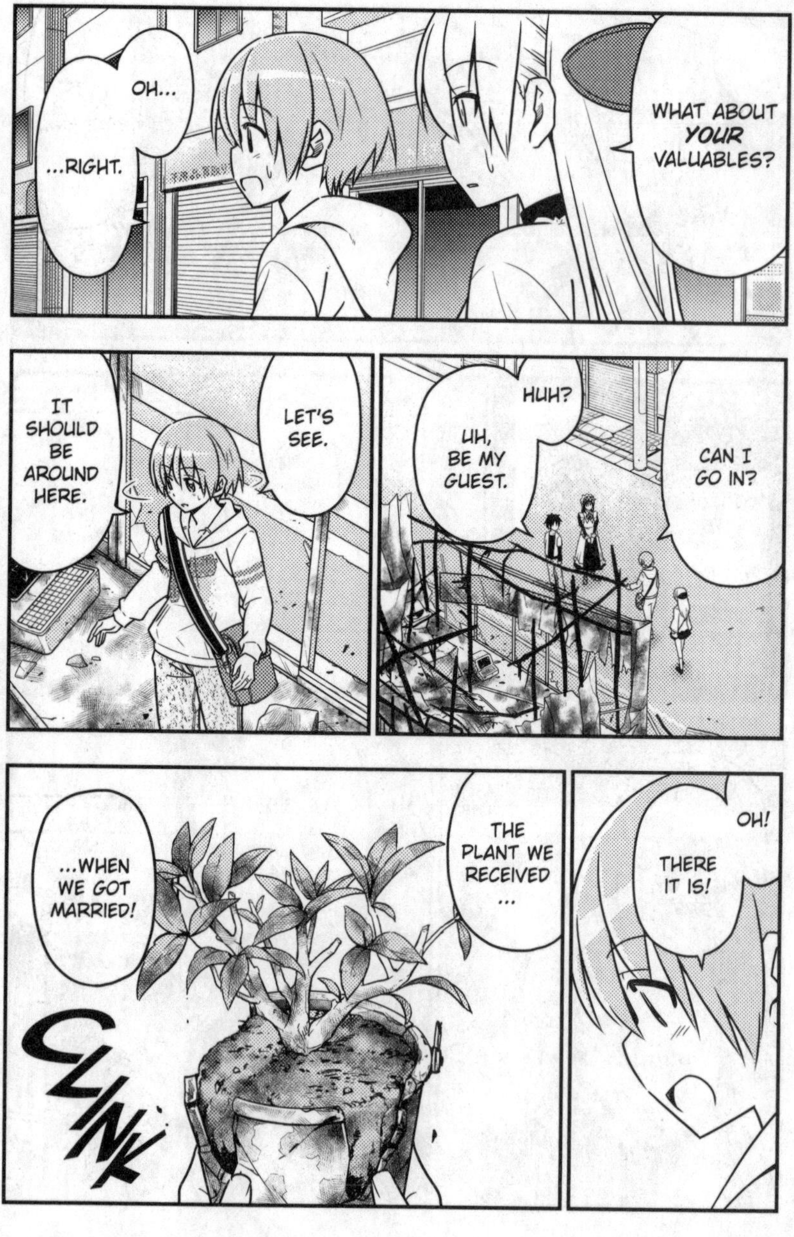
WHAT ABOUT YOUR VALUABLES?
OH...
...RIGHT.
CAN I GO IN?
HUH?
UH, BE MY GUEST.
LET'S SEE.
IT SHOULD BE AROUND HERE.
OH!
THERE IT IS!
THE PLANT WE RECEIVED ...
...WHEN WE GOT MARRIED!
CLINK

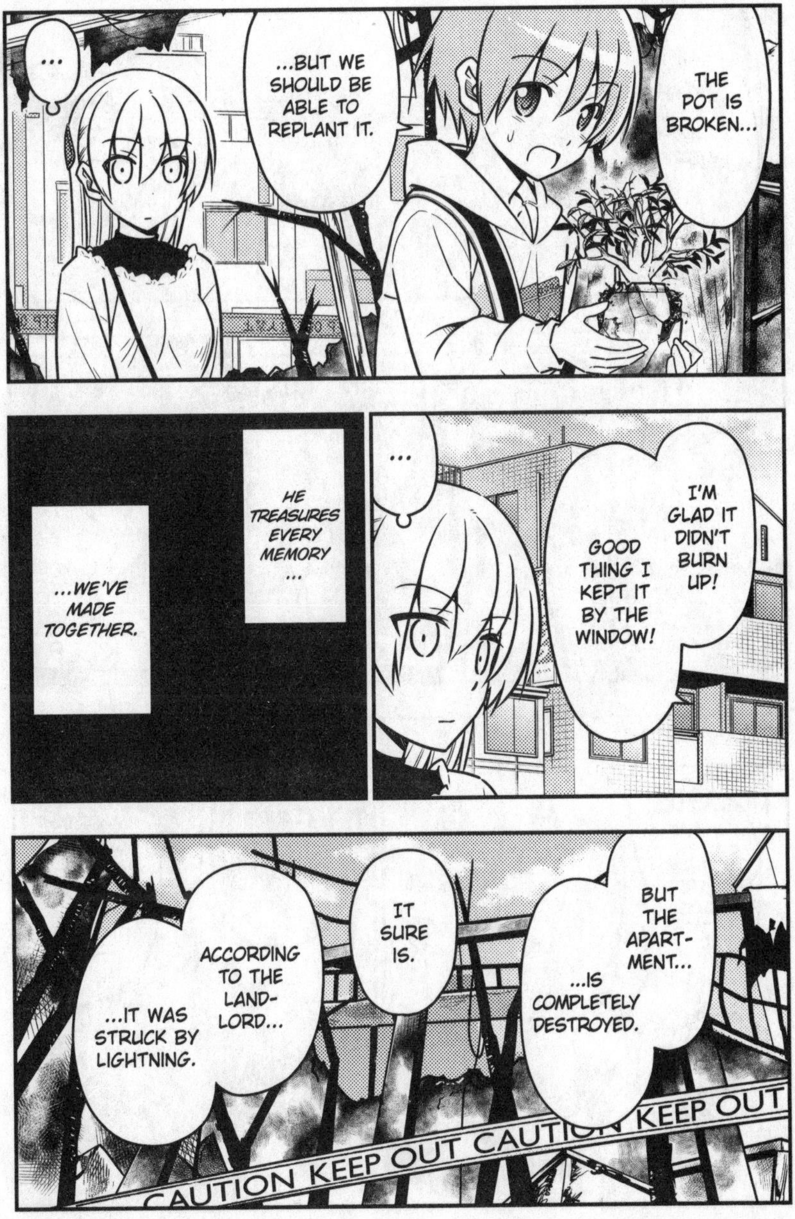
THE POT IS BROKEN...
...BUT WE SHOULD BE ABLE TO REPLANT IT.
...
I'M GLAD IT DIDN'T BURN UP!
GOOD THING I KEPT IT BY THE WINDOW!
...
HE TREASURES EVERY MEMORY...
...WE'VE MADE TOGETHER.
BUT THE APARTMENT...
...IS COMPLETELY DESTROYED.
IT SURE IS.
ACCORDING TO THE LANDLORD...
...IT WAS STRUCK BY LIGHTNING.
CAUTION KEEP OUT CAUTION KEEP OUT

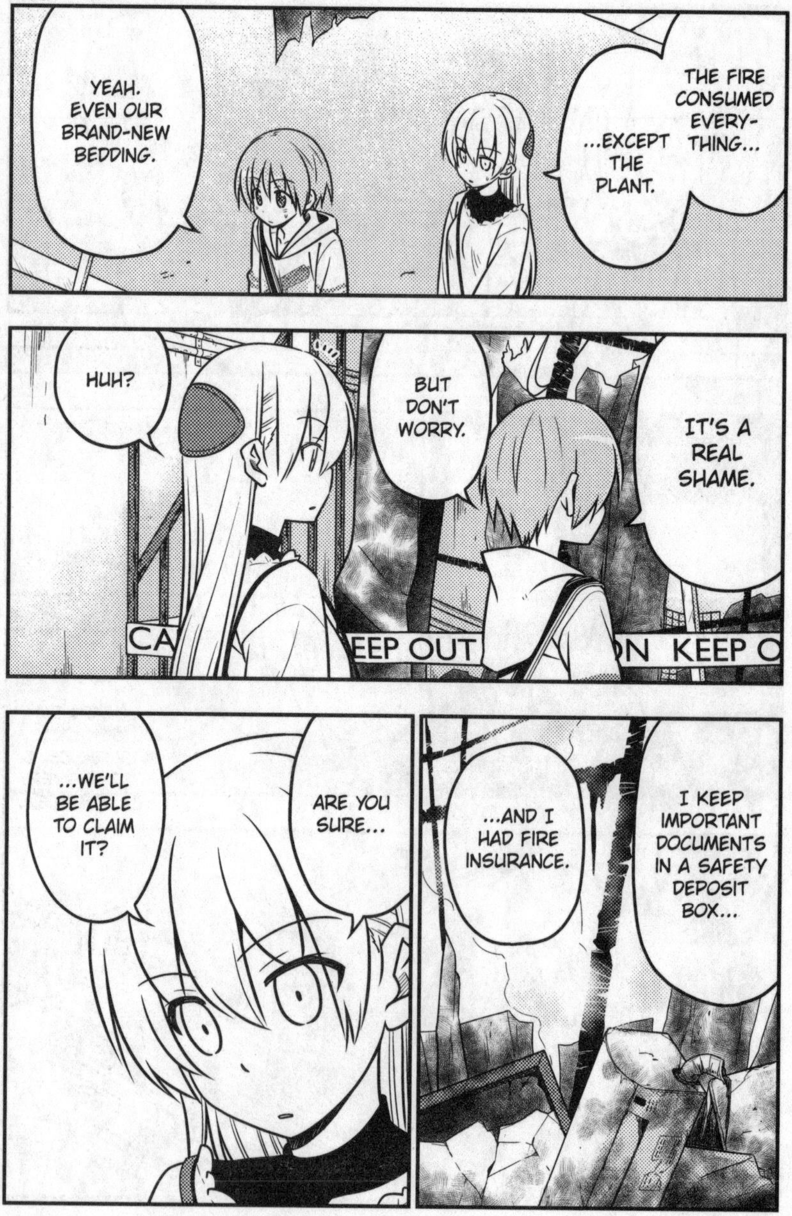
THE FIRE CONSUMED EVERY-THING...
...EXCEPT THE PLANT.
YEAH. EVEN OUR BRAND-NEW BEDDING.
IT'S A REAL SHAME.
BUT DON'T WORRY.
HUH?
I KEEP IMPORTANT DOCUMENTS IN A SAFETY DEPOSIT BOX...
...AND I HAD FIRE INSURANCE.
ARE YOU SURE...
...WE'LL BE ABLE TO CLAIM IT?

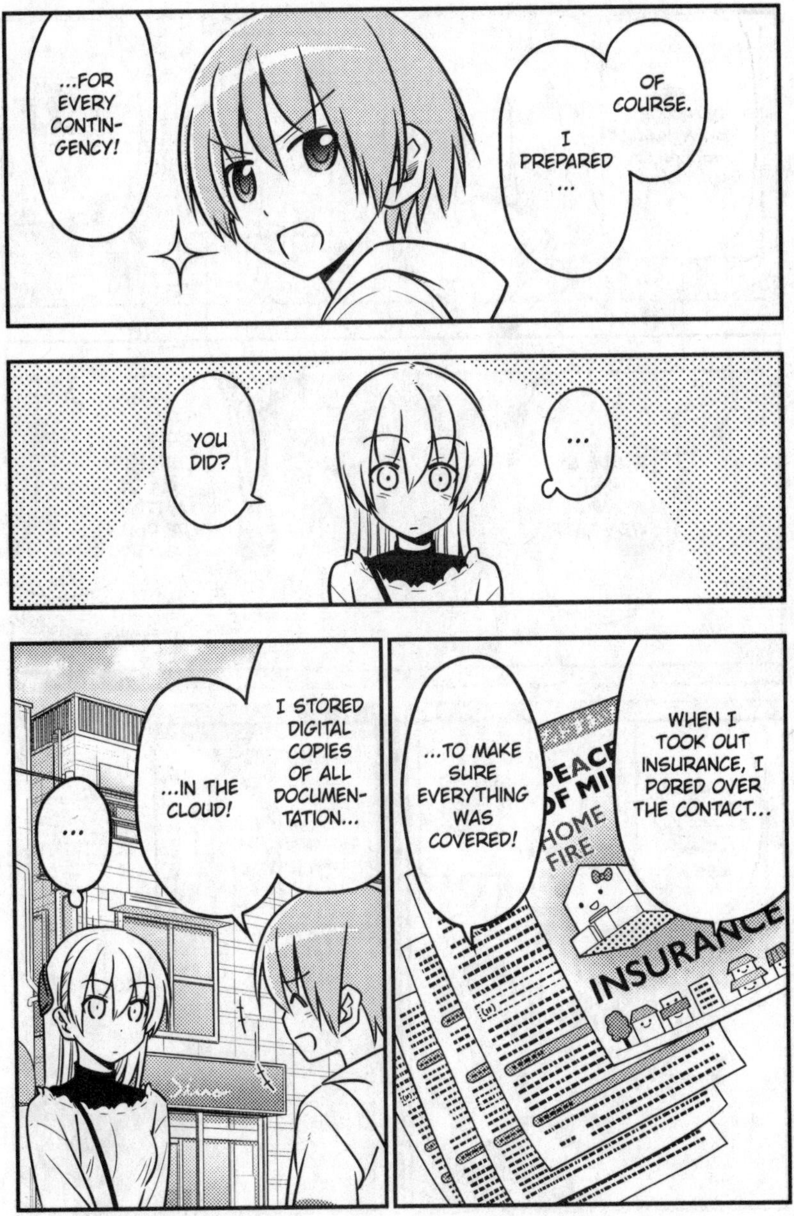
OF COURSE. I PREPARED ...
...FOR EVERY CONTIN-GENCY!
...
YOU DID?
WHEN I TOOK OUT INSURANCE, I PORED OVER THE CONTACT...
...TO MAKE SURE EVERYTHING WAS COVERED!
HOME
FIRE
INSURANCE
I STORED DIGITAL COPIES OF ALL DOCUMEN-TATION...
...IN THE CLOUD!
...

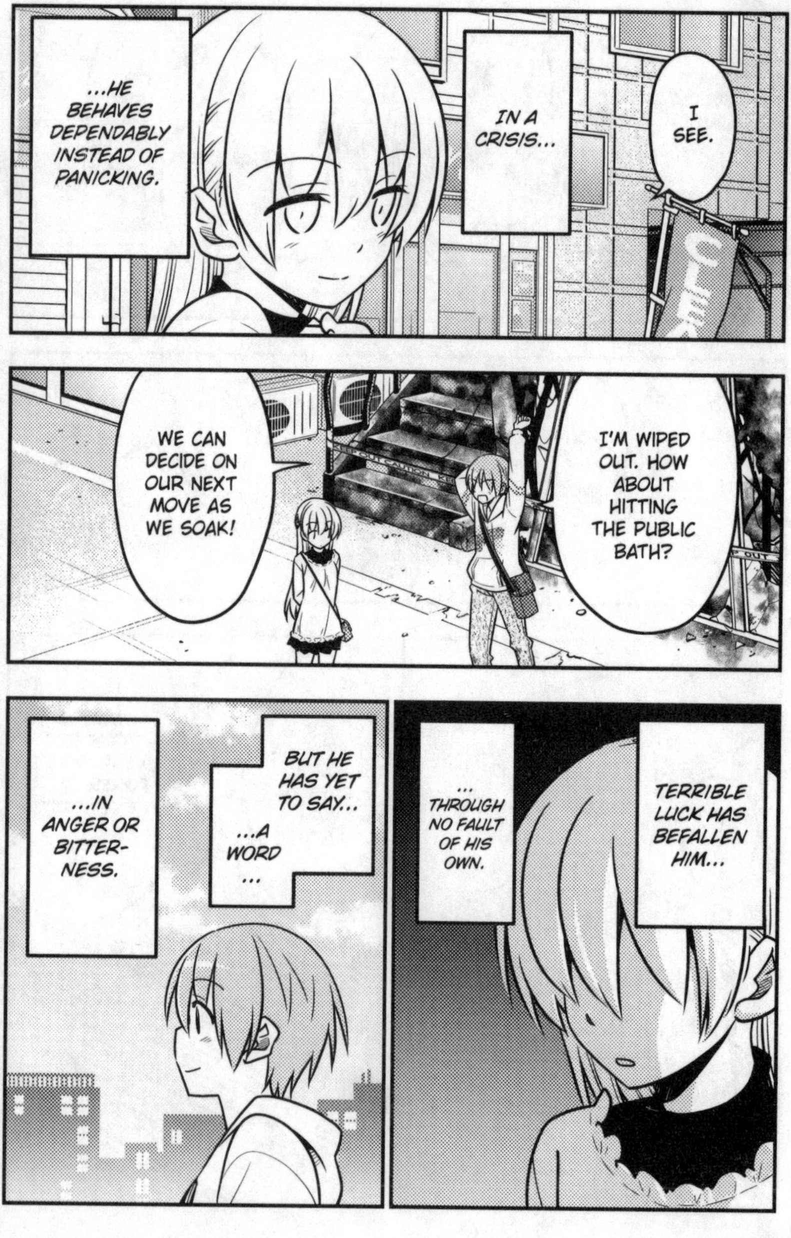
I SEE.
IN A CRISIS...
...HE BEHAVES DEPENDABLY INSTEAD OF PANICKING.
I'M WIPED OUT. HOW ABOUT HITTING THE PUBLIC BATH?
WE CAN DECIDE ON OUR NEXT MOVE AS WE SOAK!
TERRIBLE LUCK HAS BEFALLEN HIM...
...THROUGH NO FAULT OF HIS OWN.
BUT HE HAS YET TO SAY...
...A WORD...
...IN ANGER OR BITTERNESS.

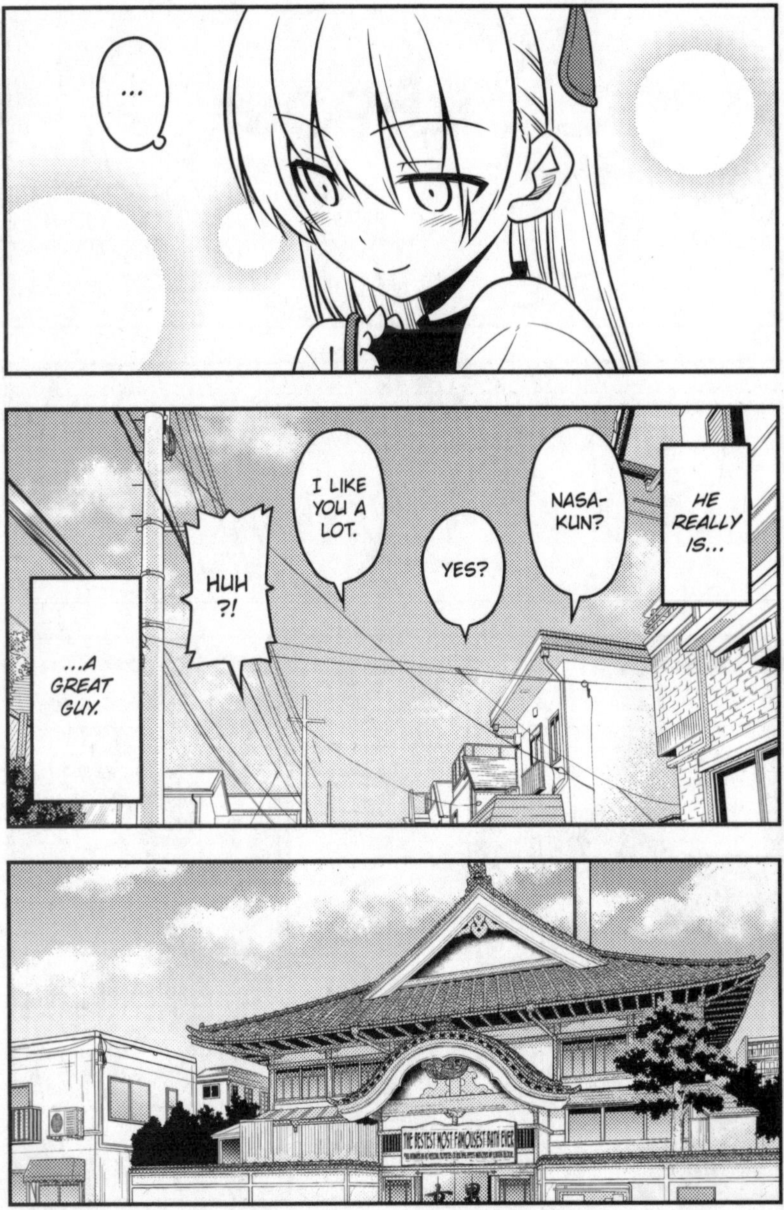
...
HE REALLY IS...
NASA-KUN?
YES?
I LIKE YOU A LOT.
HUH ?!
...A GREAT GUY.
THE BESTEST MOST FAMOUSEST BATH EVER

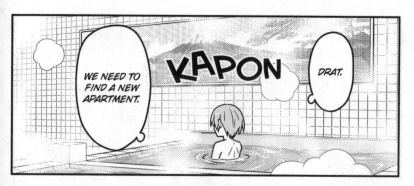

DRAT.
KAPON
WE NEED TO FIND A NEW APARTMENT.
EVEN IF WE GET LUCKY, IT'LL TAKE AT LEAST A WEEK TO MOVE.
WHERE DO WE STAY UNTIL THEN?
I GUESS WE'LL HAVE TO GET A ROOM...
...IN A CHEAP MOTEL.
...
A MOTEL?!
NOW HE PANICS.

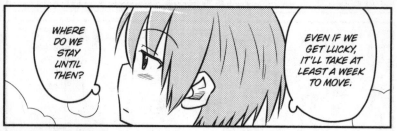

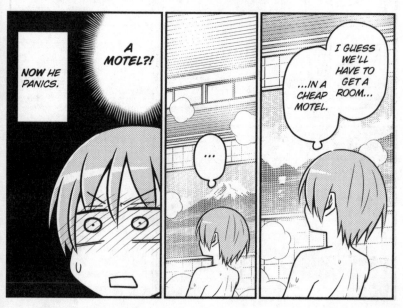

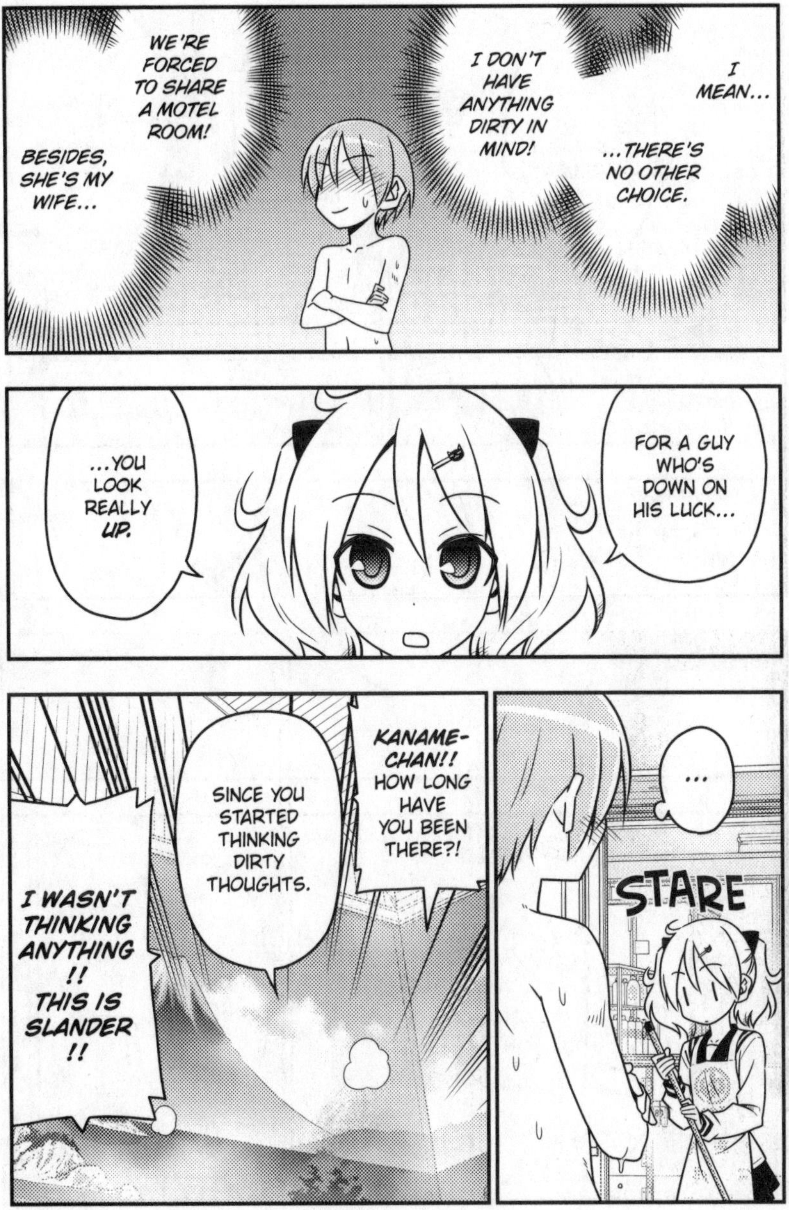
I MEAN...
...THERE'S NO OTHER CHOICE.
I DON'T HAVE ANYTHING DIRTY IN MIND!
WE'RE FORCED TO SHARE A MOTEL ROOM!
BESIDES, SHE'S MY WIFE...
FOR A GUY WHO'S DOWN ON HIS LUCK...
...YOU LOOK REALLY *UP.*
...
STARE
KANAME-CHAN!! HOW LONG HAVE YOU BEEN THERE?!
SINCE YOU STARTED THINKING DIRTY THOUGHTS.
I WASN'T THINKING ANYTHING!! THIS IS SLANDER!!

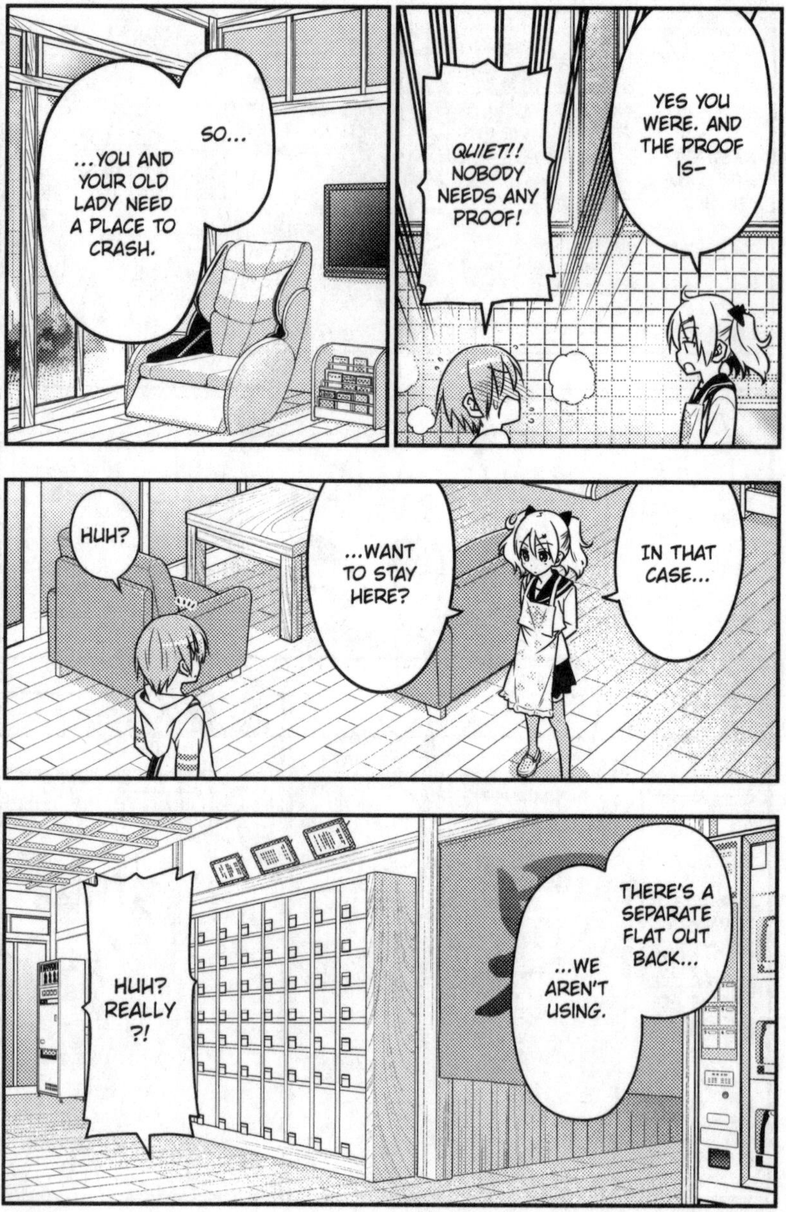
YES YOU WERE. AND THE PROOF IS-
QUIET!! NOBODY NEEDS ANY PROOF!
SO...
...YOU AND YOUR OLD LADY NEED A PLACE TO CRASH.
IN THAT CASE...
...WANT TO STAY HERE?
HUH?
THERE'S A SEPARATE FLAT OUT BACK...
...WE AREN'T USING.
HUH? REALLY ?!

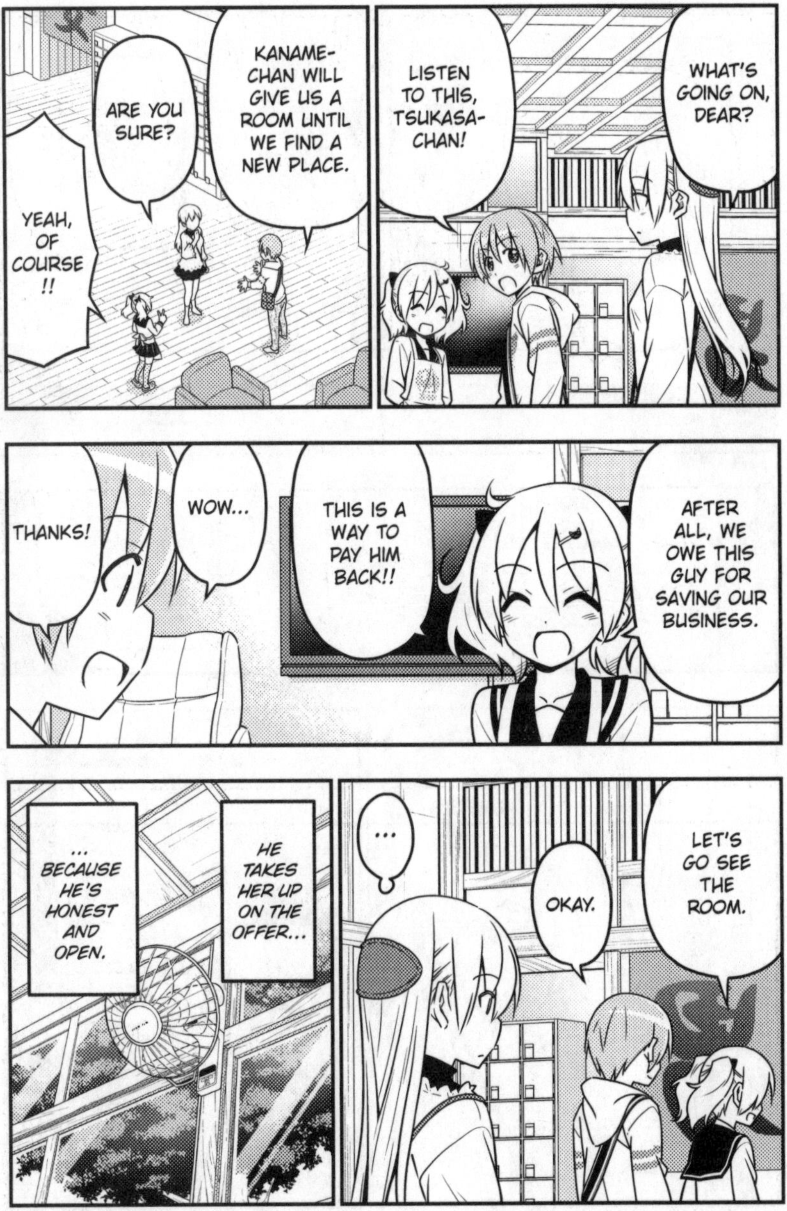
WHAT'S GOING ON, DEAR?
LISTEN TO THIS, TSUKASA-CHAN!
KANAME-CHAN WILL GIVE US A ROOM UNTIL WE FIND A NEW PLACE.
ARE YOU SURE?
YEAH, OF COURSE!!
AFTER ALL, WE OWE THIS GUY FOR SAVING OUR BUSINESS.
THIS IS A WAY TO PAY HIM BACK!!
WOW...
THANKS!
LET'S GO SEE THE ROOM.
OKAY.
...
HE TAKES HER UP ON THE OFFER...
...BECAUSE HE'S HONEST AND OPEN.

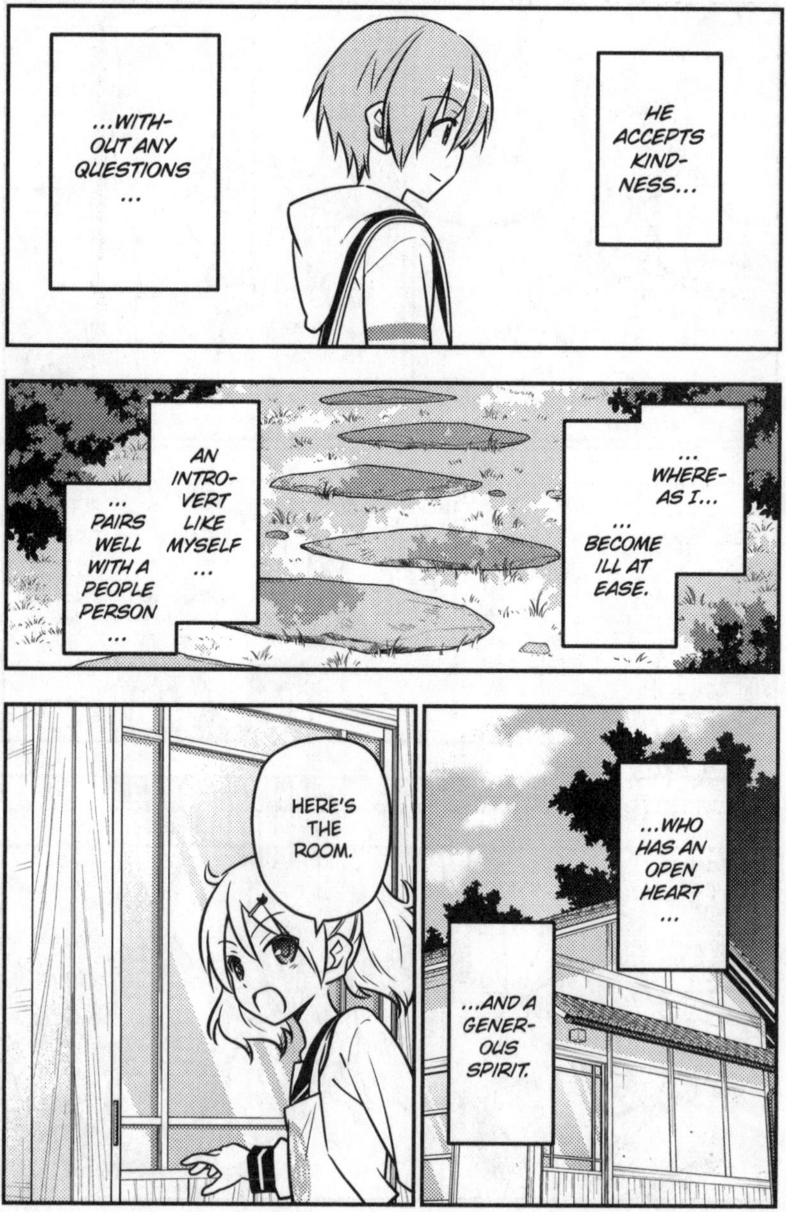
HE ACCEPTS KINDNESS...
...WITHOUT ANY QUESTIONS...
...WHEREAS I...
...BECOME ILL AT EASE.
AN INTROVERT LIKE MYSELF...
...PAIRS WELL WITH A PEOPLE PERSON...
...WHO HAS AN OPEN HEART...
...AND A GENEROUS SPIRIT.
HERE'S THE ROOM.

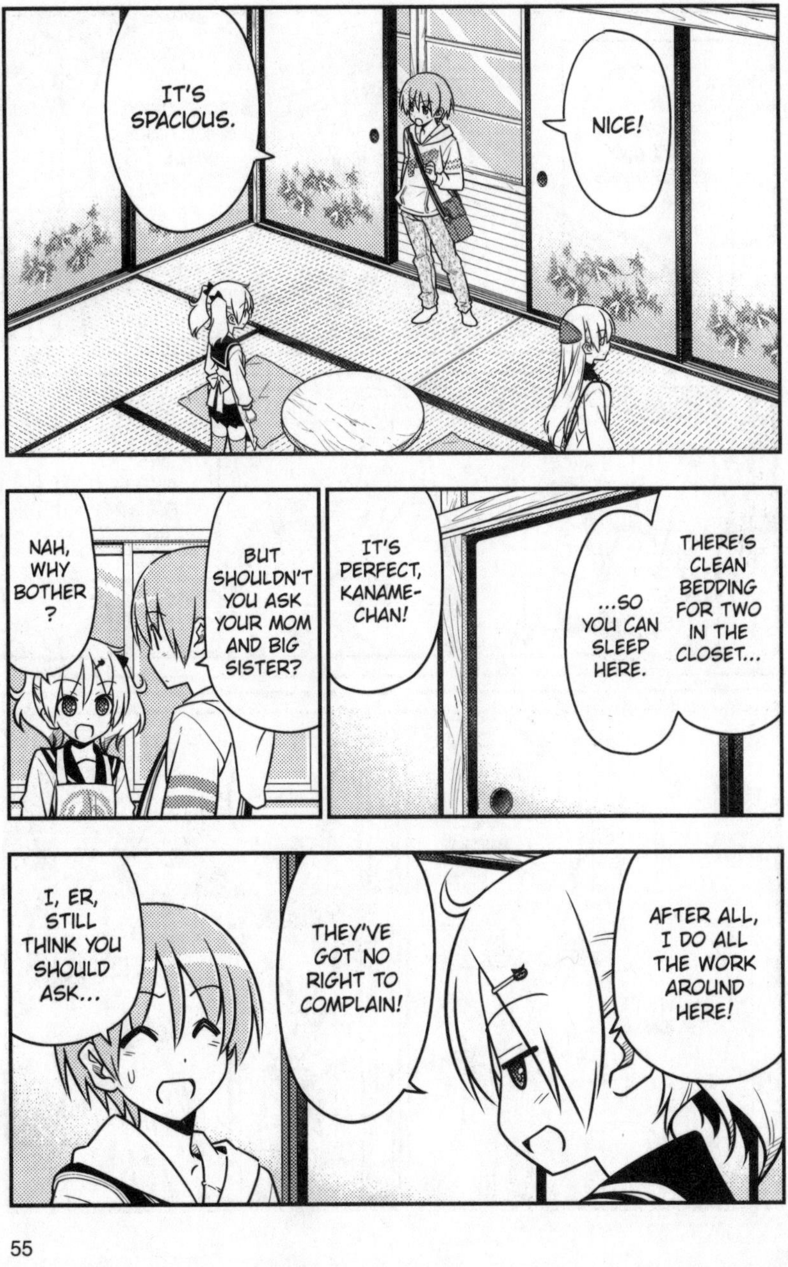
NICE!
IT'S SPACIOUS.
THERE'S CLEAN BEDDING FOR TWO IN THE CLOSET...
...SO YOU CAN SLEEP HERE.
IT'S PERFECT, KANAME-CHAN!
BUT SHOULDN'T YOU ASK YOUR MOM AND BIG SISTER?
NAH, WHY BOTHER?
AFTER ALL, I DO ALL THE WORK AROUND HERE!
THEY'VE GOT NO RIGHT TO COMPLAIN!
I, ER, STILL THINK YOU SHOULD ASK...

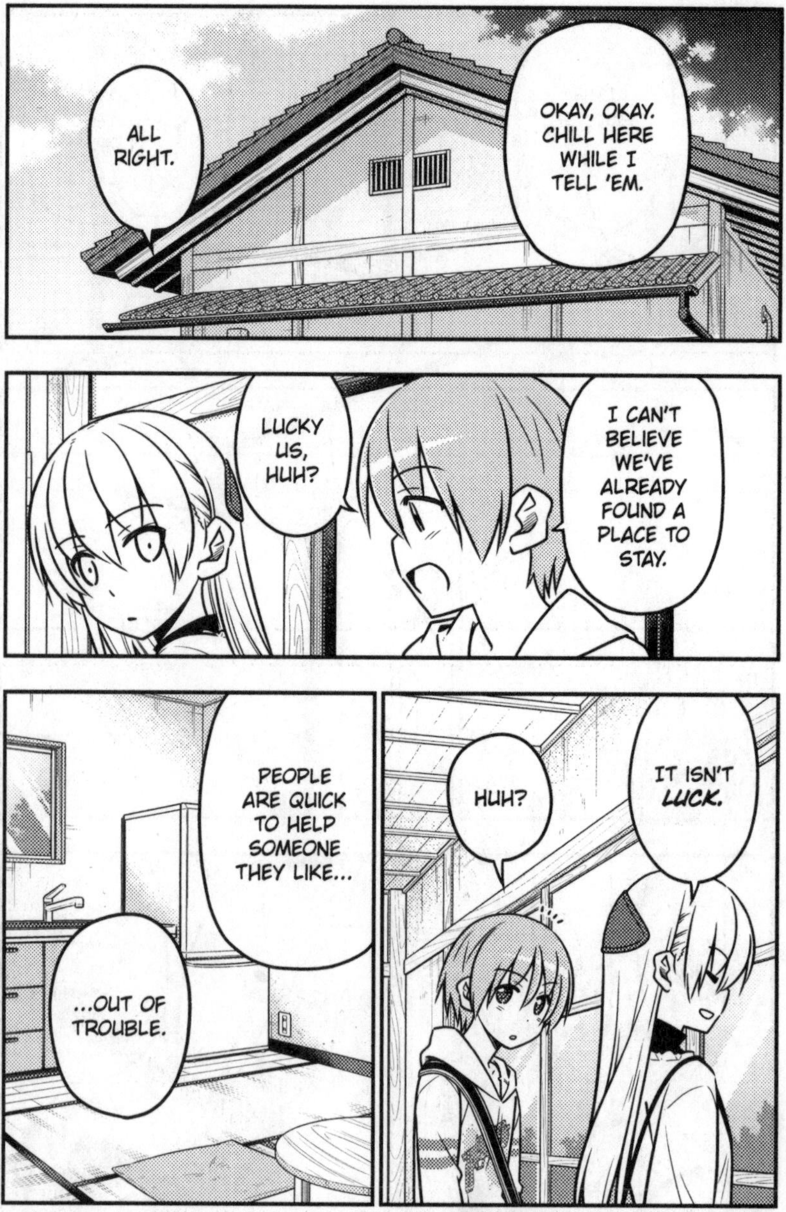
OKAY, OKAY. CHILL HERE WHILE I TELL 'EM.
ALL RIGHT.
I CAN'T BELIEVE WE'VE ALREADY FOUND A PLACE TO STAY.
LUCKY US, HUH?
IT ISN'T *LUCK.*
HUH?
PEOPLE ARE QUICK TO HELP SOMEONE THEY LIKE...
...OUT OF TROUBLE.

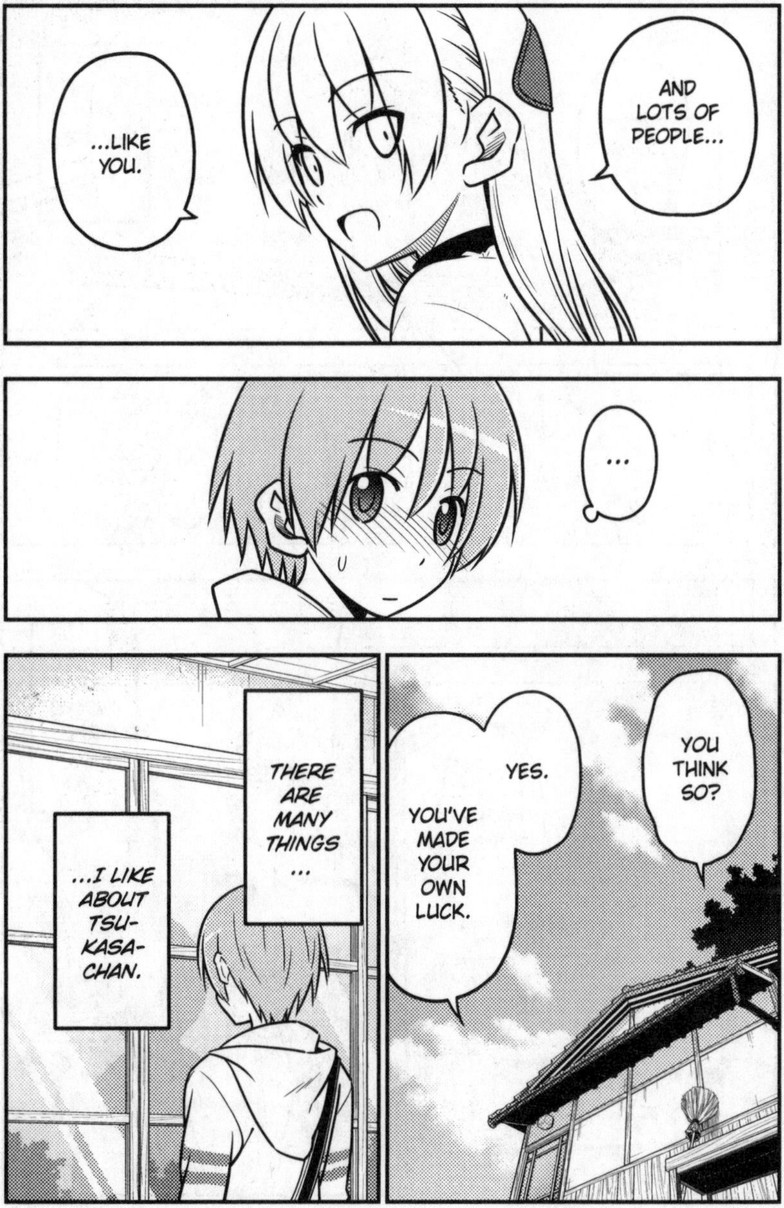
AND LOTS OF PEOPLE...
...LIKE YOU.
...
YOU THINK SO?
YES.
YOU'VE MADE YOUR OWN LUCK.
THERE ARE MANY THINGS...
...I LIKE ABOUT TSU-KASA-CHAN.

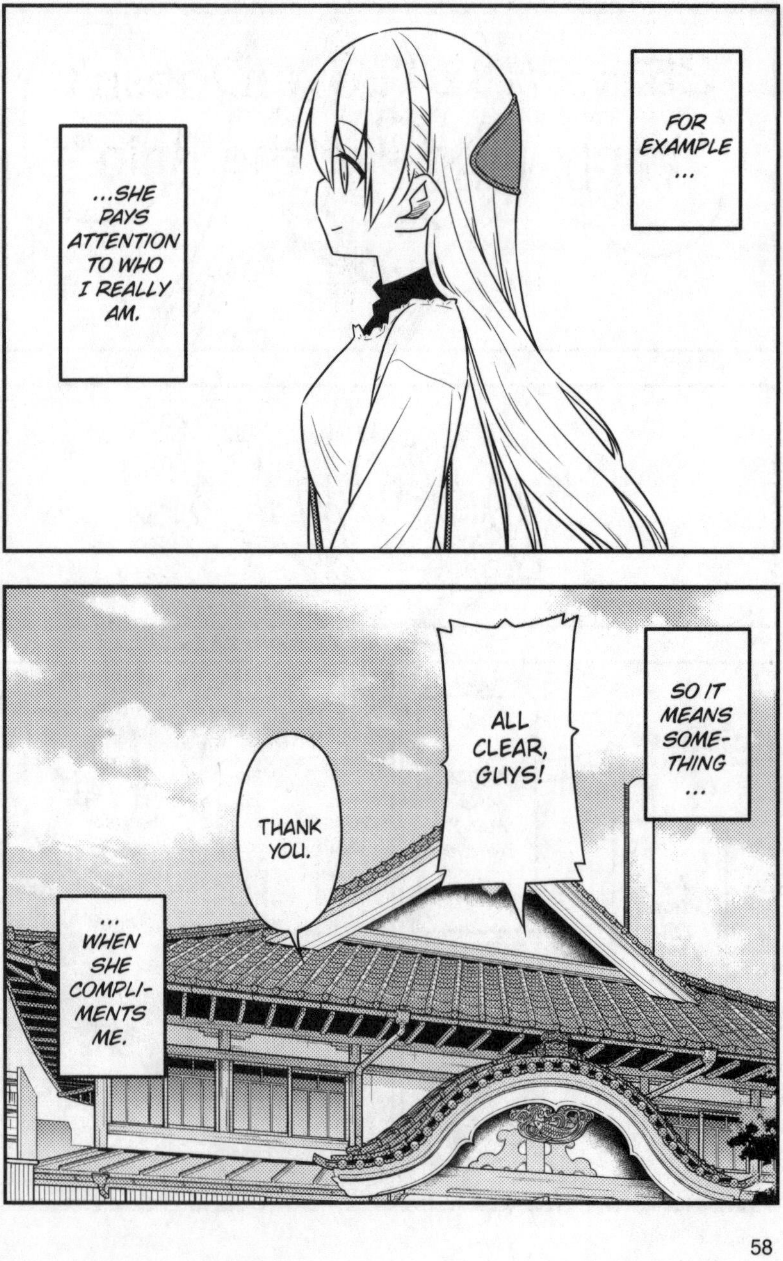
FOR EXAMPLE ...
...SHE PAYS ATTENTION TO WHO I REALLY AM.
SO IT MEANS SOME-THING ...
ALL CLEAR, GUYS!
THANK YOU.
... WHEN SHE COMPLI-MENTS ME.

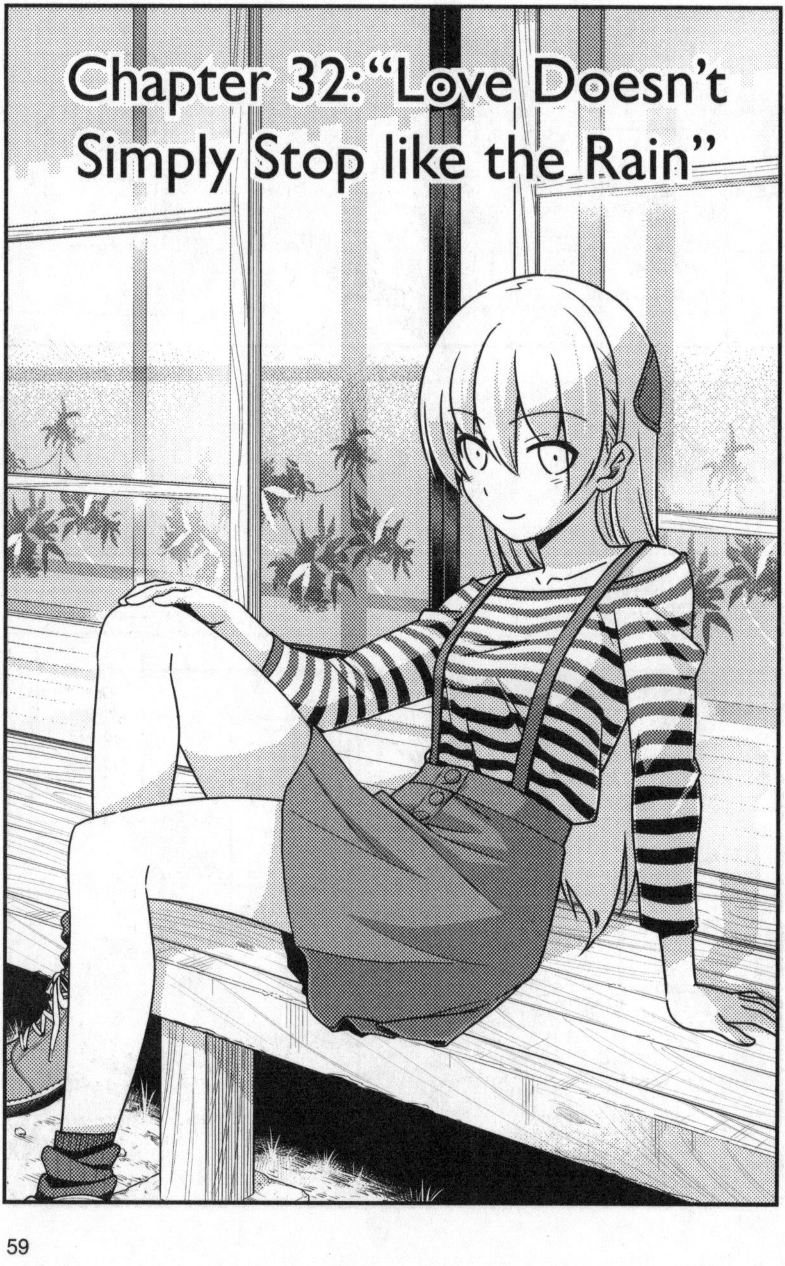
Chapter 32: "Love Doesn't Simply Stop like the Rain"

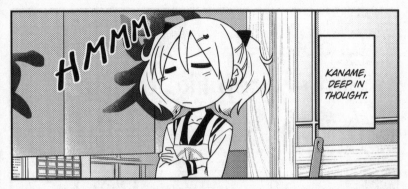

KANAME, DEEP IN THOUGHT.
HMMM
I WANNA HELP THAT NERD OUT...
...BUT WHAT ABOUT MY SISTER AYA?
AFTER ALL ...
... SHE'S INTO HIM.
... BUT ...
...SHE'S SUCH A DIMWIT...
...SHE HASN'T FIGURED OUT HE'S MARRIED.
...! ASTONISHING!
THIS MAN IS...
ARI-MAN

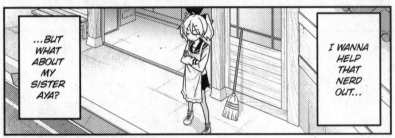

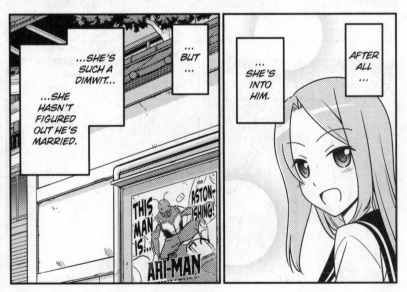

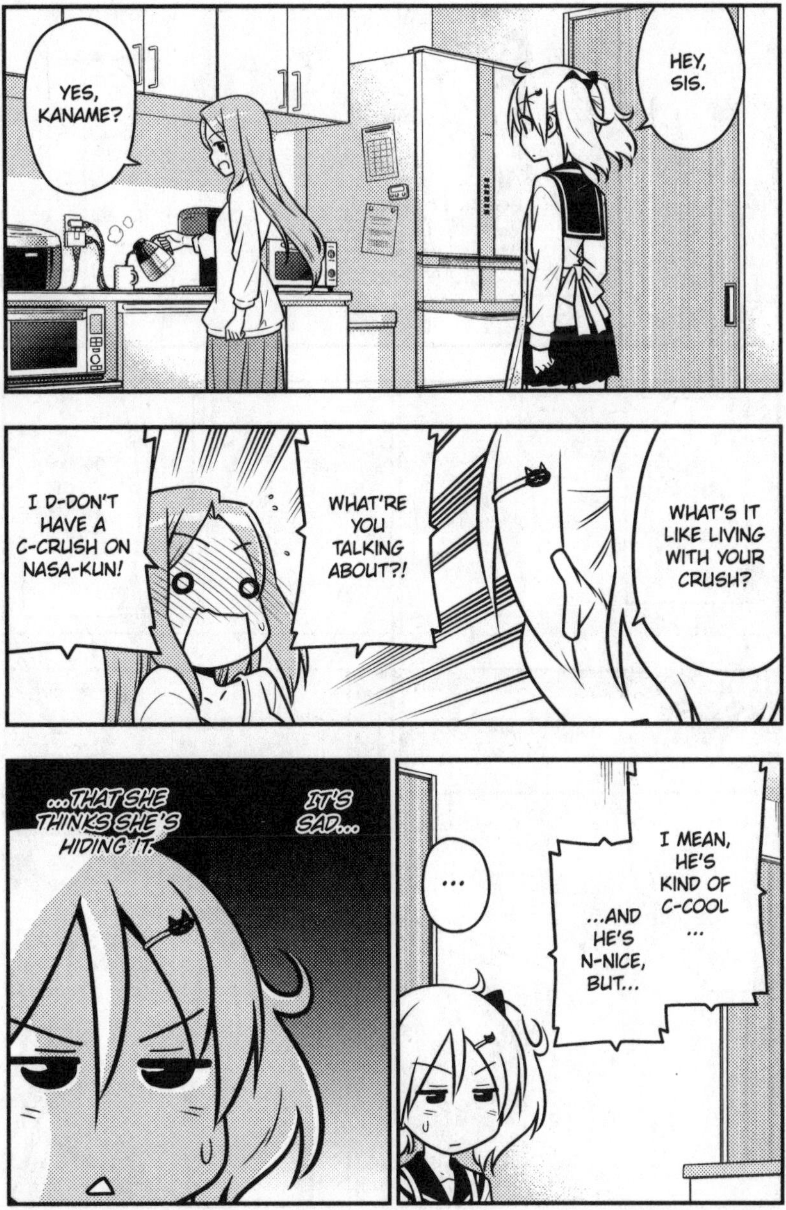
HEY, SIS.
YES, KANAME?
WHAT'S IT LIKE LIVING WITH YOUR CRUSH?
WHAT'RE YOU TALKING ABOUT?!
I D-DON'T HAVE A C-CRUSH ON NASA-KUN!
I MEAN, HE'S KIND OF C-COOL ...
...AND HE'S N-NICE, BUT...
...
IT'S SAD...
...THAT SHE THINKS SHE'S HIDING IT.

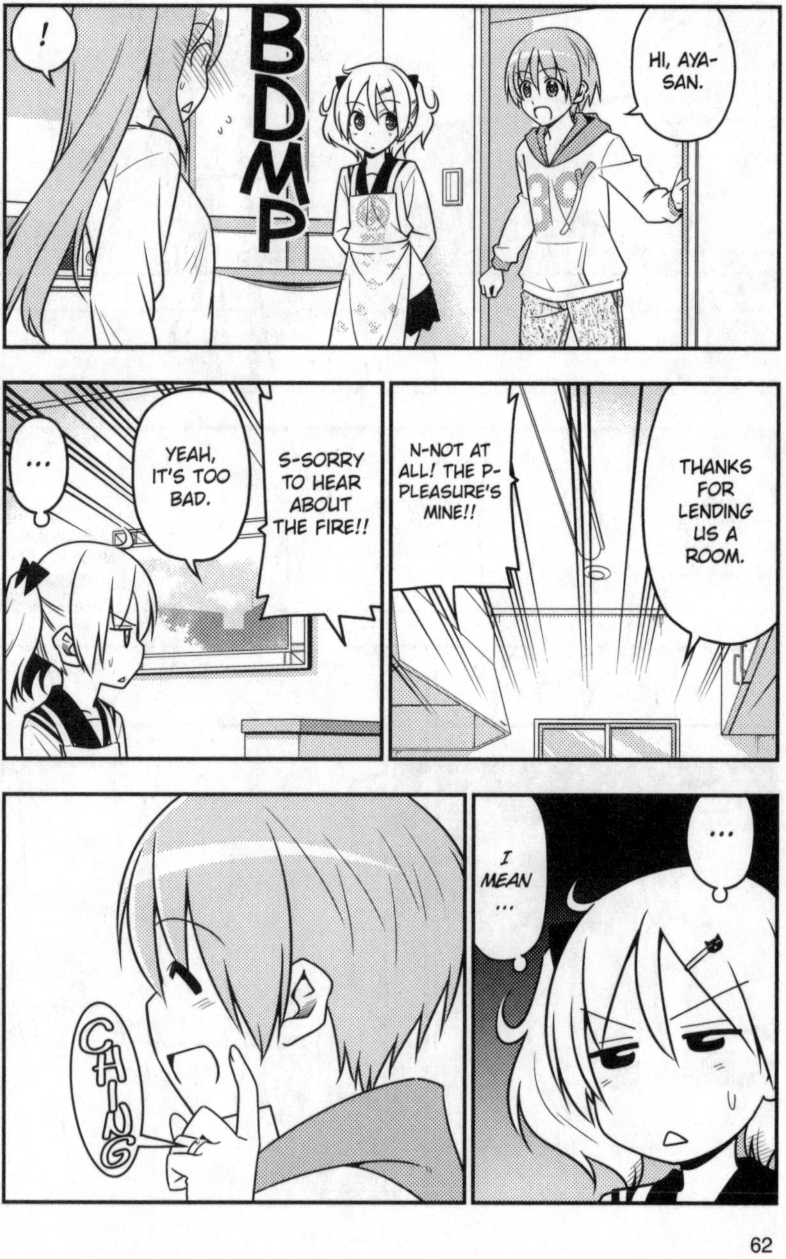
HI, AYA-SAN.
BDMP
!
THANKS FOR LENDING US A ROOM.
N-NOT AT ALL! THE P-PLEASURE'S MINE!!
S-SORRY TO HEAR ABOUT THE FIRE!!
YEAH, IT'S TOO BAD.
...
...
I MEAN ...
CHING

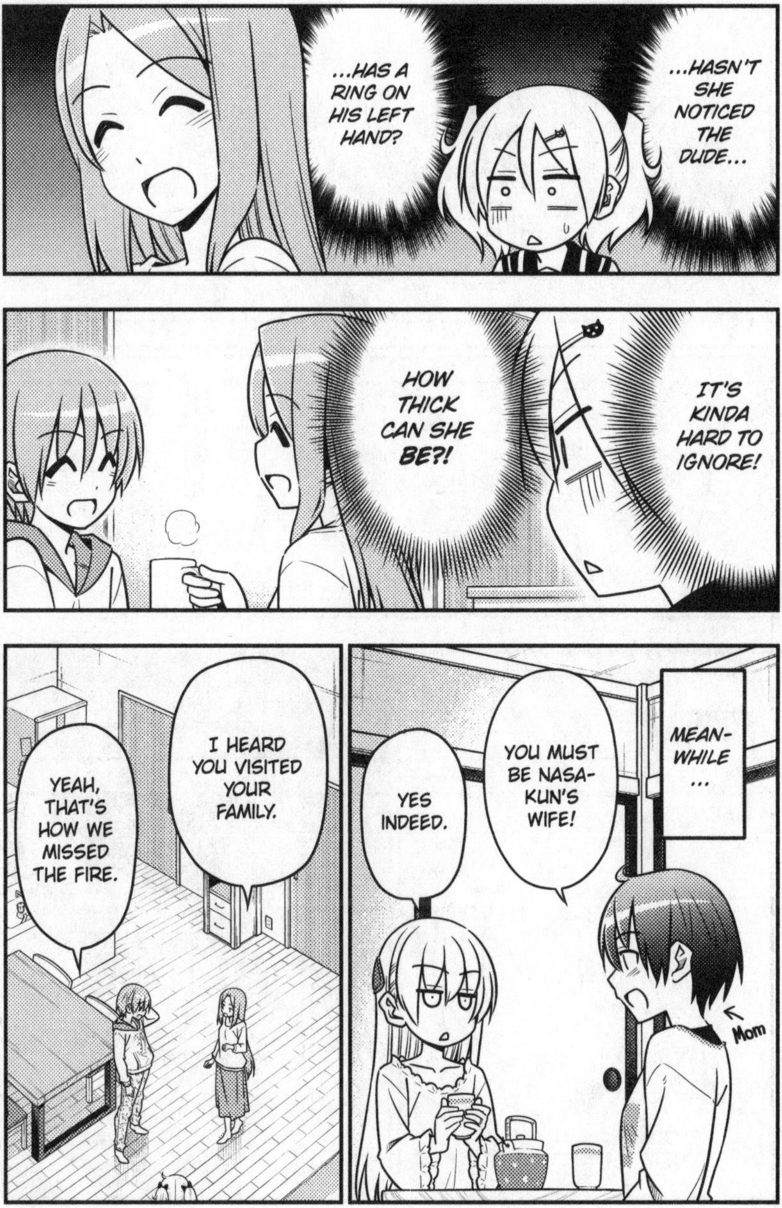
...HASN'T SHE NOTICED THE DUDE...
...HAS A RING ON HIS LEFT HAND?
IT'S KINDA HARD TO IGNORE!
HOW THICK CAN SHE BE?!
MEAN-WHILE ...
YOU MUST BE NASA-KUN'S WIFE!
YES INDEED.
Mom
I HEARD YOU VISITED YOUR FAMILY.
YEAH, THAT'S HOW WE MISSED THE FIRE.

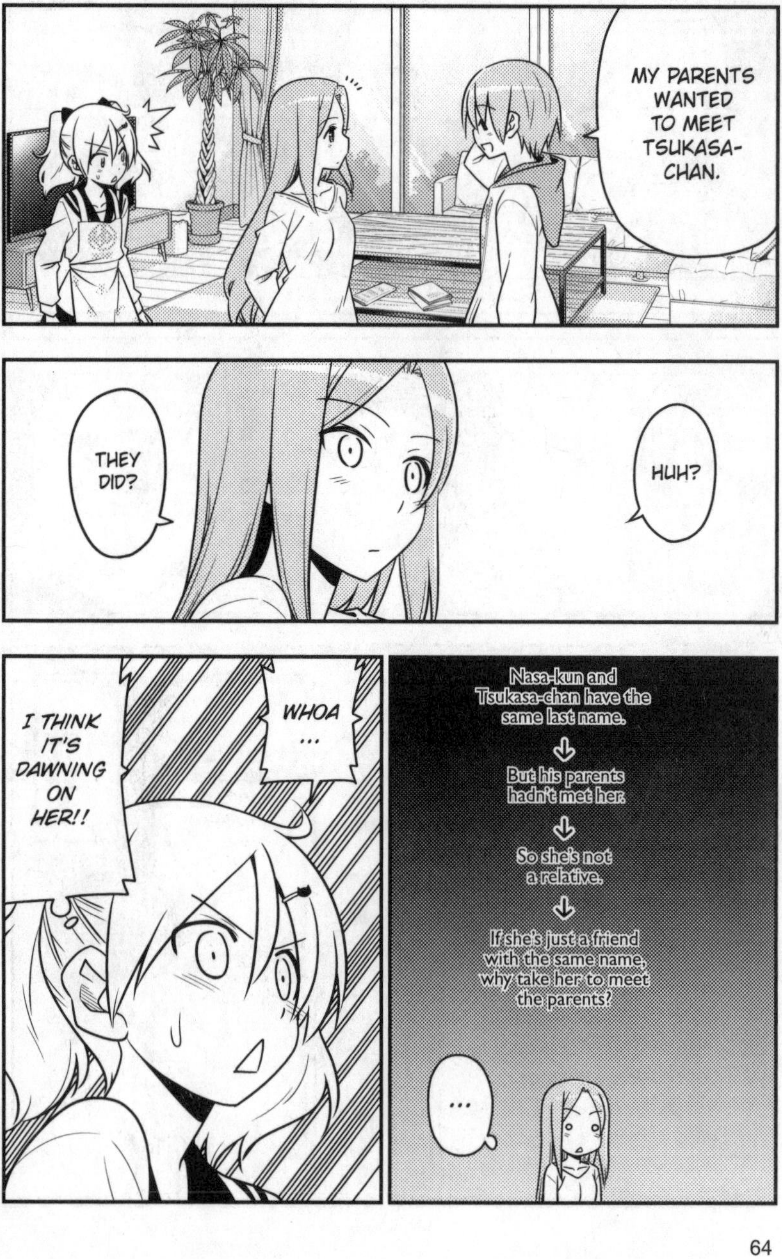
MY PARENTS WANTED TO MEET TSUKASA-CHAN.
HUH?
THEY DID?
Nasa-kun and Tsukasa-chan have the same last name.
But his parents hadn't met her.
So she's not a relative.
If she's just a friend with the same name, why take her to meet the parents?
...
WHOA ...
I THINK IT'S DAWNING ON HER!!

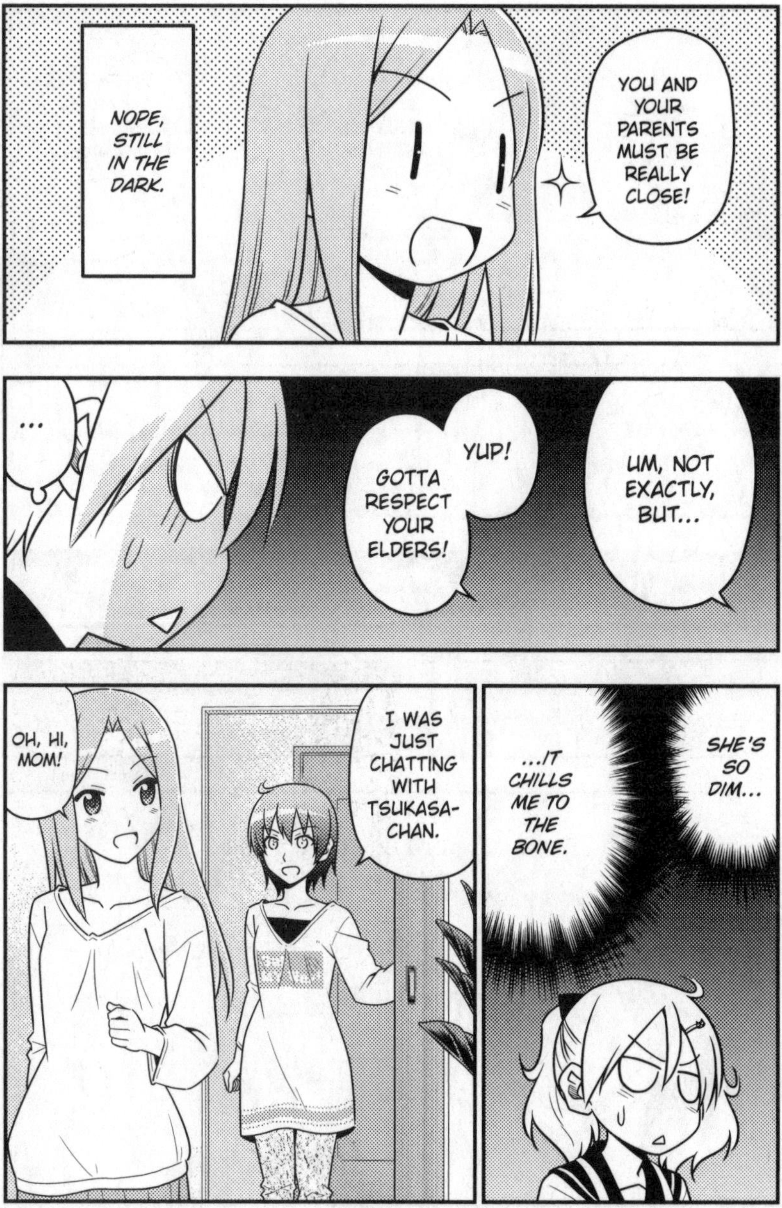
YOU AND YOUR PARENTS MUST BE REALLY CLOSE!
NOPE, STILL IN THE DARK.
UM, NOT EXACTLY, BUT...
YUP! GOTTA RESPECT YOUR ELDERS!
...
SHE'S SO DIM...
...IT CHILLS ME TO THE BONE.
I WAS JUST CHATTING WITH TSUKASA-CHAN.
OH, HI, MOM!

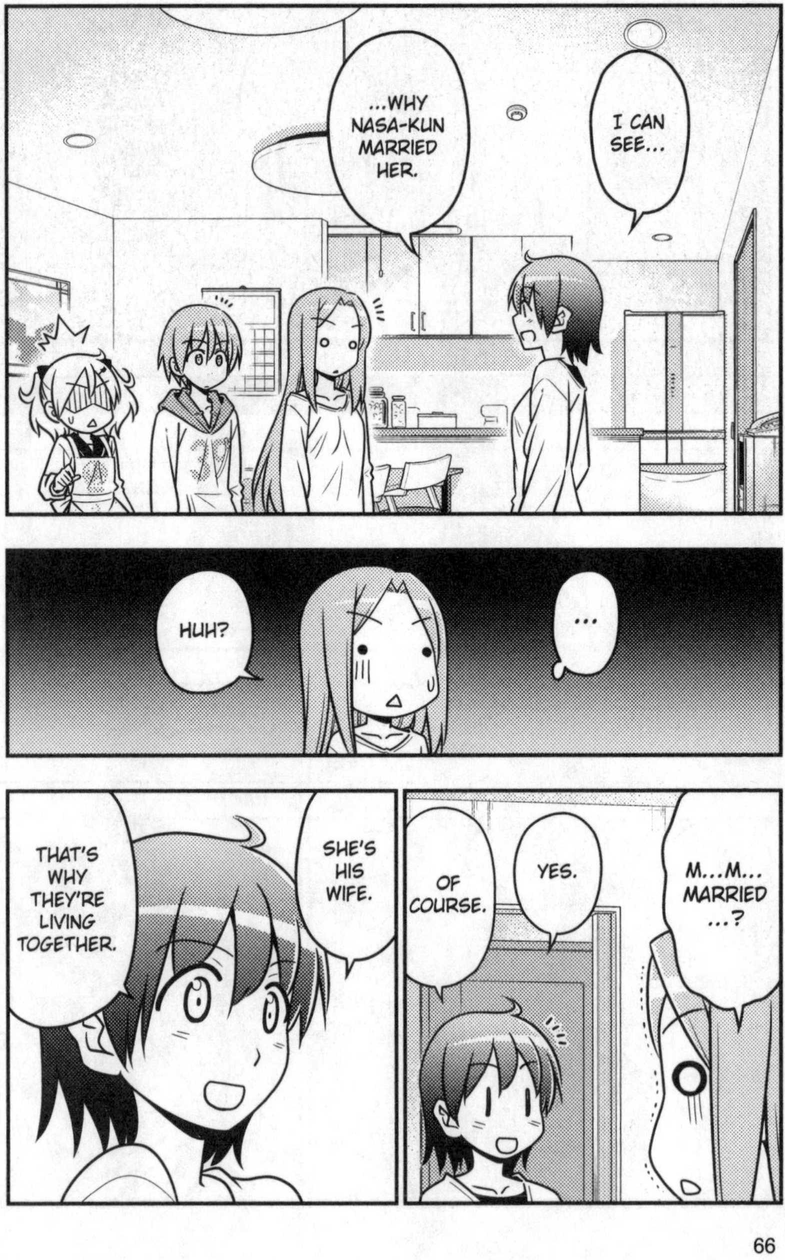
I CAN SEE...
...WHY NASA-KUN MARRIED HER.
...
HUH?
M...M... MARRIED ...?
YES.
OF COURSE.
SHE'S HIS WIFE.
THAT'S WHY THEY'RE LIVING TOGETHER.

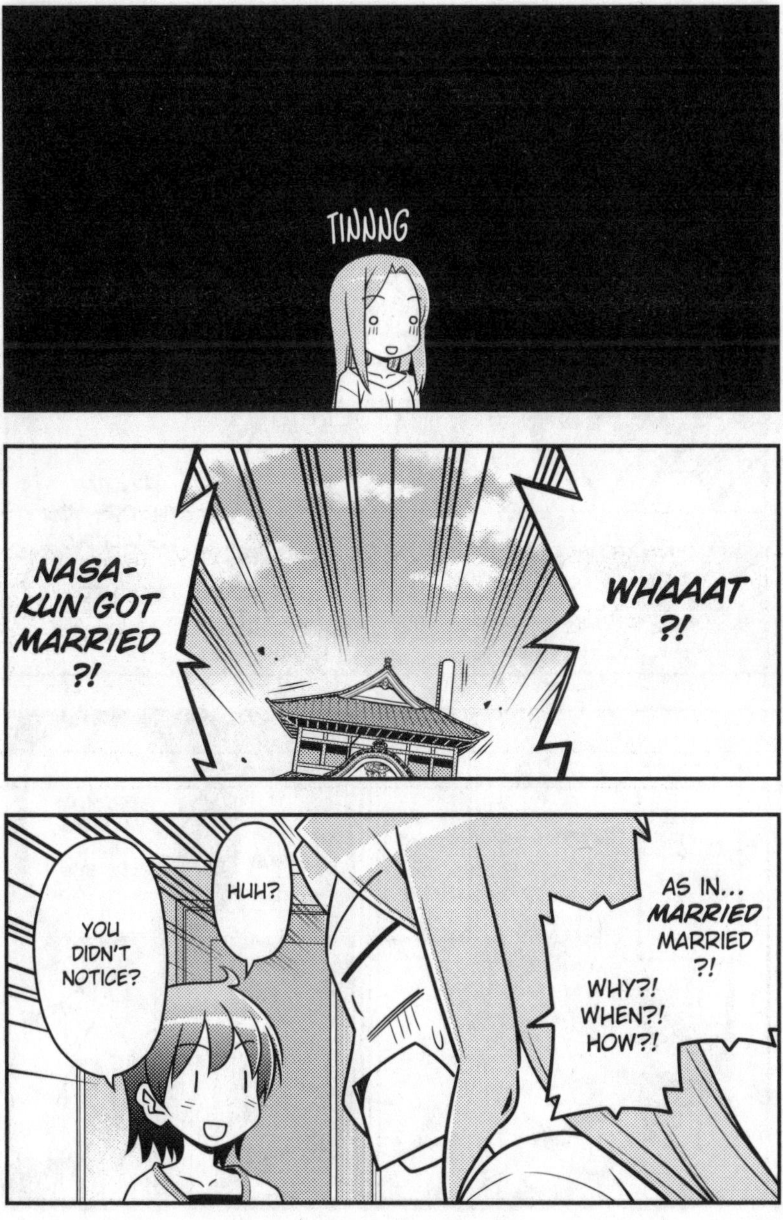
TINNNG
WHAAAT ?!
NASA-KUN GOT MARRIED ?!
AS IN... MARRIED MARRIED ?!
WHY?! WHEN?! HOW?!
HUH?
YOU DIDN'T NOTICE?

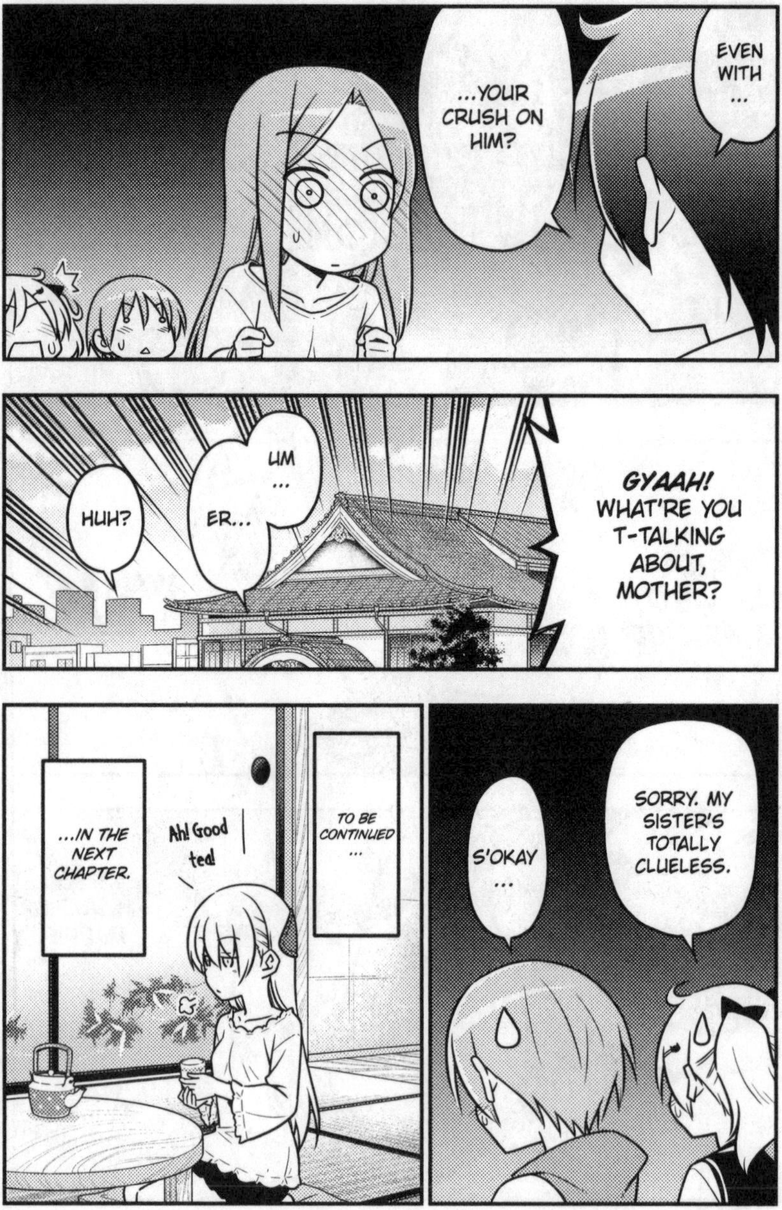
EVEN WITH ...
...YOUR CRUSH ON HIM?
GYAAH! WHAT'RE YOU T-TALKING ABOUT, MOTHER?
UM ... ER...
HUH?
SORRY. MY SISTER'S TOTALLY CLUELESS.
S'OKAY ...
TO BE CONTINUED ...
Ah! Good tea!
...IN THE NEXT CHAPTER.

# Chapter 33: "Not a Dream! Not an Imaginary Story! The Romantic Tension Is Over!"

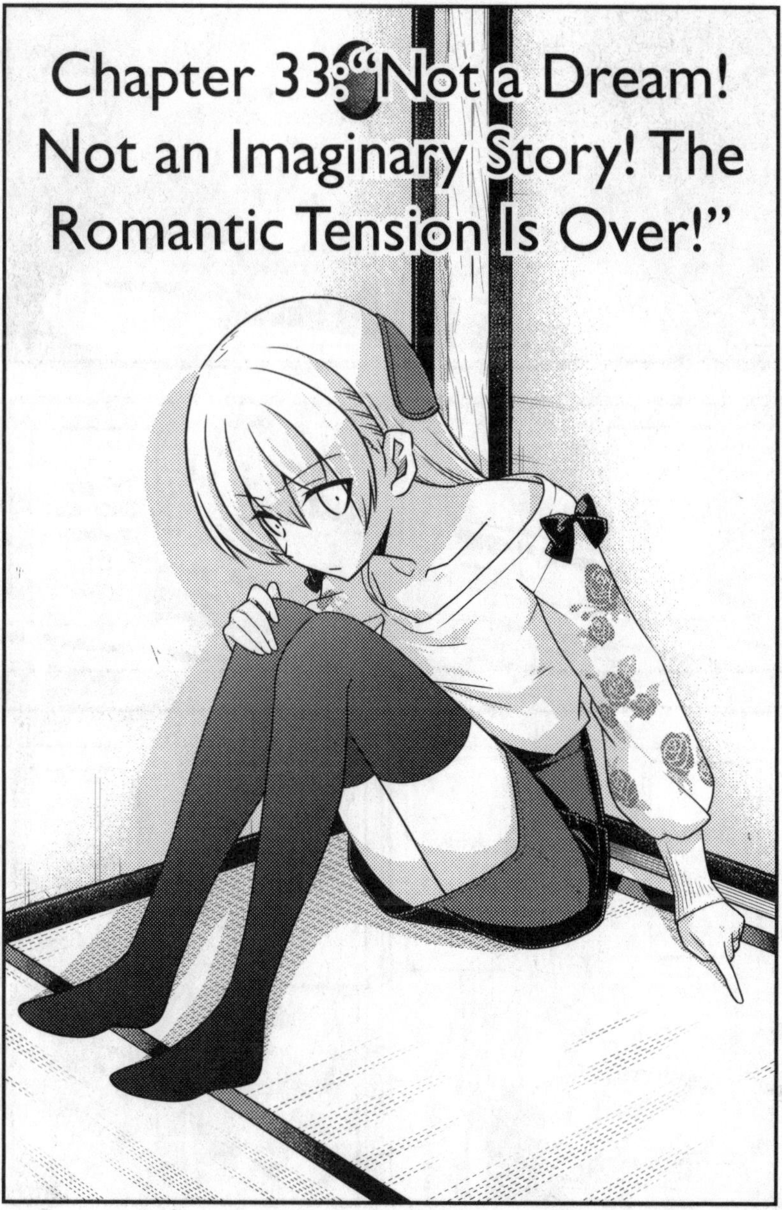

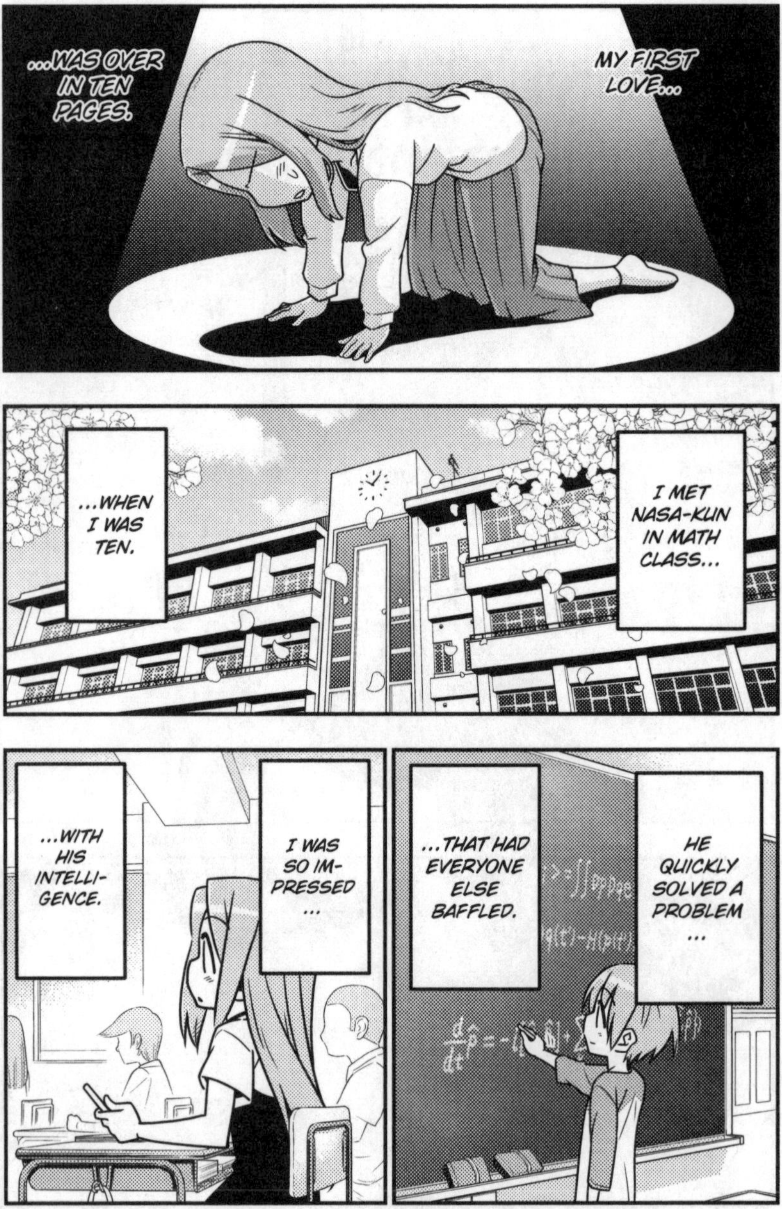
MY FIRST LOVE...
...WAS OVER IN TEN PAGES.
I MET NASA-KUN IN MATH CLASS...
...WHEN I WAS TEN.
HE QUICKLY SOLVED A PROBLEM ...
...THAT HAD EVERYONE ELSE BAFFLED.
I WAS SO IM-PRESSED ...
...WITH HIS INTELLI-GENCE.

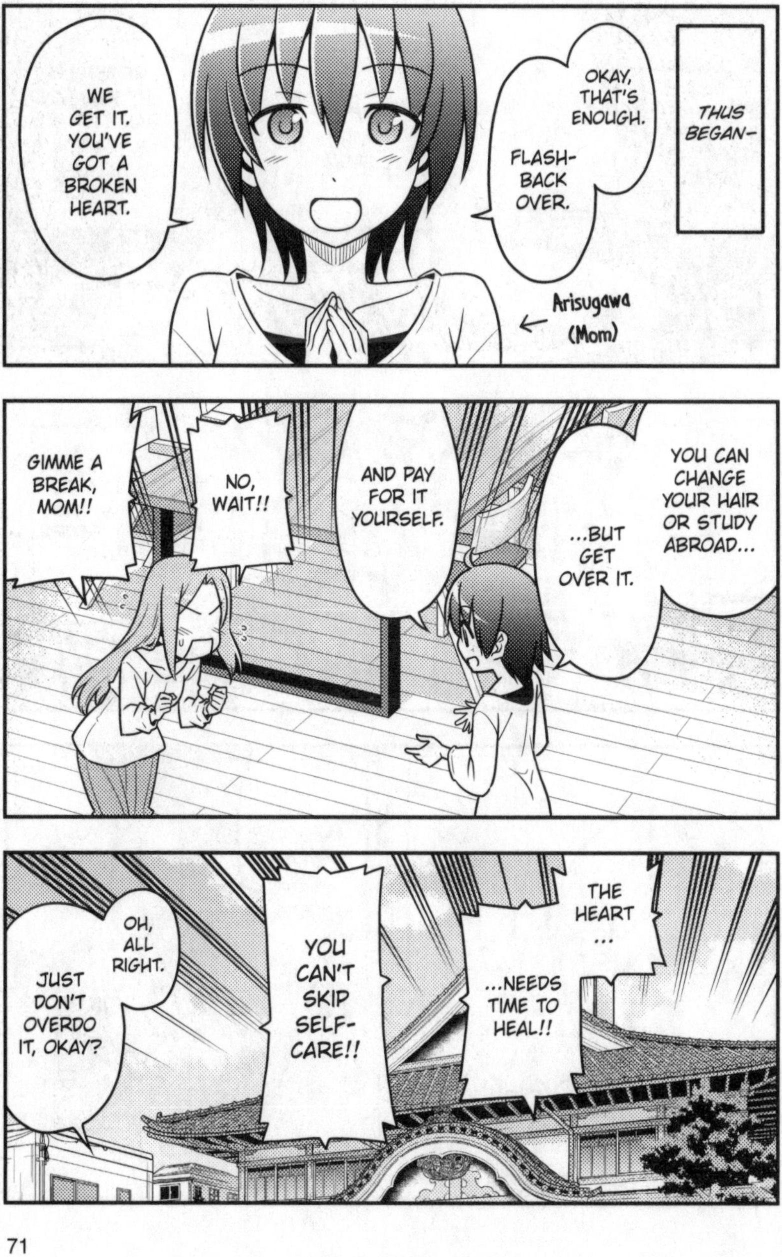
THUS BEGAN-
OKAY, THAT'S ENOUGH.
FLASH-BACK OVER.
Arisugawa (Mom)
WE GET IT. YOU'VE GOT A BROKEN HEART.
YOU CAN CHANGE YOUR HAIR OR STUDY ABROAD...
...BUT GET OVER IT.
AND PAY FOR IT YOURSELF.
NO, WAIT!!
GIMME A BREAK, MOM!!
THE HEART ...
...NEEDS TIME TO HEAL!!
YOU CAN'T SKIP SELF-CARE!!
OH, ALL RIGHT.
JUST DON'T OVERDO IT, OKAY?

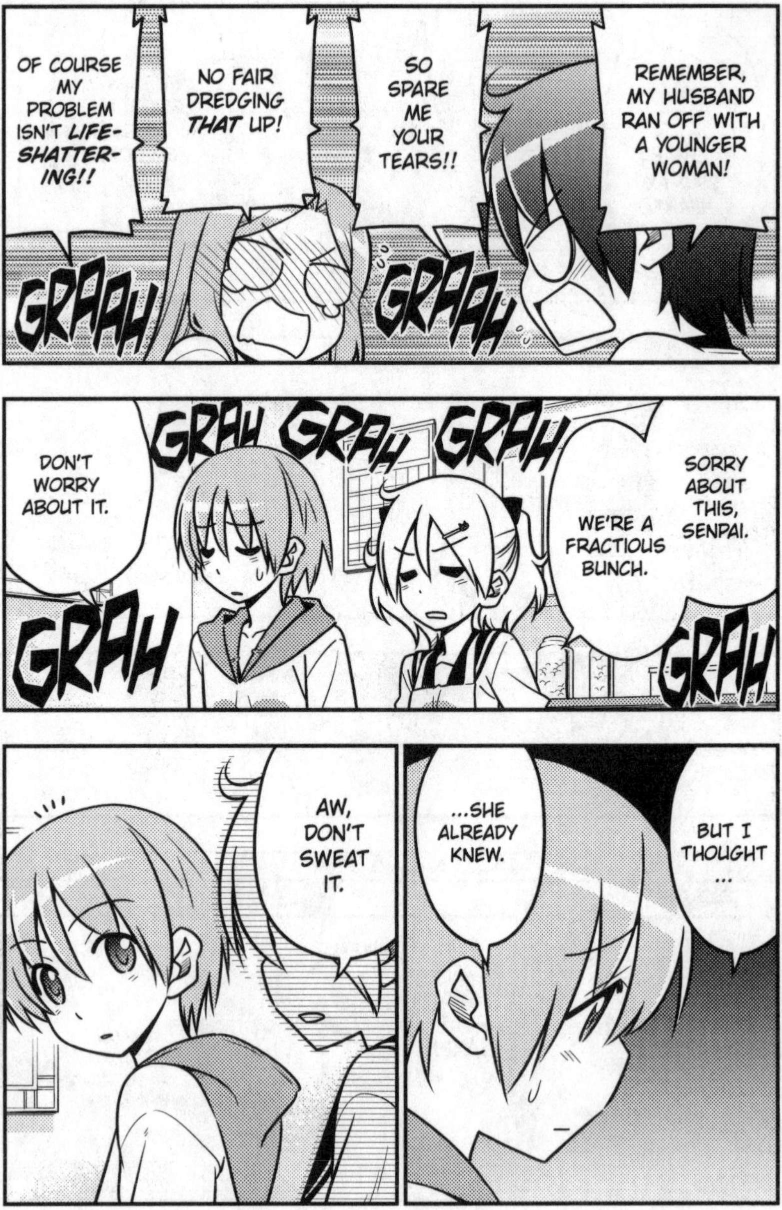
REMEMBER, MY HUSBAND RAN OFF WITH A YOUNGER WOMAN!
SO SPARE ME YOUR TEARS!!
GRAAH
NO FAIR DREDGING *THAT* UP!
OF COURSE MY PROBLEM ISN'T *LIFE-SHATTERING!!*
GRAAH
SORRY ABOUT THIS, SENPAI.
WE'RE A FRACTIOUS BUNCH.
GRAH
GRAH GRAH GRAH
DON'T WORRY ABOUT IT.
GRAH
BUT I THOUGHT...
...SHE ALREADY KNEW.
AW, DON'T SWEAT IT.

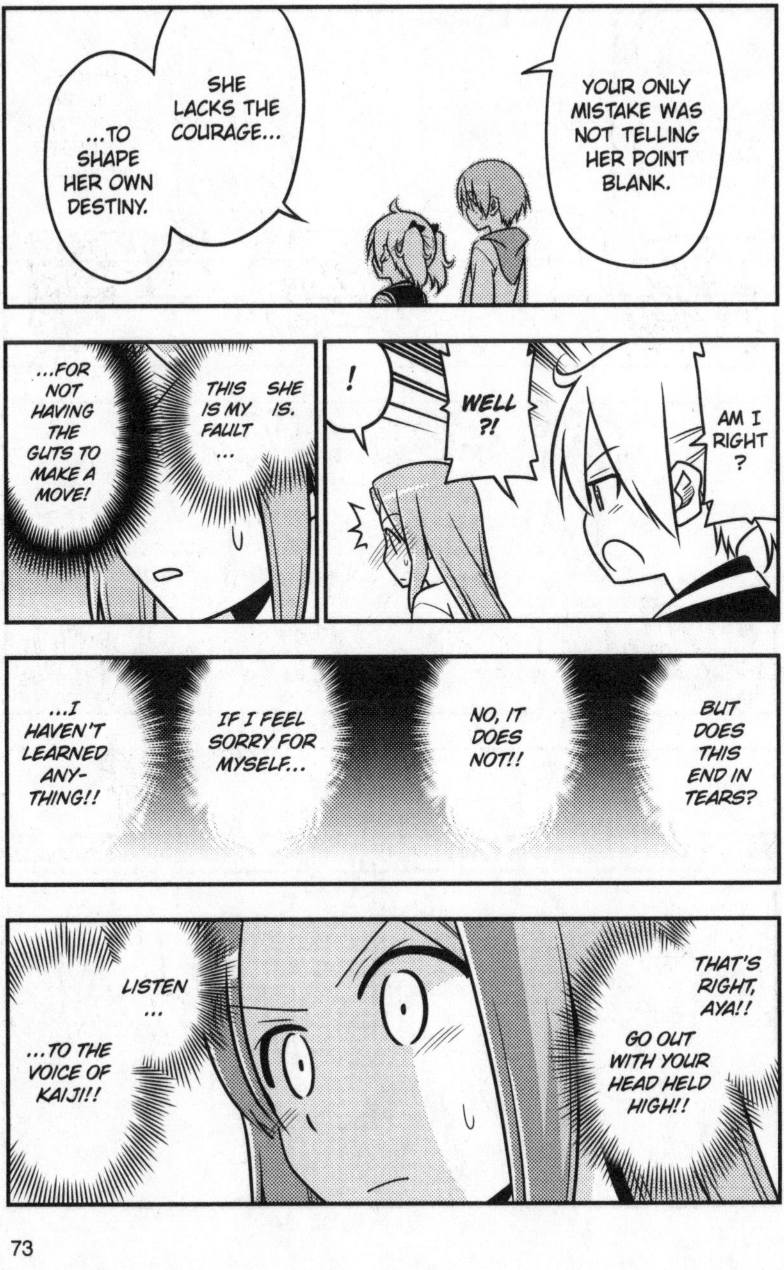
YOUR ONLY MISTAKE WAS NOT TELLING HER POINT BLANK.
SHE LACKS THE COURAGE...
...TO SHAPE HER OWN DESTINY.
AM I RIGHT?
WELL?!
!
SHE IS.
THIS IS MY FAULT...
...FOR NOT HAVING THE GUTS TO MAKE A MOVE!
BUT DOES THIS END IN TEARS?
NO, IT DOES NOT!!
IF I FEEL SORRY FOR MYSELF...
...I HAVEN'T LEARNED ANYTHING!!
THAT'S RIGHT, AYA!!
GO OUT WITH YOUR HEAD HELD HIGH!!
LISTEN...
...TO THE VOICE OF KAIJI!!

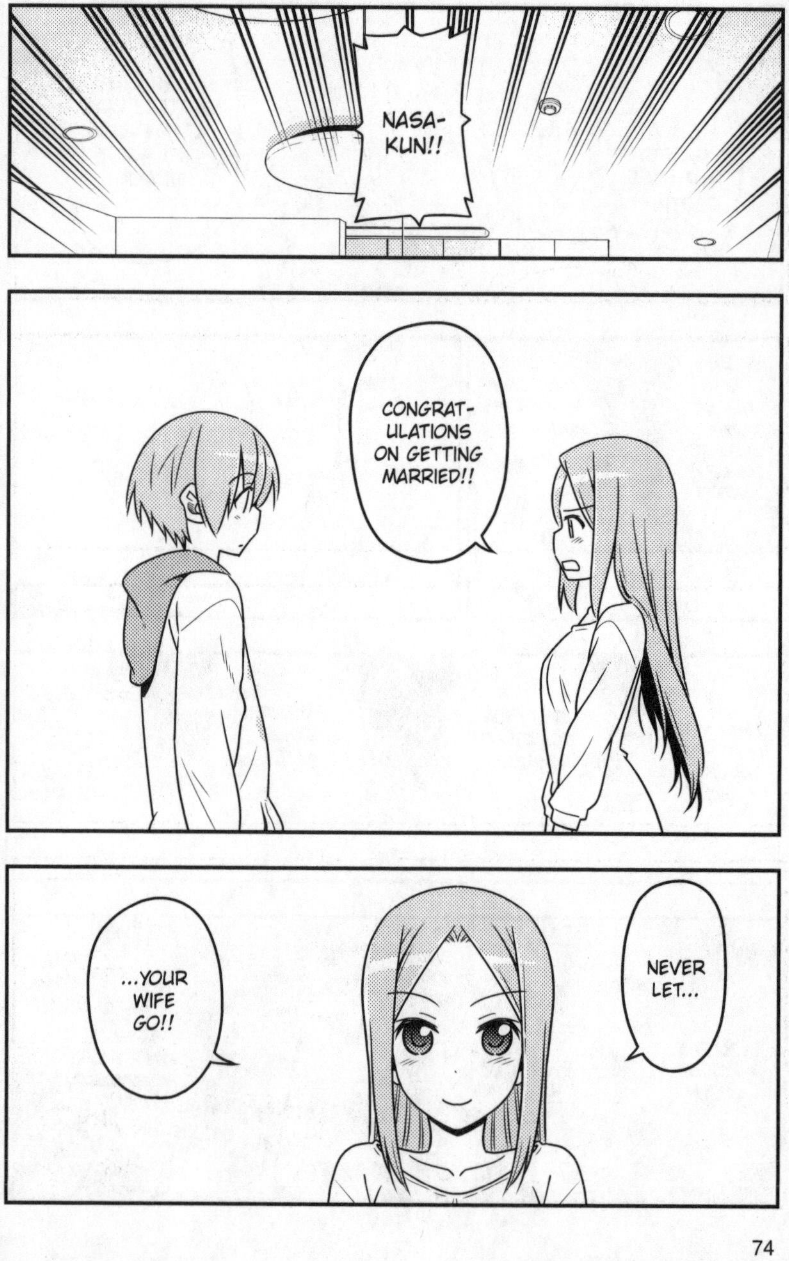
NASA-KUN!!
CONGRAT-ULATIONS ON GETTING MARRIED!!
NEVER LET...
...YOUR WIFE GO!!

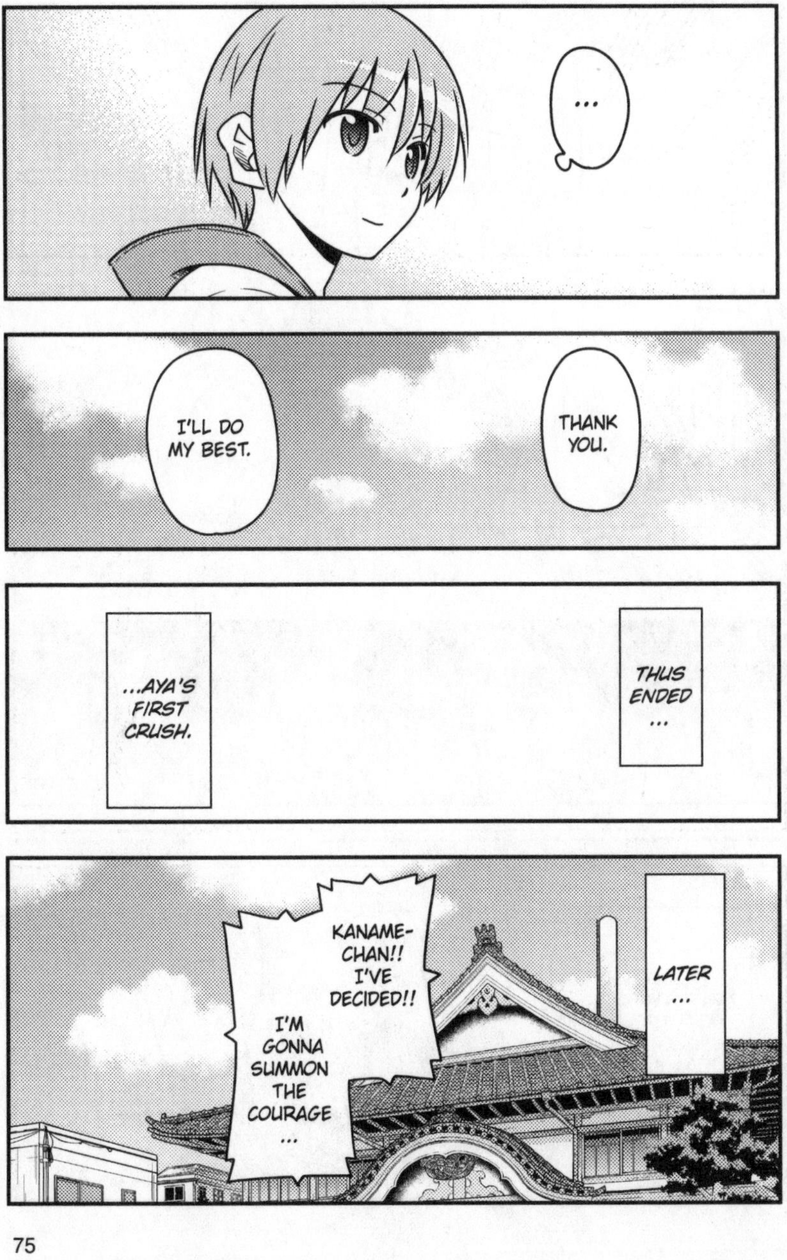
...
THANK YOU.
I'LL DO MY BEST.
THUS ENDED ...
...AYA'S FIRST CRUSH.
LATER ...
KANAME-CHAN!! I'VE DECIDED!!
I'M GONNA SUMMON THE COURAGE ...

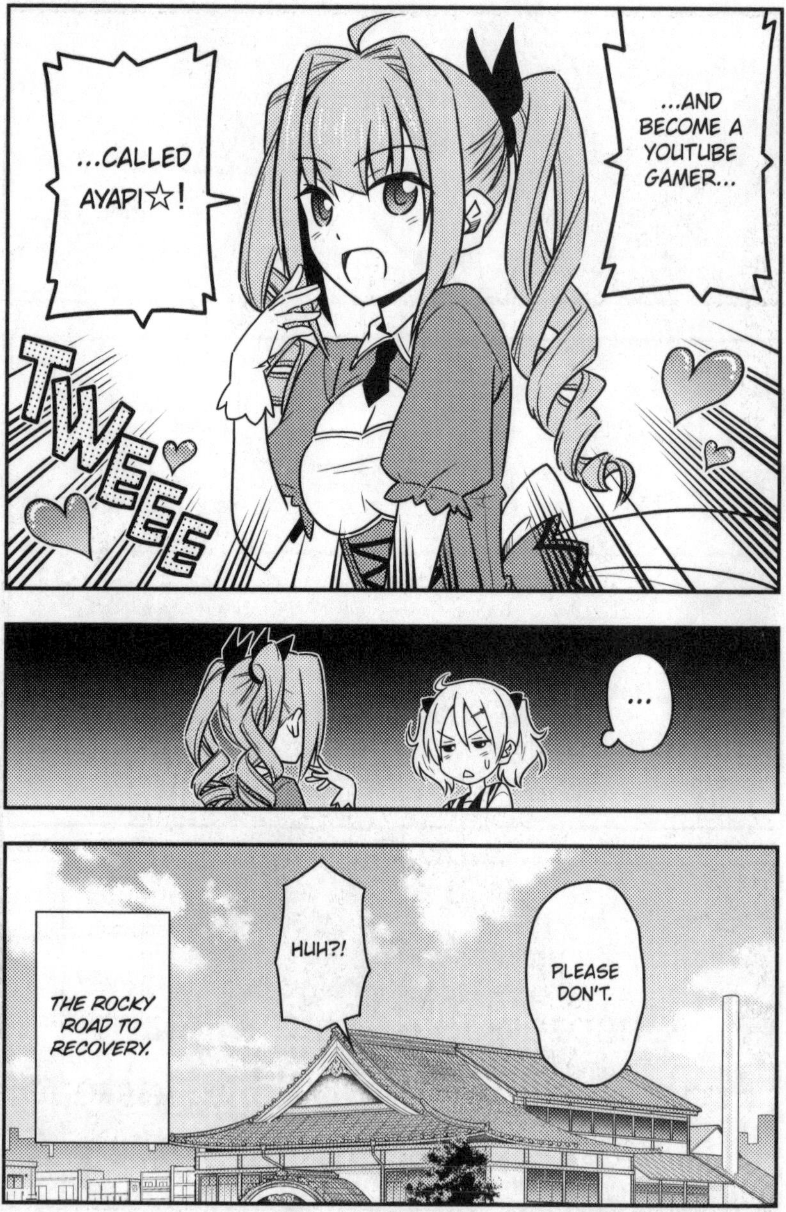
...AND BECOME A YOUTUBE GAMER...
...CALLED AYAPI☆!
TWEEEE
...
PLEASE DON'T.
HUH?!
THE ROCKY ROAD TO RECOVERY.

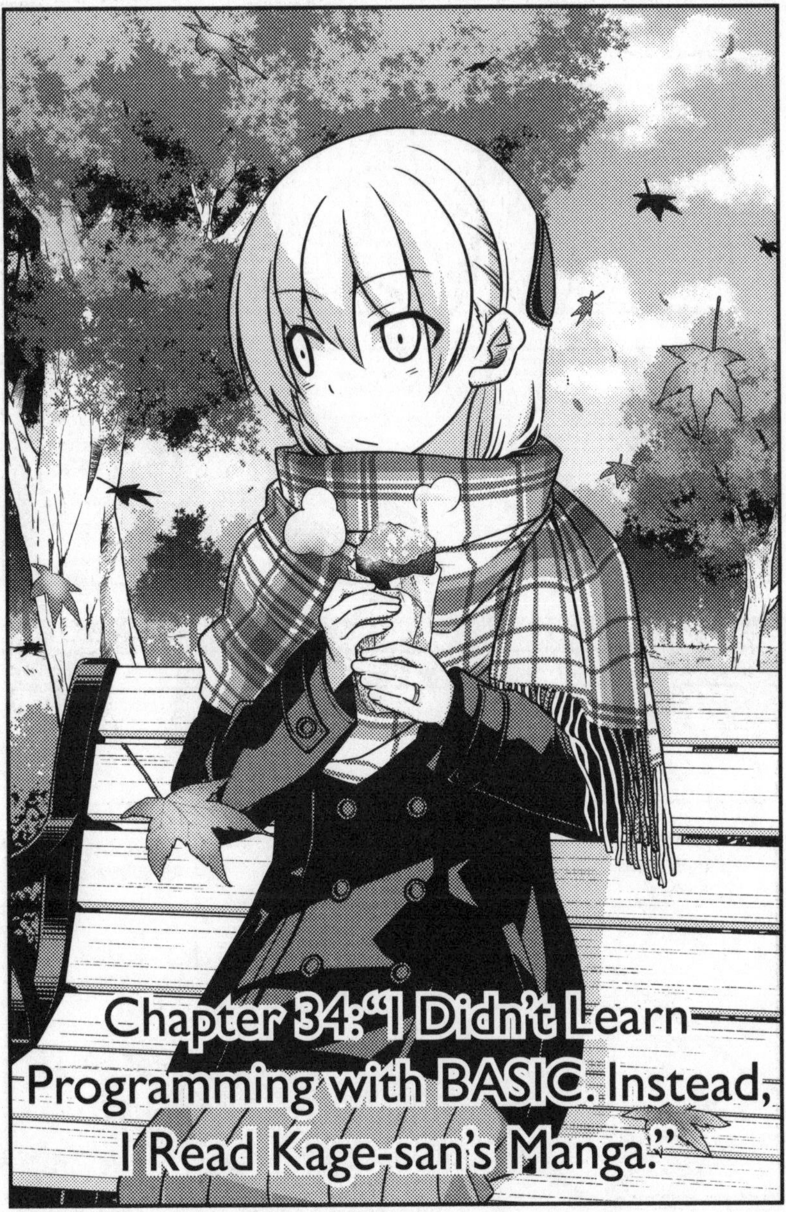
Chapter 34: "I Didn't Learn Programming with BASIC. Instead, I Read Kage-san's Manga."

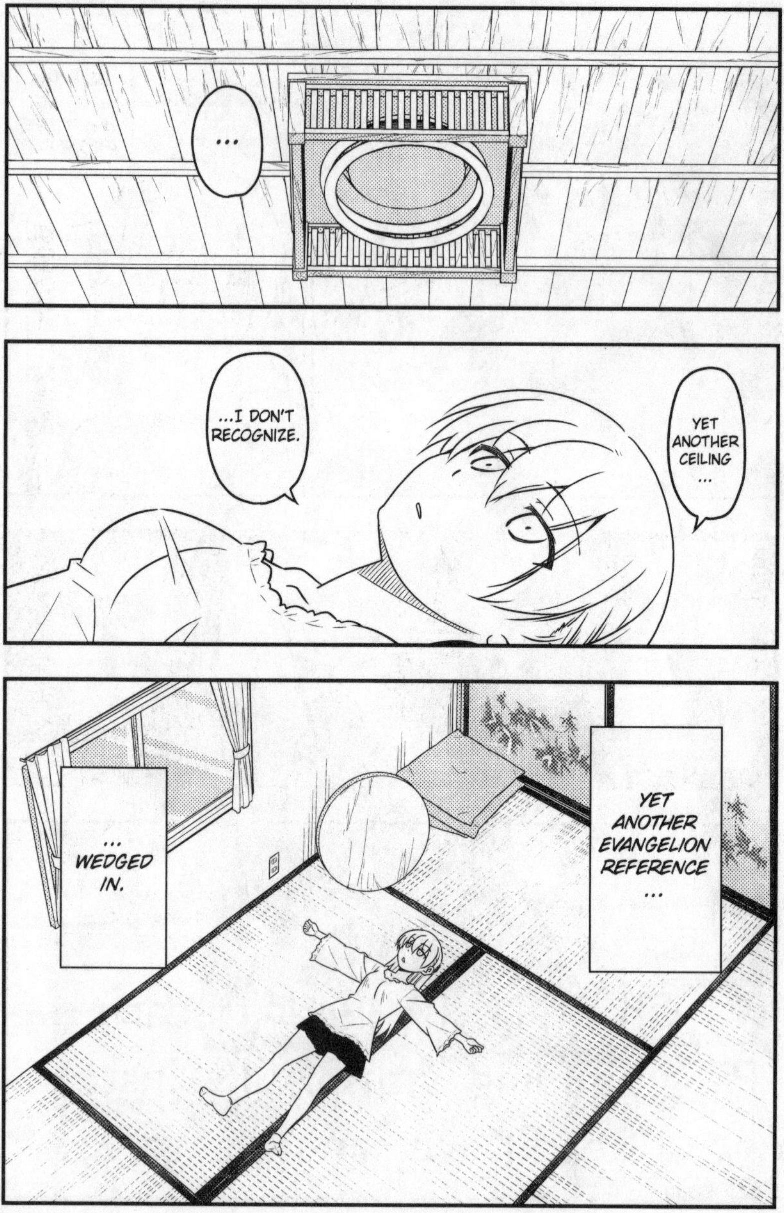
...
YET ANOTHER CEILING ...
...I DON'T RECOGNIZE.
YET ANOTHER EVANGELION REFERENCE ...
... WEDGED IN.

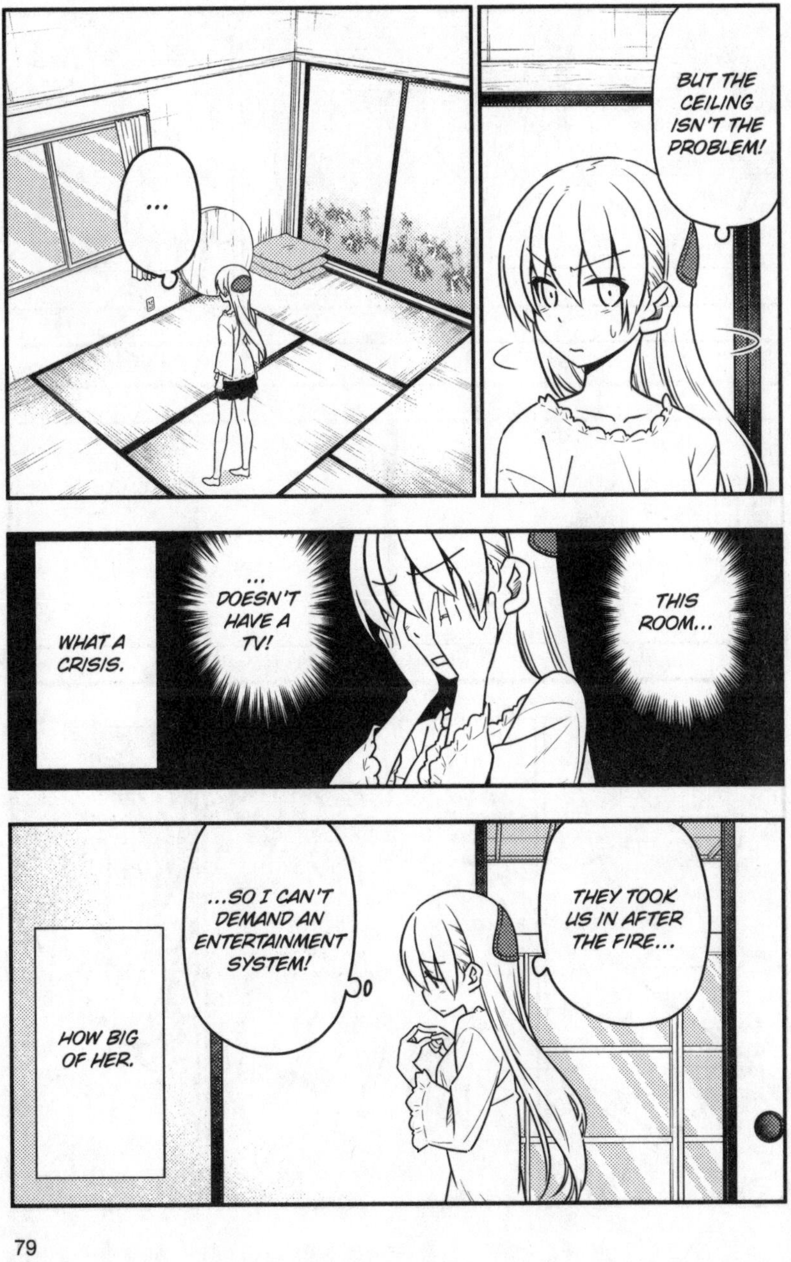
BUT THE CEILING ISN'T THE PROBLEM!
...
THIS ROOM...
... DOESN'T HAVE A TV!
WHAT A CRISIS.
THEY TOOK US IN AFTER THE FIRE...
...SO I CAN'T DEMAND AN ENTERTAINMENT SYSTEM!
HOW BIG OF HER.

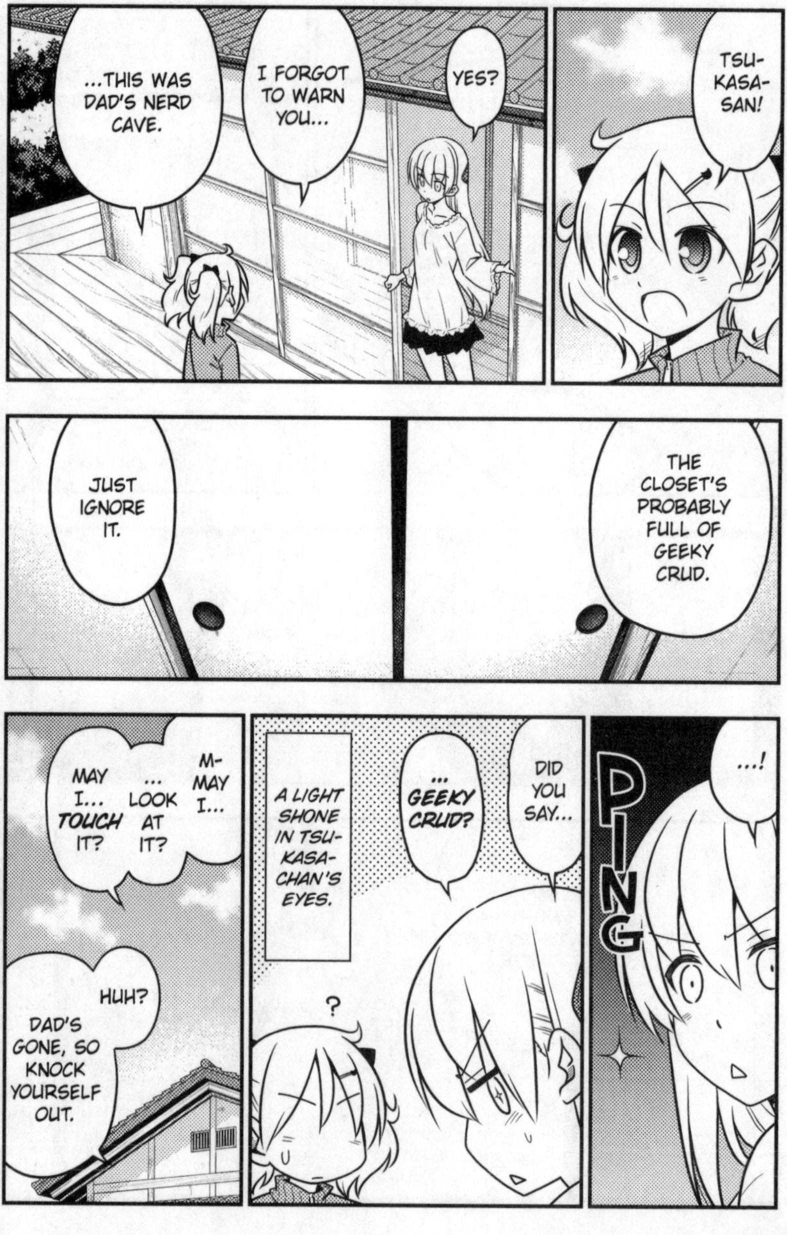
TSU-KASA-SAN!
YES?
I FORGOT TO WARN YOU...
...THIS WAS DAD'S NERD CAVE.
THE CLOSET'S PROBABLY FULL OF GEEKY CRUD.
JUST IGNORE IT.
...!
PING
DID YOU SAY...
...GEEKY CRUD?
A LIGHT SHONE IN TSUKASA-CHAN'S EYES.
?
M-MAY I...
...LOOK AT IT?
MAY I... TOUCH IT?
HUH?
DAD'S GONE, SO KNOCK YOURSELF OUT.

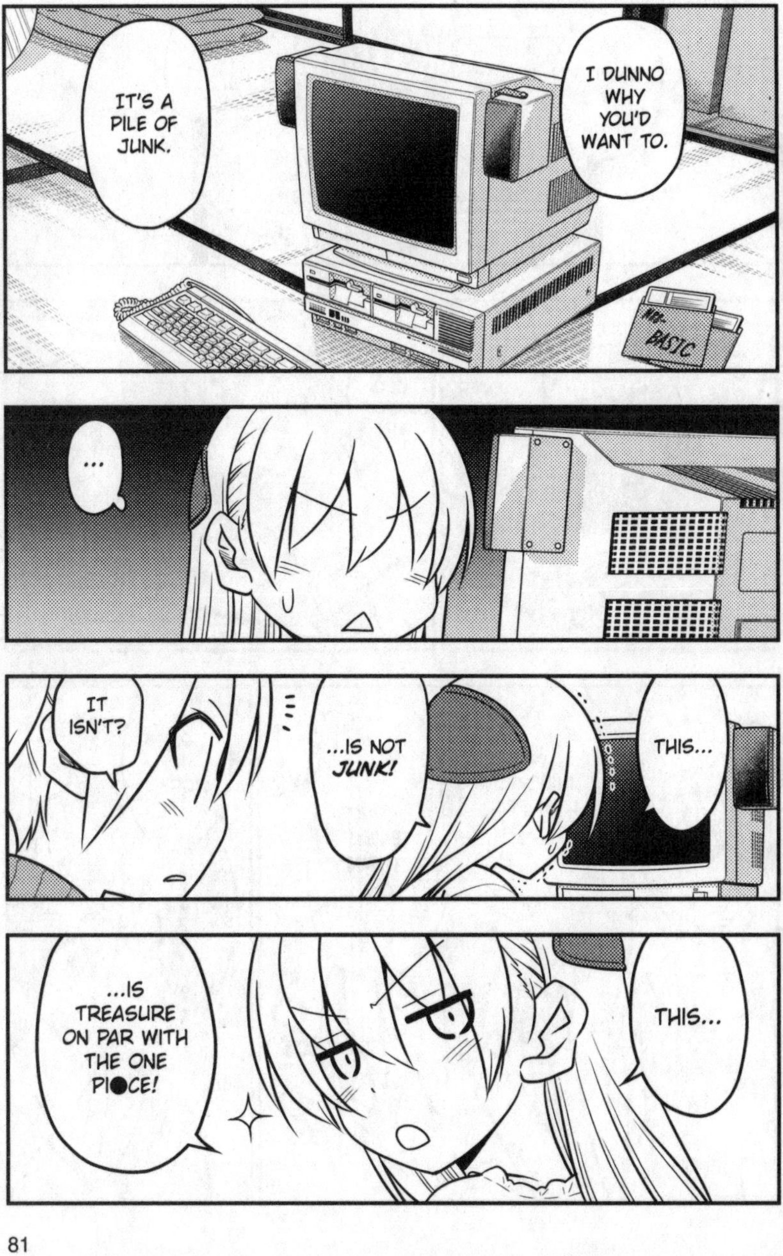
I DUNNO WHY YOU'D WANT TO.
IT'S A PILE OF JUNK.
BASIC
...
THIS...
...IS NOT JUNK!
IT ISN'T?
THIS...
...IS TREASURE ON PAR WITH THE ONE PI●CE!

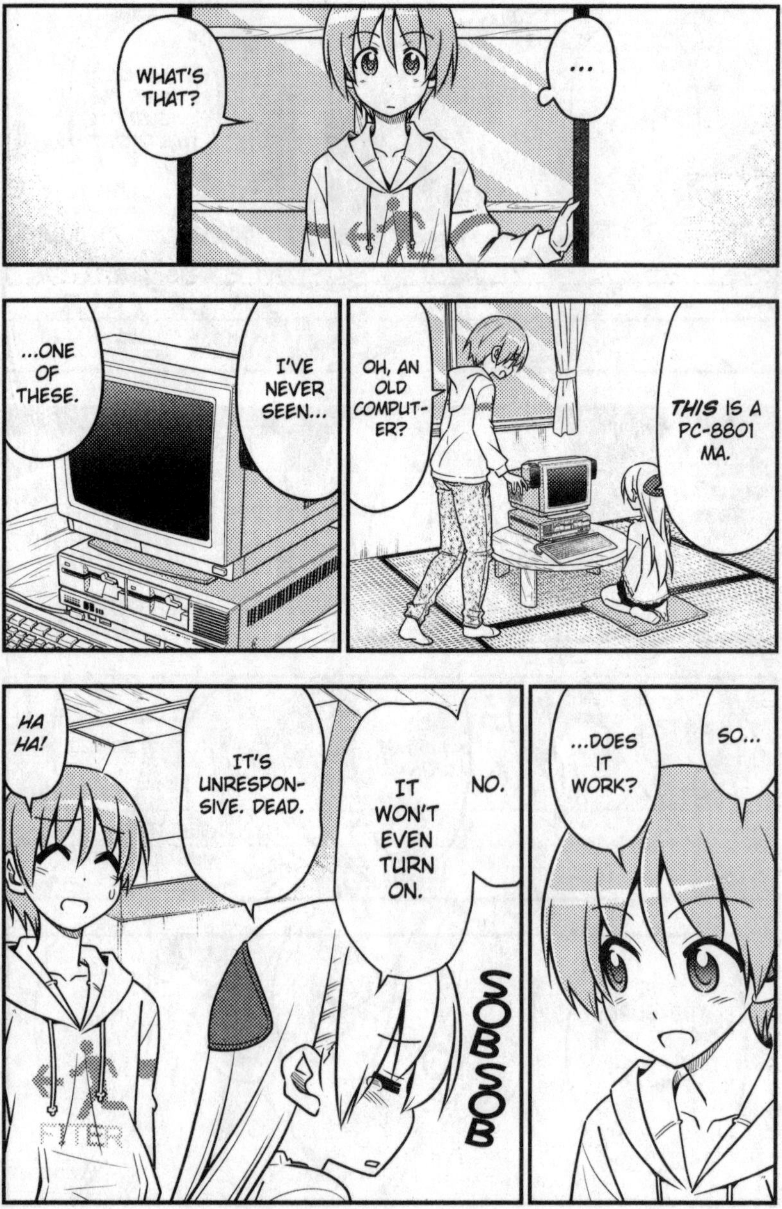
...
WHAT'S THAT?
THIS IS A PC-8801 MA.
OH, AN OLD COMPUTER?
I'VE NEVER SEEN...
...ONE OF THESE.
SO...
...DOES IT WORK?
NO.
IT WON'T EVEN TURN ON.
SOBSOB
IT'S UNRESPONSIVE. DEAD.
HA HA!

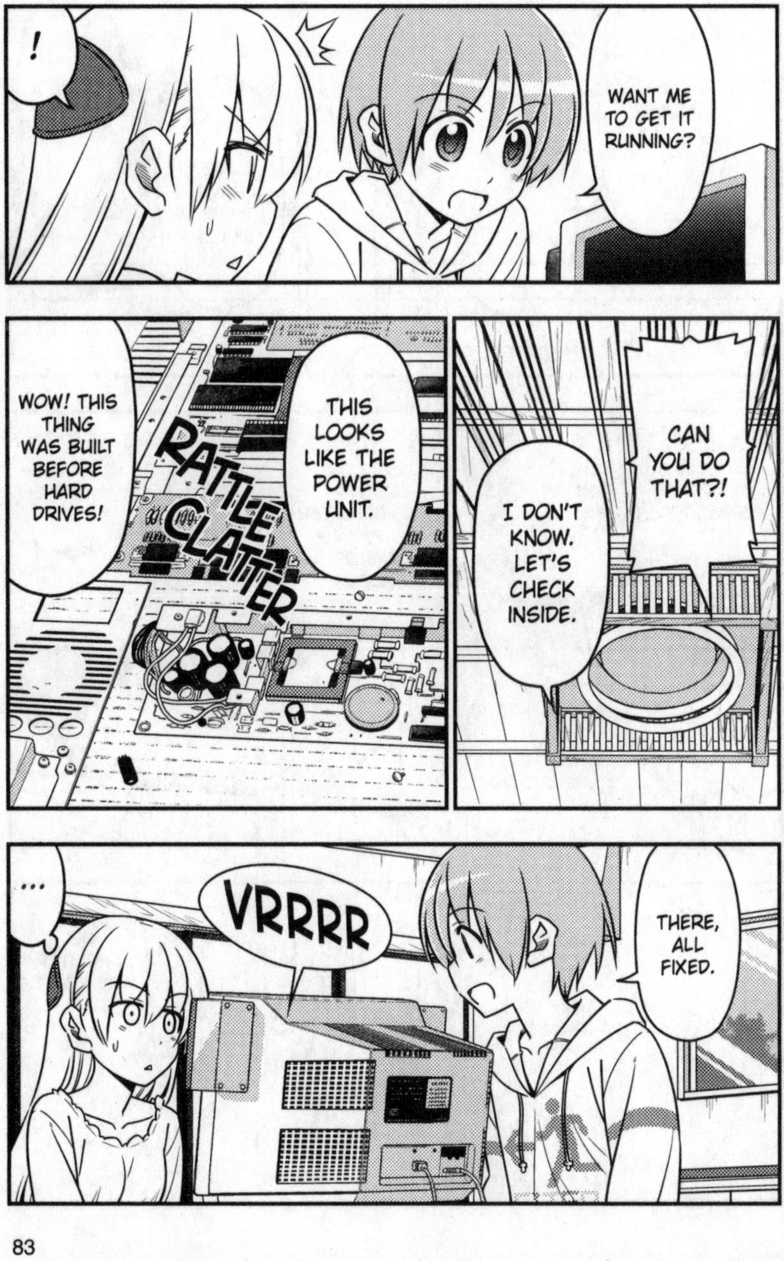
WANT ME TO GET IT RUNNING?
!
CAN YOU DO THAT?!
I DON'T KNOW. LET'S CHECK INSIDE.
THIS LOOKS LIKE THE POWER UNIT.
RATTLE CLATTER
WOW! THIS THING WAS BUILT BEFORE HARD DRIVES!
THERE, ALL FIXED.
VRRRR
...

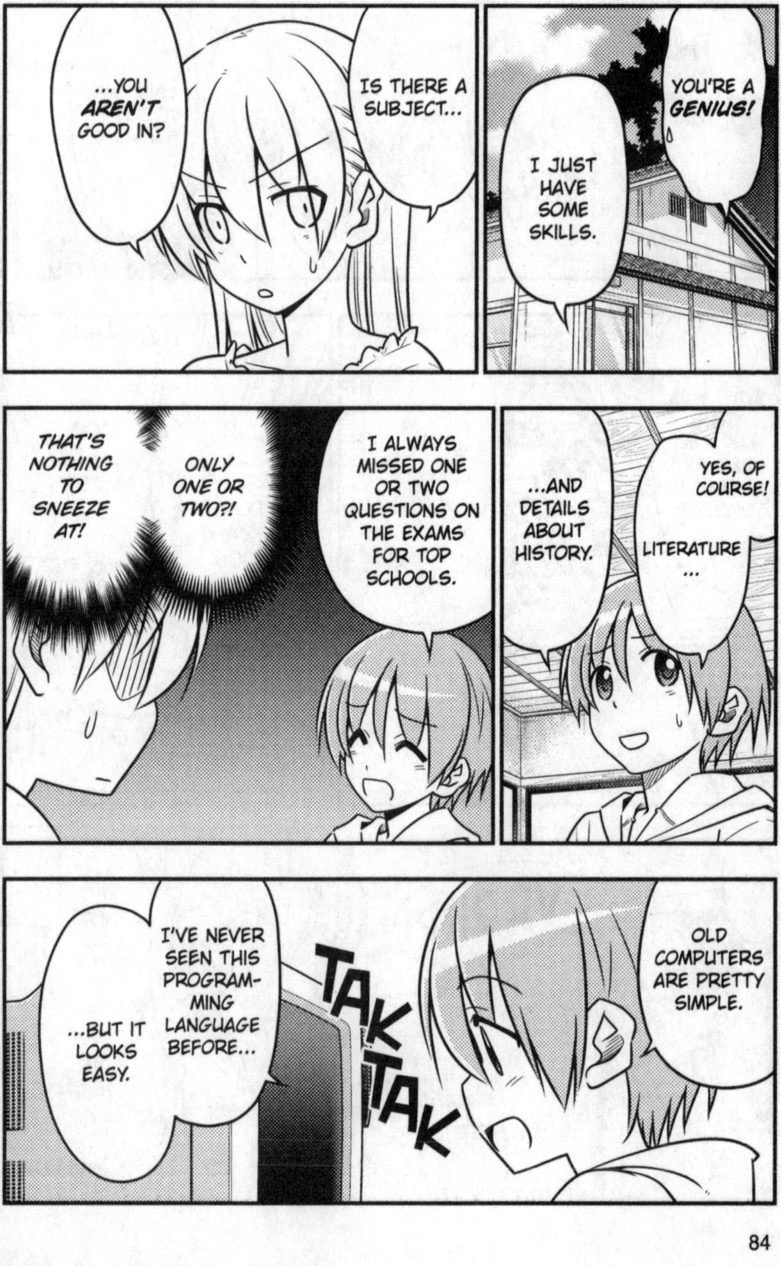
YOU'RE A GENIUS!
I JUST HAVE SOME SKILLS.
IS THERE A SUBJECT...
...YOU AREN'T GOOD IN?
YES, OF COURSE!
LITERATURE ...
...AND DETAILS ABOUT HISTORY.
I ALWAYS MISSED ONE OR TWO QUESTIONS ON THE EXAMS FOR TOP SCHOOLS.
ONLY ONE OR TWO?!
THAT'S NOTHING TO SNEEZE AT!
OLD COMPUTERS ARE PRETTY SIMPLE.
TAK TAK
I'VE NEVER SEEN THIS PROGRAM-MING LANGUAGE BEFORE...
...BUT IT LOOKS EASY.

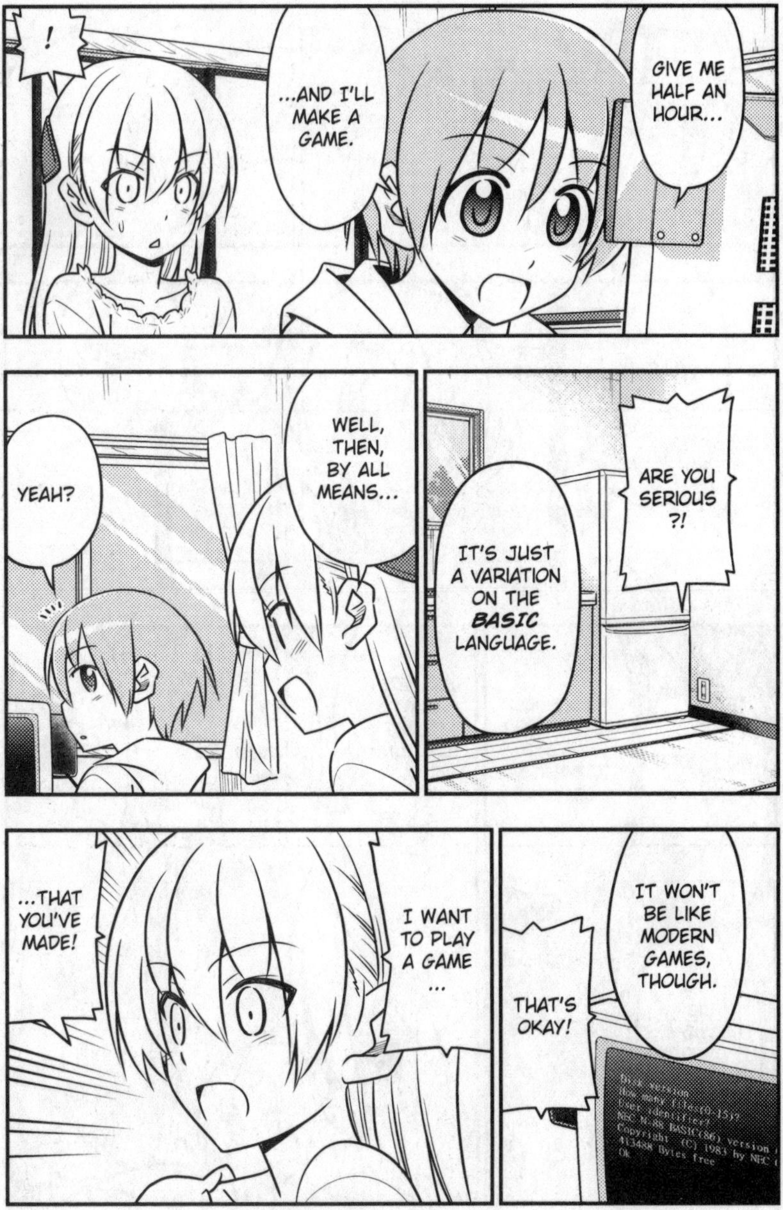
GIVE ME HALF AN HOUR...
...AND I'LL MAKE A GAME.
!
ARE YOU SERIOUS ?!
IT'S JUST A VARIATION ON THE BASIC LANGUAGE.
WELL, THEN, BY ALL MEANS...
YEAH?
IT WON'T BE LIKE MODERN GAMES, THOUGH.
THAT'S OKAY!
I WANT TO PLAY A GAME ...
...THAT YOU'VE MADE!

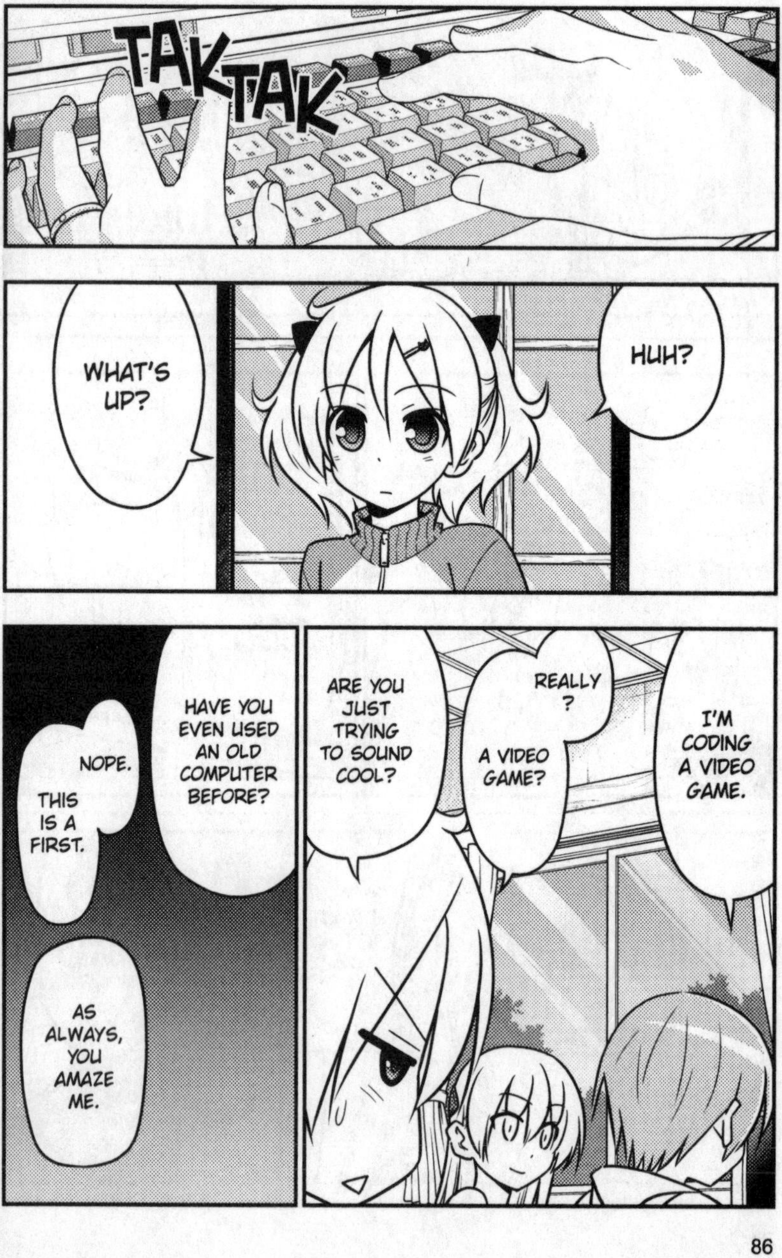
TAKTAK
HUH?
WHAT'S UP?
I'M CODING A VIDEO GAME.
REALLY? A VIDEO GAME?
ARE YOU JUST TRYING TO SOUND COOL?
HAVE YOU EVEN USED AN OLD COMPUTER BEFORE?
NOPE. THIS IS A FIRST.
AS ALWAYS, YOU AMAZE ME.

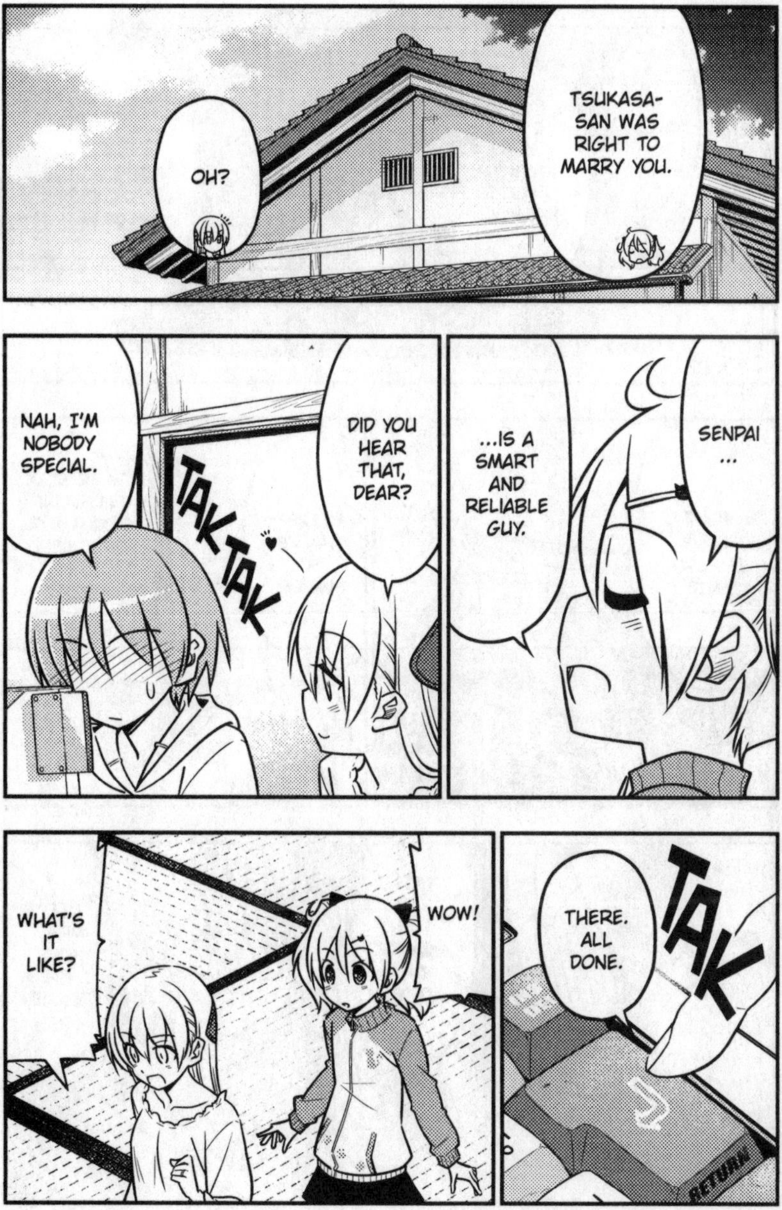
TSUKASA-SAN WAS RIGHT TO MARRY YOU.
OH?
SENPAI ...
...IS A SMART AND RELIABLE GUY.
DID YOU HEAR THAT, DEAR?
TAK TAK
NAH, I'M NOBODY SPECIAL.
TAK
THERE. ALL DONE.
RETURN
WOW!
WHAT'S IT LIKE?

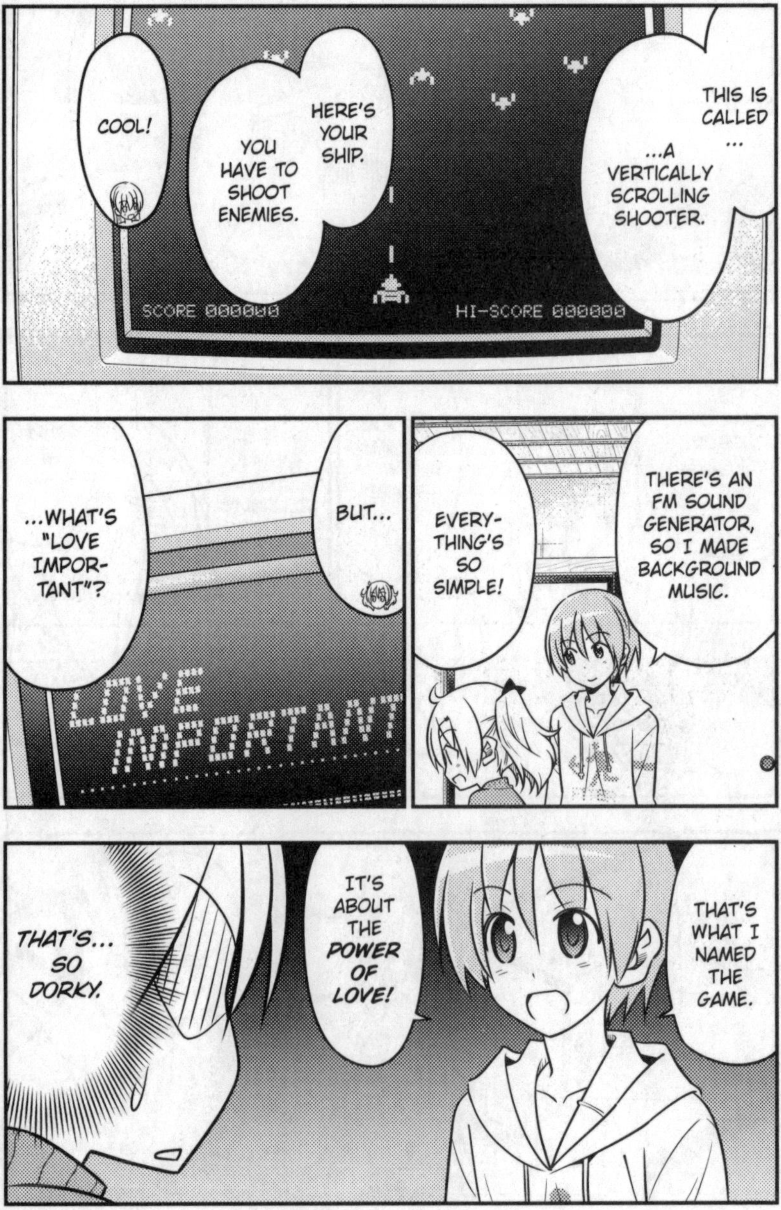
THIS IS CALLED ...
...A VERTICALLY SCROLLING SHOOTER.
HERE'S YOUR SHIP.
YOU HAVE TO SHOOT ENEMIES.
COOL!
SCORE 000000
HI-SCORE 000000
THERE'S AN FM SOUND GENERATOR, SO I MADE BACKGROUND MUSIC.
EVERY-THING'S SO SIMPLE!
BUT...
...WHAT'S "LOVE IMPOR-TANT"?
LOVE IMPORTANT
THAT'S WHAT I NAMED THE GAME.
IT'S ABOUT THE *POWER OF LOVE!*
*THAT'S... SO DORKY.*

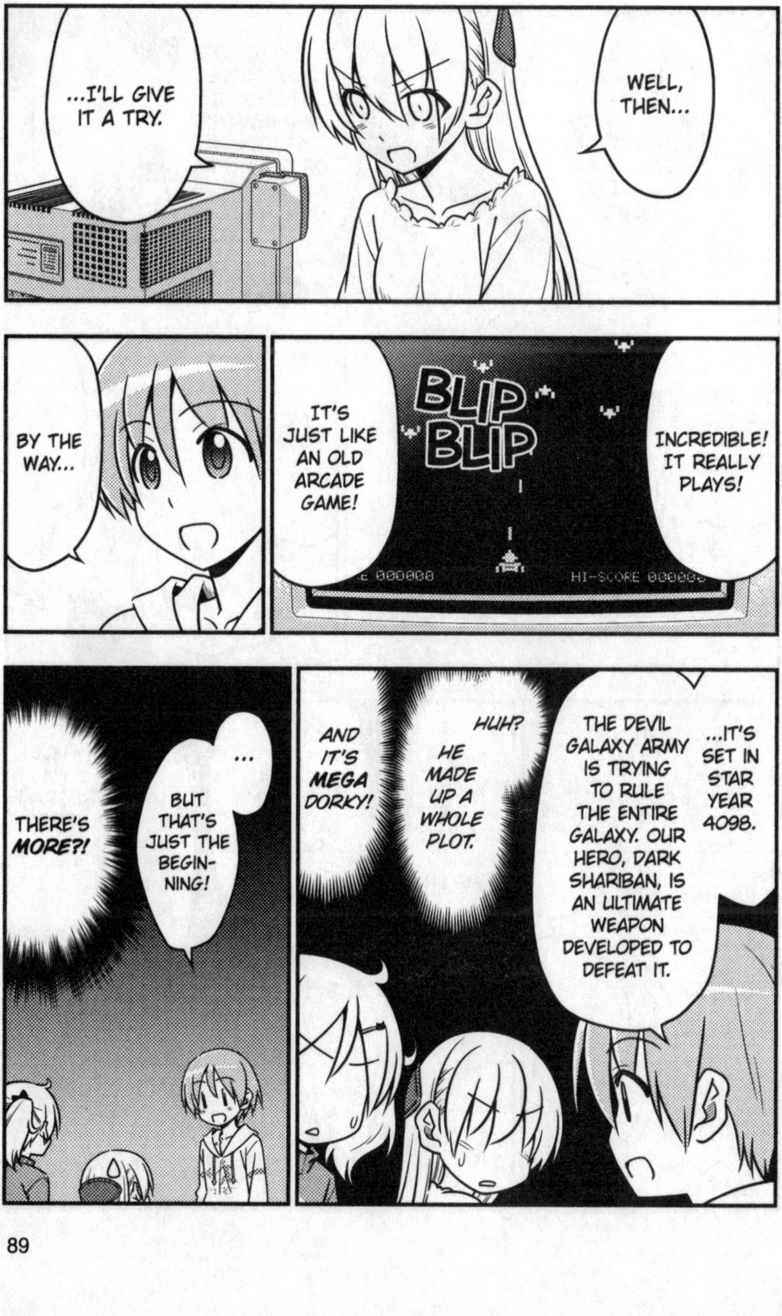
WELL, THEN...
...I'LL GIVE IT A TRY.
INCREDIBLE! IT REALLY PLAYS!
BLIP BLIP
IT'S JUST LIKE AN OLD ARCADE GAME!
BY THE WAY...
...IT'S SET IN STAR YEAR 4098.
THE DEVIL GALAXY ARMY IS TRYING TO RULE THE ENTIRE GALAXY. OUR HERO, DARK SHARIBAN, IS AN ULTIMATE WEAPON DEVELOPED TO DEFEAT IT.
HUH? HE MADE UP A WHOLE PLOT.
AND IT'S MEGA DORKY!
...
BUT THAT'S JUST THE BEGIN- NING!
THERE'S MORE?!

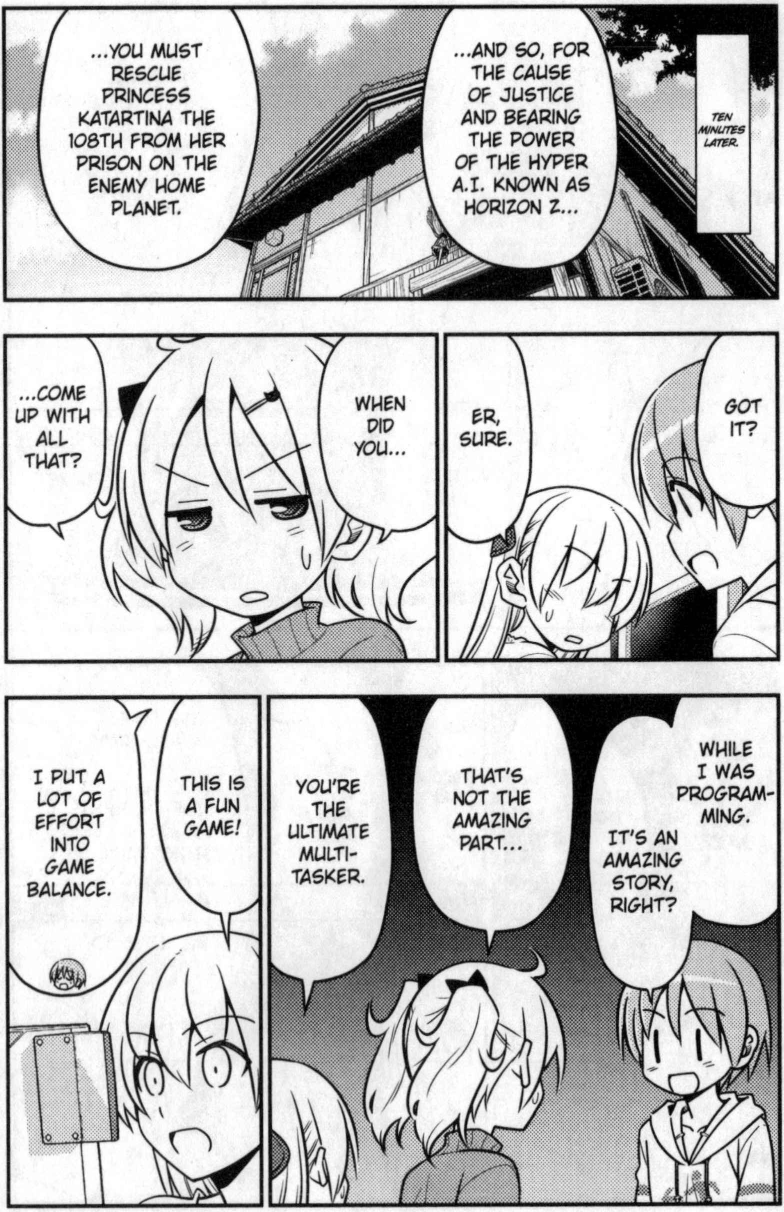
TEN MINUTES LATER.
...AND SO, FOR THE CAUSE OF JUSTICE AND BEARING THE POWER OF THE HYPER A.I. KNOWN AS HORIZON Z...
...YOU MUST RESCUE PRINCESS KATARTINA THE 108TH FROM HER PRISON ON THE ENEMY HOME PLANET.
GOT IT?
ER, SURE.
WHEN DID YOU...
...COME UP WITH ALL THAT?
WHILE I WAS PROGRAM-MING.
IT'S AN AMAZING STORY, RIGHT?
THAT'S NOT THE AMAZING PART...
YOU'RE THE ULTIMATE MULTI-TASKER.
THIS IS A FUN GAME!
I PUT A LOT OF EFFORT INTO GAME BALANCE.

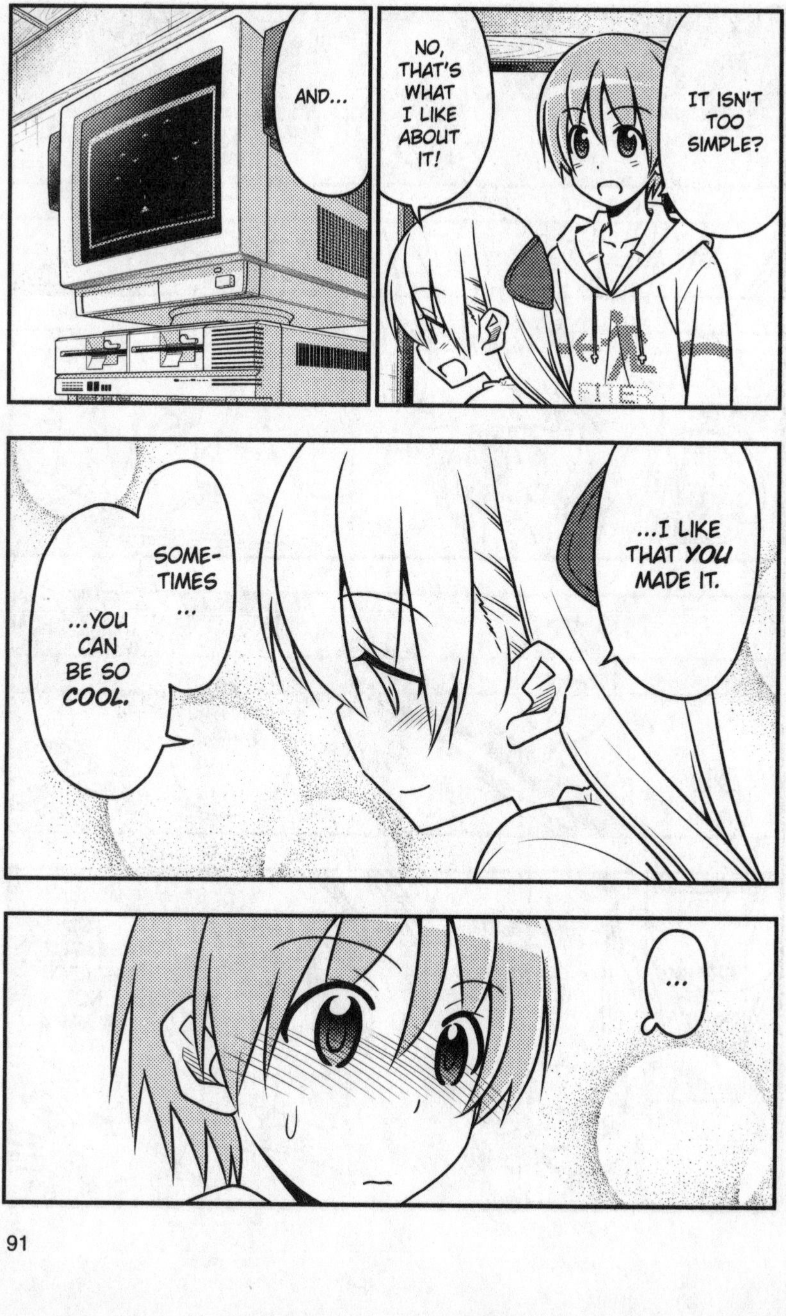
IT ISN'T TOO SIMPLE?
NO, THAT'S WHAT I LIKE ABOUT IT!
AND...
...I LIKE THAT YOU MADE IT.
SOME-TIMES ...
...YOU CAN BE SO COOL.
...

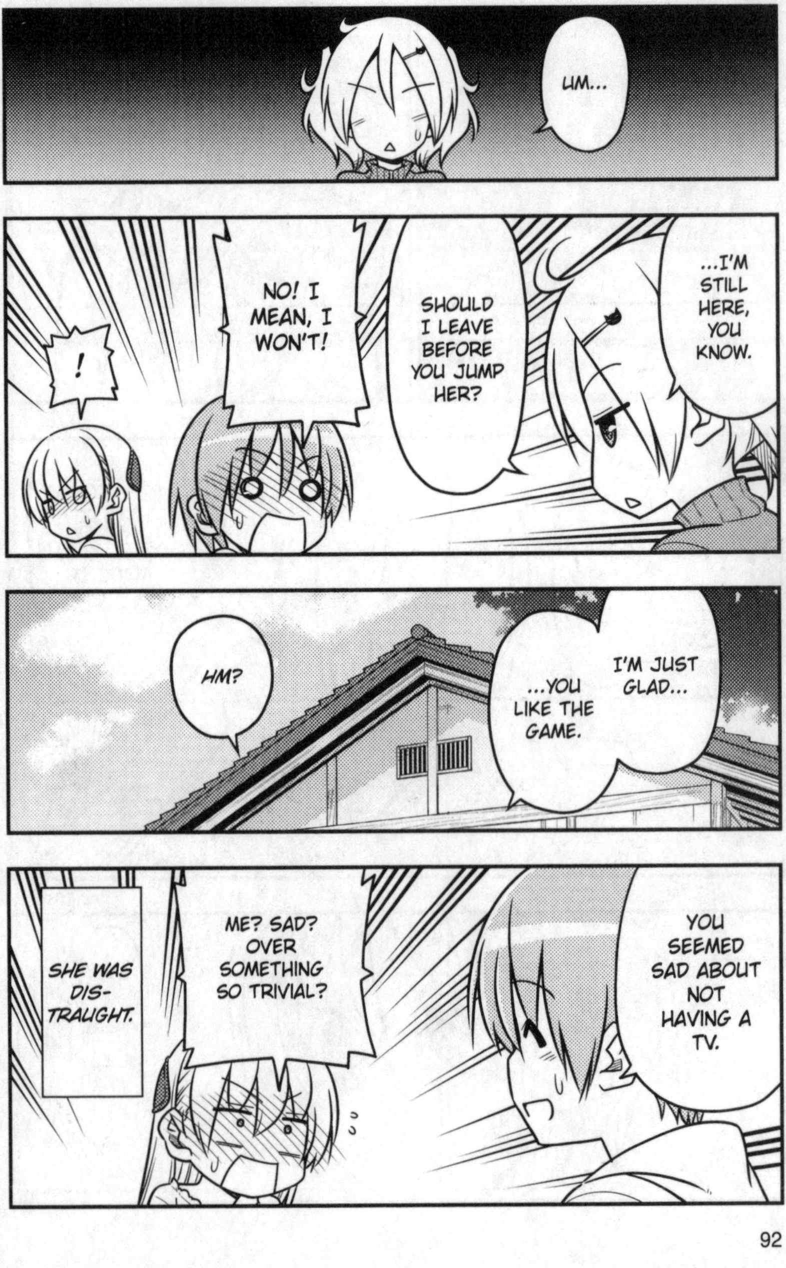
UM...
...I'M STILL HERE, YOU KNOW.
SHOULD I LEAVE BEFORE YOU JUMP HER?
NO! I MEAN, I WON'T!
!
I'M JUST GLAD...
...YOU LIKE THE GAME.
HM?
YOU SEEMED SAD ABOUT NOT HAVING A TV.
ME? SAD? OVER SOMETHING SO TRIVIAL?
SHE WAS DIS-TRAUGHT.

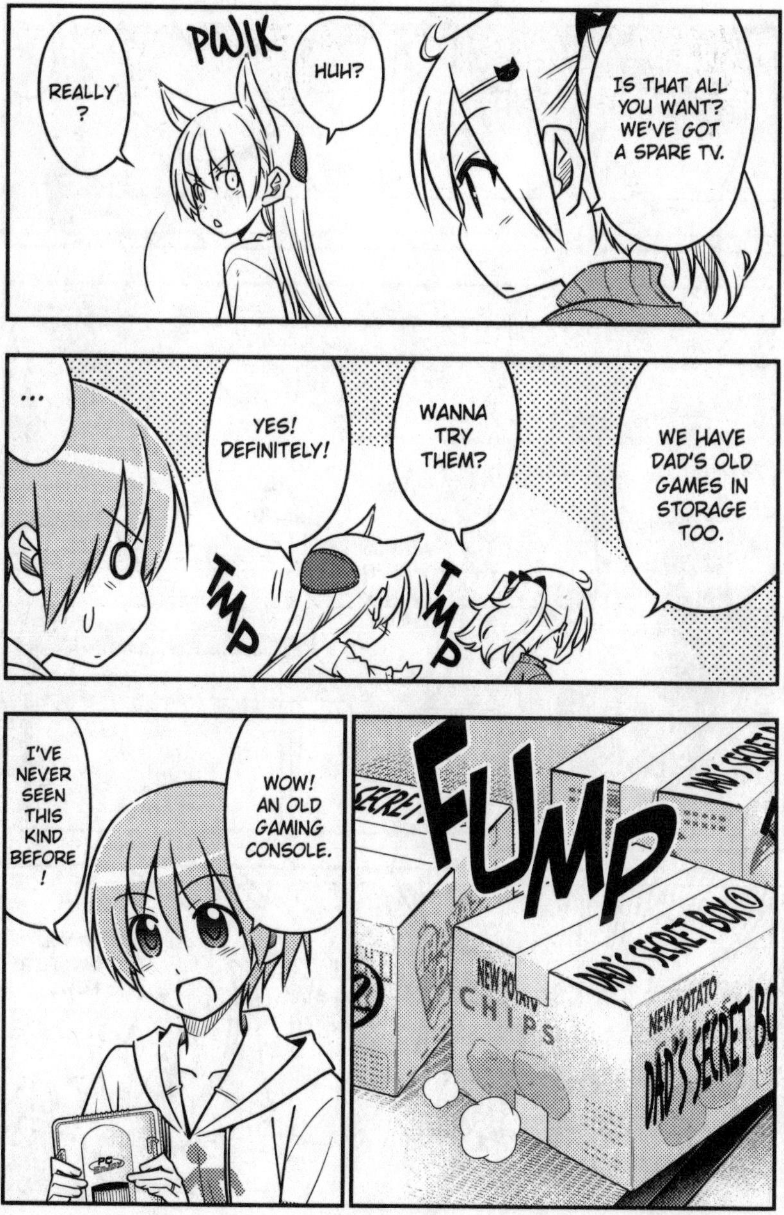
IS THAT ALL YOU WANT? WE'VE GOT A SPARE TV.
HUH?
PWIK
REALLY?
WE HAVE DAD'S OLD GAMES IN STORAGE TOO.
WANNA TRY THEM?
YES! DEFINITELY!
TMP
TMP
...
FUMP
DAD'S SECRET BOX ①
NEW POTATO CHIPS
NEW POTATO
WOW! AN OLD GAMING CONSOLE.
I'VE NEVER SEEN THIS KIND BEFORE!

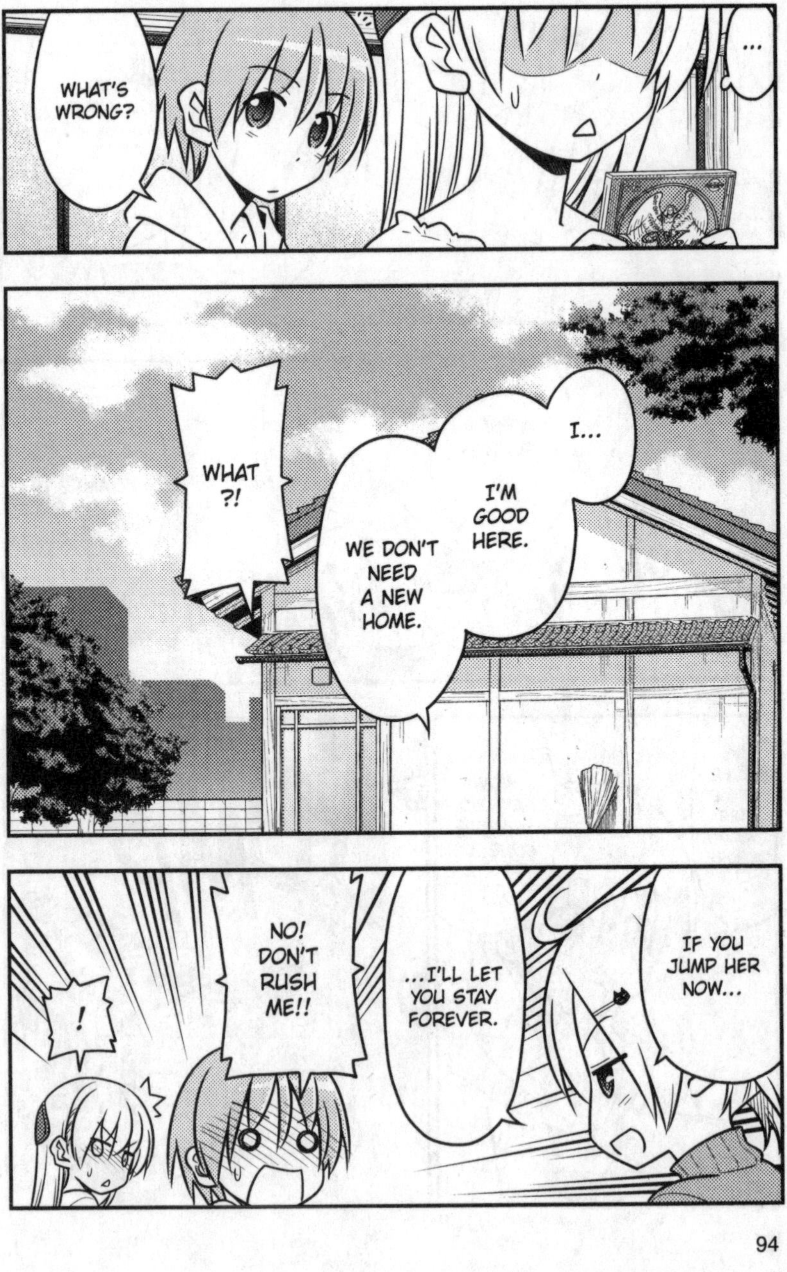
...
WHAT'S WRONG?
I...
I'M GOOD HERE.
WE DON'T NEED A NEW HOME.
WHAT ?!
IF YOU JUMP HER NOW...
...I'LL LET YOU STAY FOREVER.
NO! DON'T RUSH ME!!
!

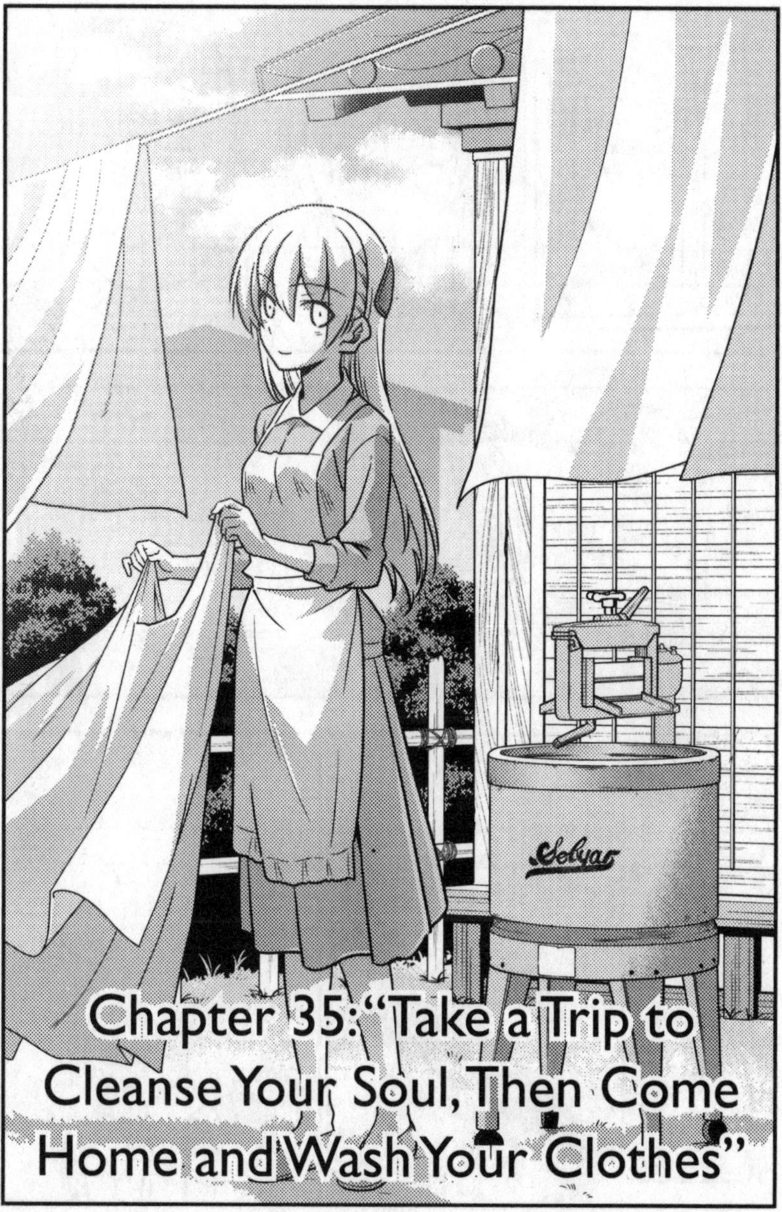
Chapter 35: "Take a Trip to Cleanse Your Soul, Then Come Home and Wash Your Clothes"

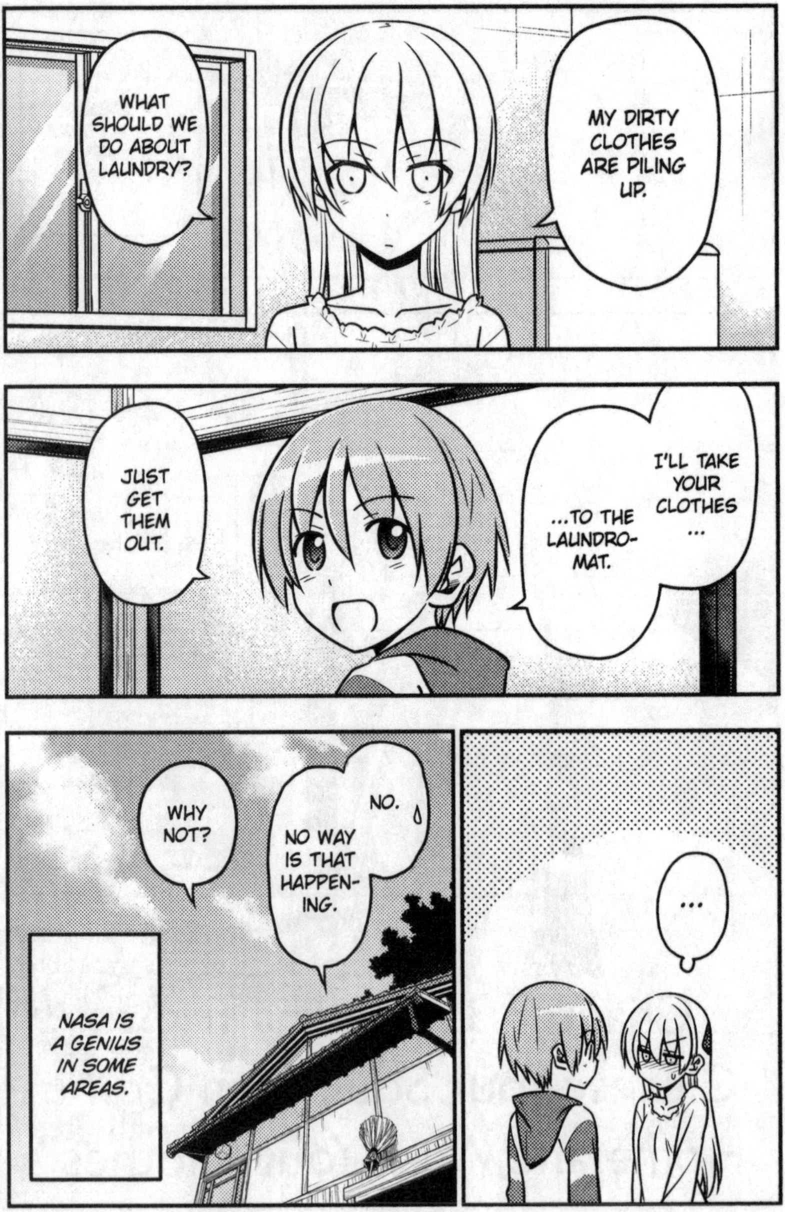
MY DIRTY CLOTHES ARE PILING UP.
WHAT SHOULD WE DO ABOUT LAUNDRY?
I'LL TAKE YOUR CLOTHES ...
...TO THE LAUNDROMAT.
JUST GET THEM OUT.
...
NO.
NO WAY IS THAT HAPPENING.
WHY NOT?
NASA IS A GENIUS IN SOME AREAS.

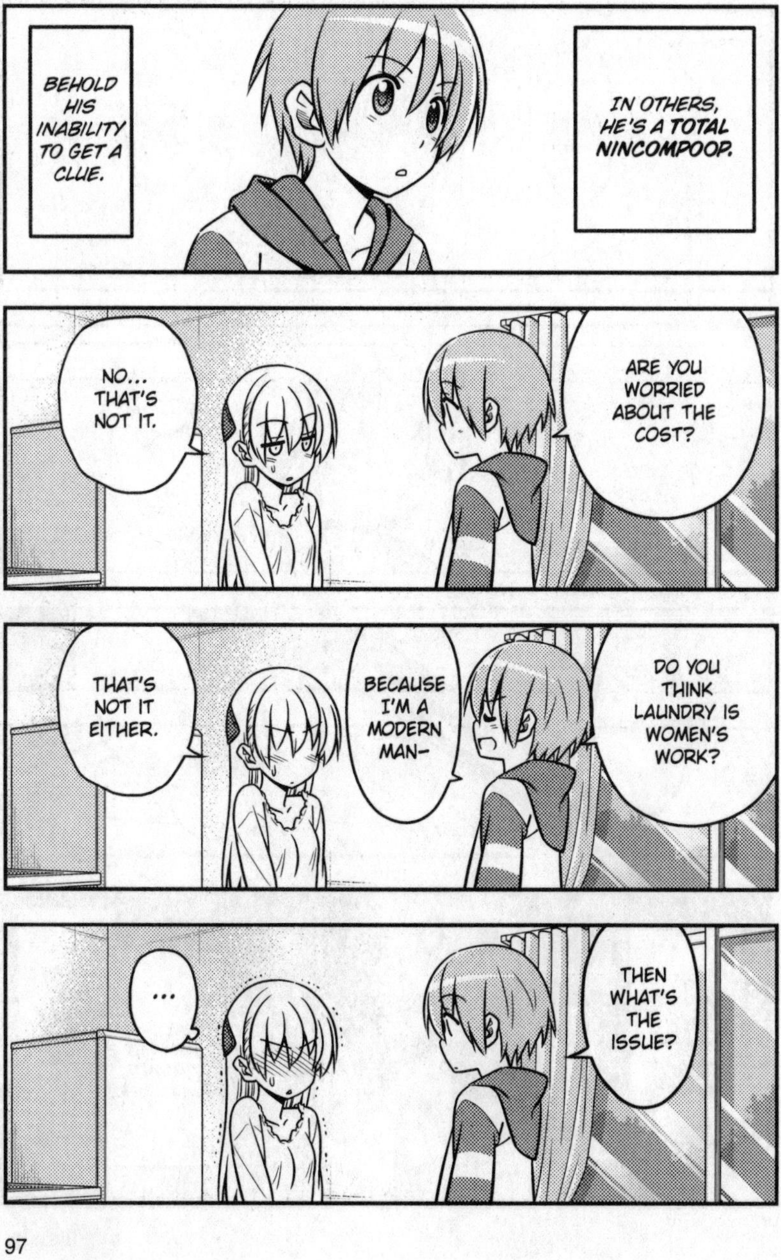
IN OTHERS, HE'S A TOTAL NINCOMPOOP.
BEHOLD HIS INABILITY TO GET A CLUE.
ARE YOU WORRIED ABOUT THE COST?
NO... THAT'S NOT IT.
DO YOU THINK LAUNDRY IS WOMEN'S WORK?
BECAUSE I'M A MODERN MAN-
THAT'S NOT IT EITHER.
THEN WHAT'S THE ISSUE?
...

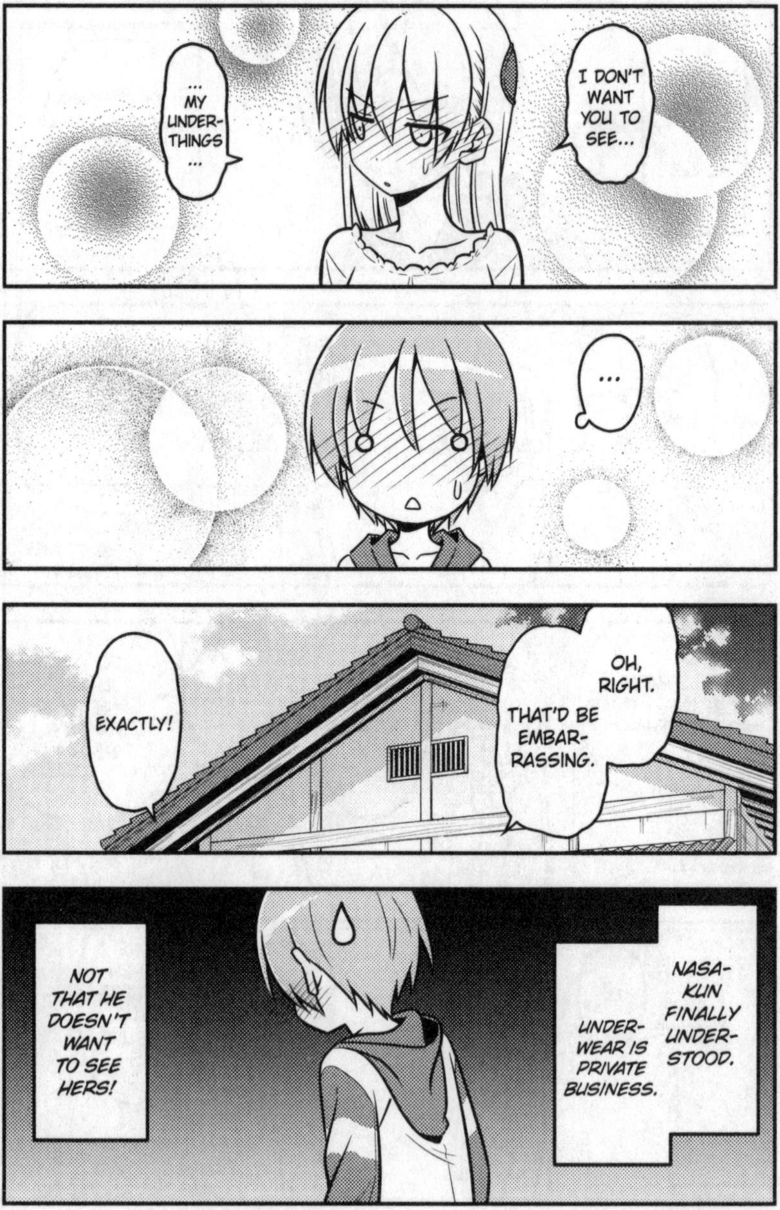
I DON'T WANT YOU TO SEE...
... MY UNDERTHINGS ...
...
OH, RIGHT.
THAT'D BE EMBARRASSING.
EXACTLY!
NASA-KUN FINALLY UNDERSTOOD.
UNDERWEAR IS PRIVATE BUSINESS.
NOT THAT HE DOESN'T WANT TO SEE HERS!

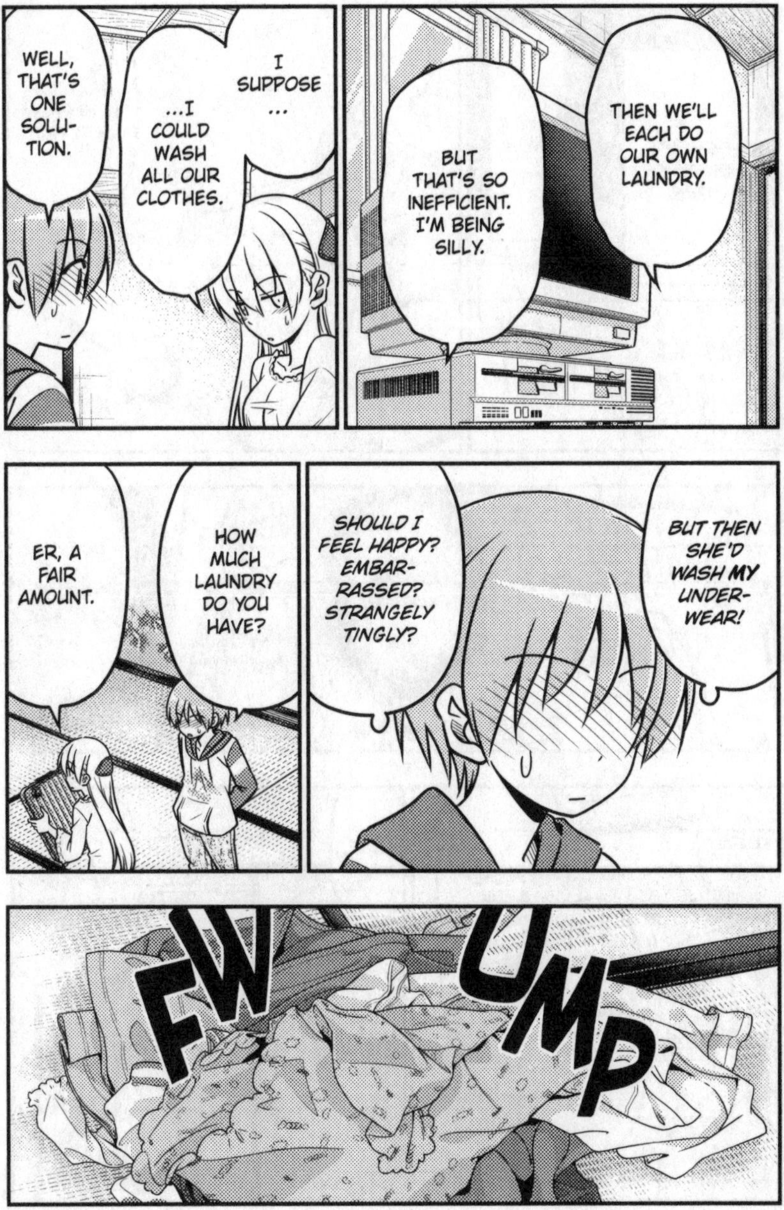
THEN WE'LL EACH DO OUR OWN LAUNDRY.
BUT THAT'S SO INEFFICIENT. I'M BEING SILLY.
I SUPPOSE ...
...I COULD WASH ALL OUR CLOTHES.
WELL, THAT'S ONE SOLU-TION.
BUT THEN SHE'D WASH MY UNDER-WEAR!
SHOULD I FEEL HAPPY? EMBAR-RASSED? STRANGELY TINGLY?
HOW MUCH LAUNDRY DO YOU HAVE?
ER, A FAIR AMOUNT.
FWUMP

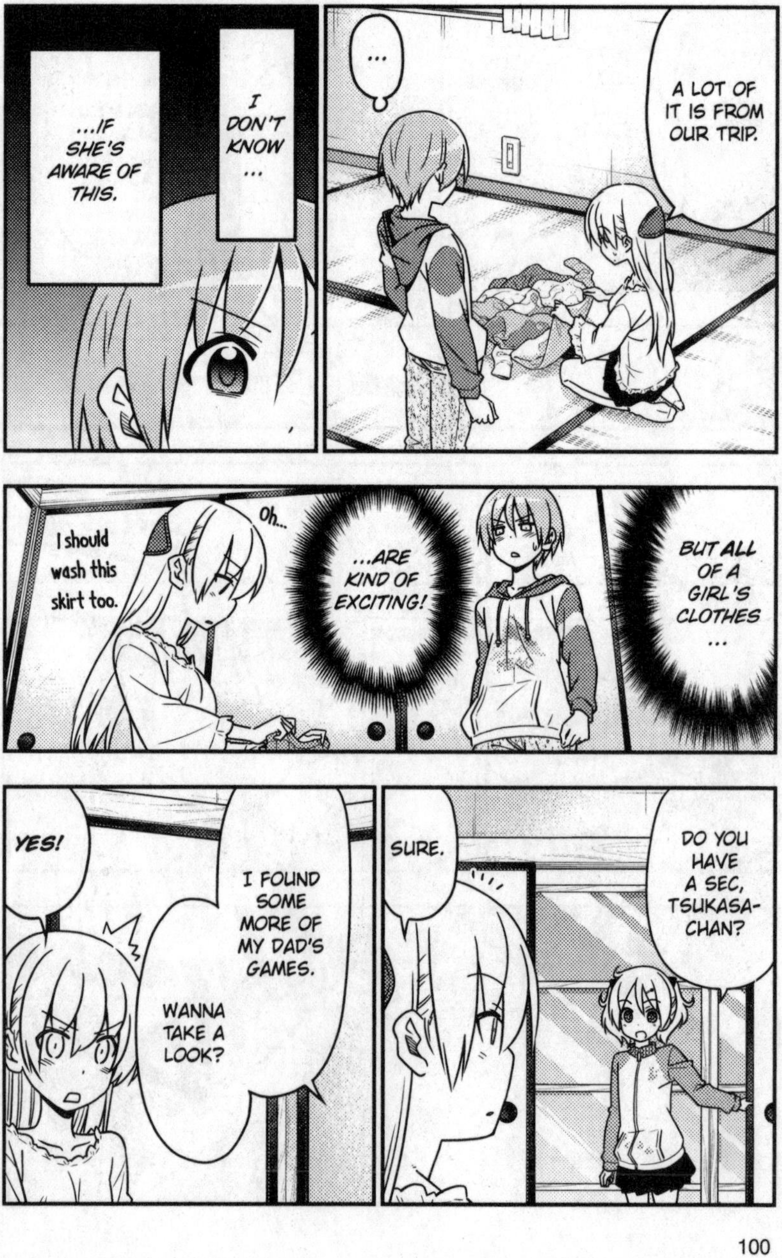
A LOT OF IT IS FROM OUR TRIP.
...
I DON'T KNOW...
...IF SHE'S AWARE OF THIS.
BUT ALL OF A GIRL'S CLOTHES...
...ARE KIND OF EXCITING!
Oh...
I should wash this skirt too.
DO YOU HAVE A SEC, TSUKASA-CHAN?
SURE.
I FOUND SOME MORE OF MY DAD'S GAMES.
WANNA TAKE A LOOK?
YES!

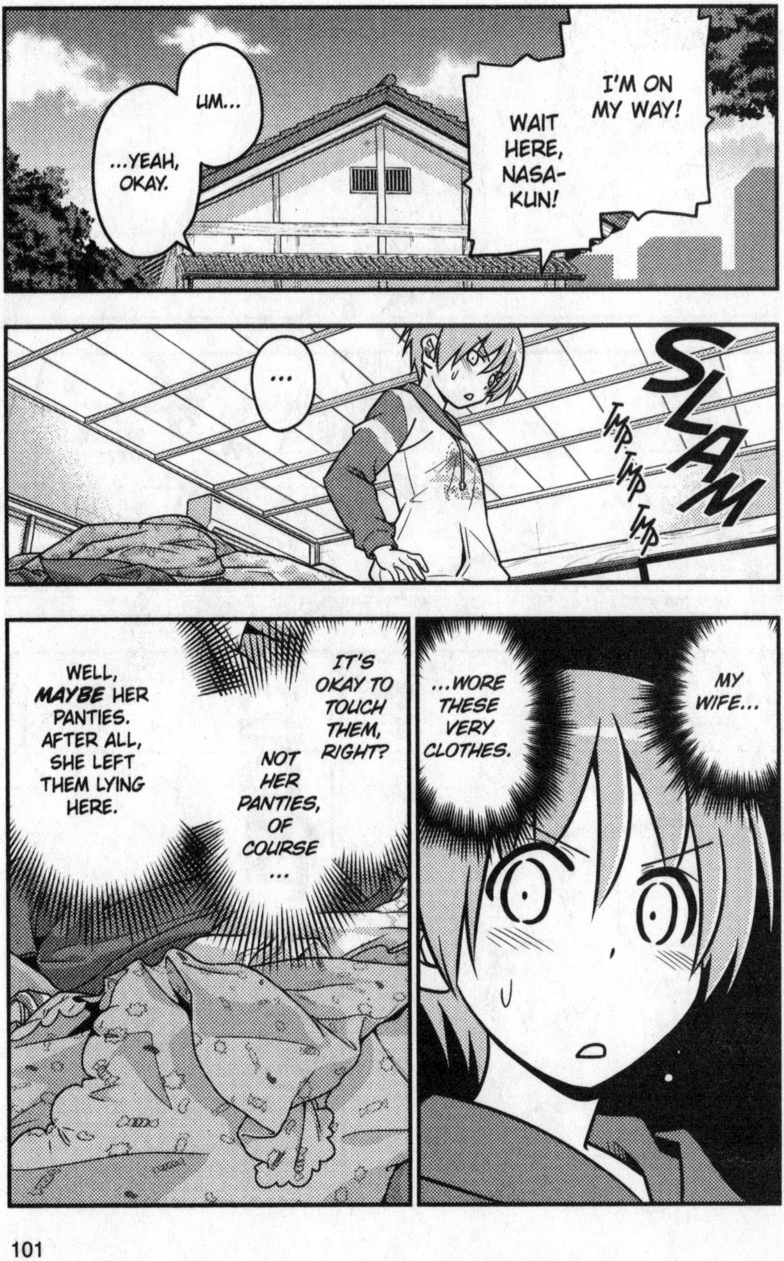
I'M ON MY WAY!
WAIT HERE, NASA-KUN!
UM...
...YEAH, OKAY.
SLAM
TMP TMP TMP TMP
...
MY WIFE...
...WORE THESE VERY CLOTHES.
IT'S OKAY TO TOUCH THEM, RIGHT?
NOT HER PANTIES, OF COURSE...
WELL, MAYBE HER PANTIES. AFTER ALL, SHE LEFT THEM LYING HERE.

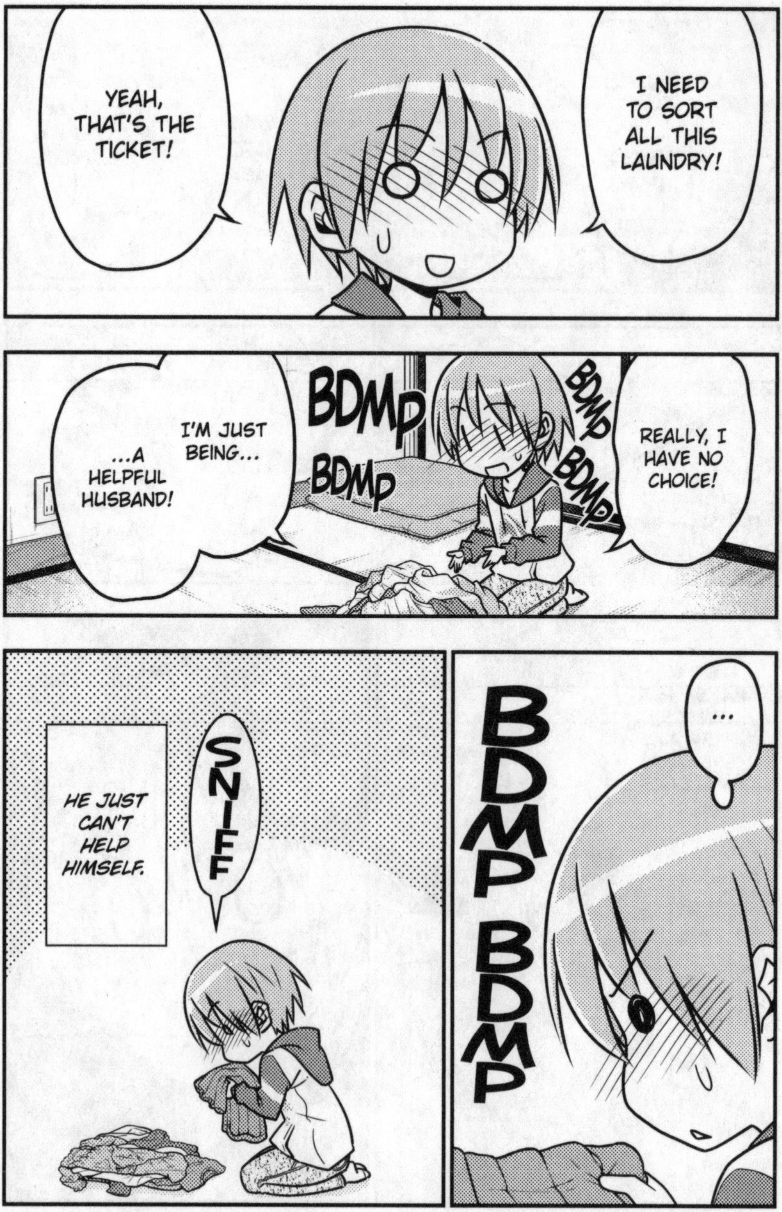

I NEED TO SORT ALL THIS LAUNDRY!
YEAH, THAT'S THE TICKET!
REALLY, I HAVE NO CHOICE!
BDMP BDMP
BDMP BDMP
I'M JUST BEING...
...A HELPFUL HUSBAND!
...
BDMP BDMP
SNIFF
HE JUST CAN'T HELP HIMSELF.

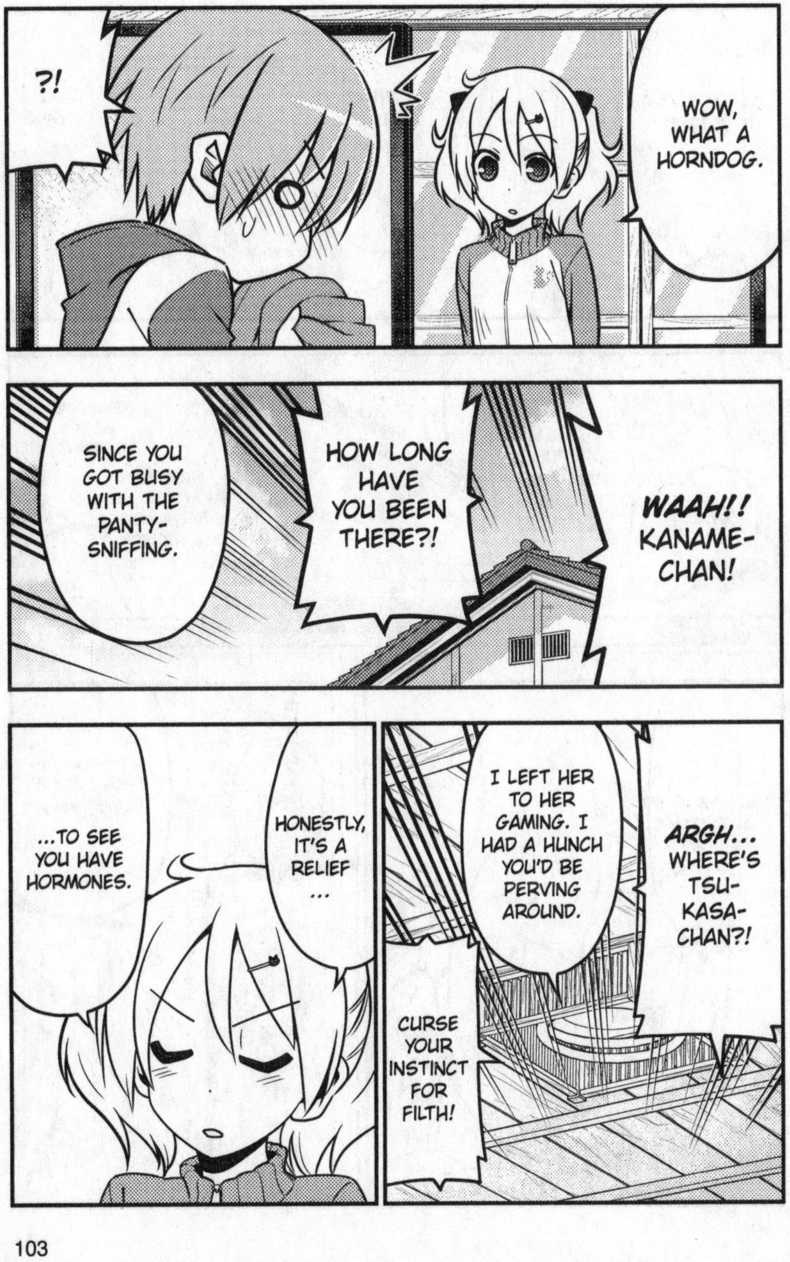
WOW, WHAT A HORNDOG.
?!
WAAH!! KANAME-CHAN!
HOW LONG HAVE YOU BEEN THERE?!
SINCE YOU GOT BUSY WITH THE PANTY-SNIFFING.
ARGH... WHERE'S TSU-KASA-CHAN?!
I LEFT HER TO HER GAMING. I HAD A HUNCH YOU'D BE PERVING AROUND.
CURSE YOUR INSTINCT FOR FILTH!
HONESTLY, IT'S A RELIEF...
...TO SEE YOU HAVE HORMONES.

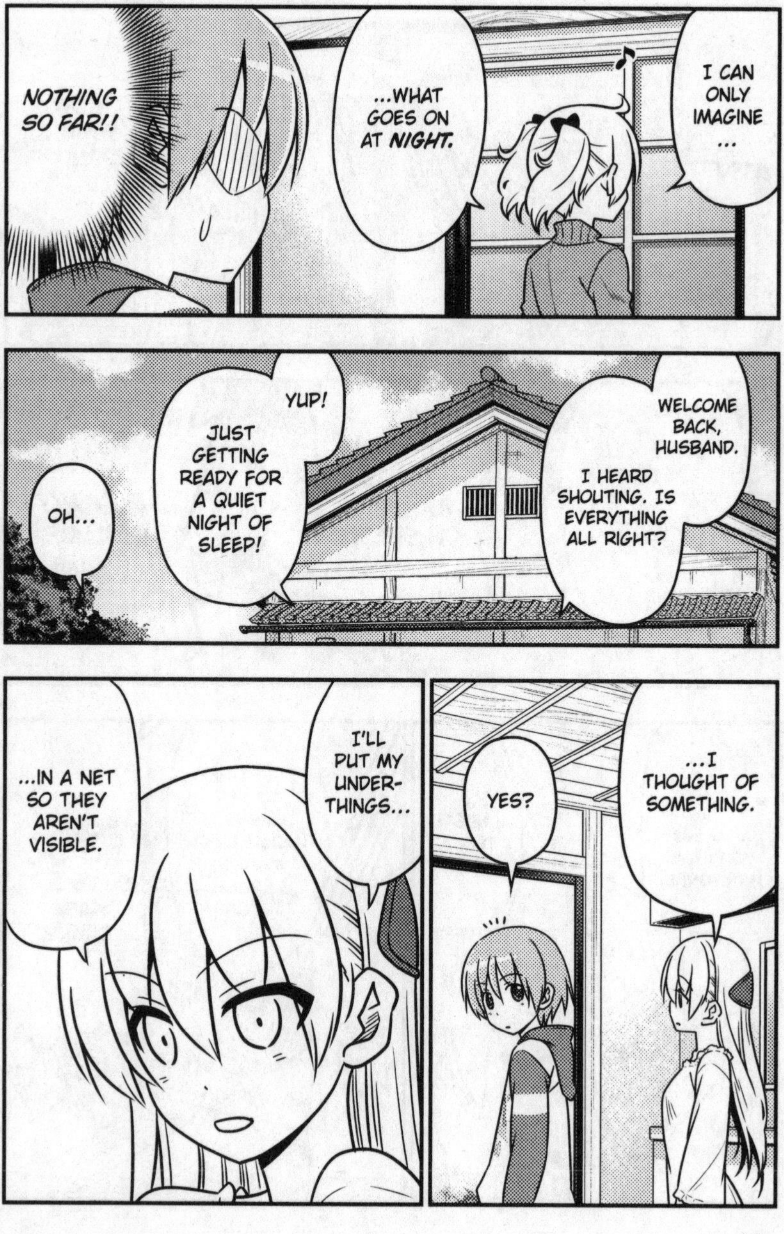
I CAN ONLY IMAGINE ...
...WHAT GOES ON AT NIGHT.
NOTHING SO FAR!!
WELCOME BACK, HUSBAND.
I HEARD SHOUTING. IS EVERYTHING ALL RIGHT?
YUP!
JUST GETTING READY FOR A QUIET NIGHT OF SLEEP!
OH...
...I THOUGHT OF SOMETHING.
YES?
I'LL PUT MY UNDER-THINGS...
...IN A NET SO THEY AREN'T VISIBLE.

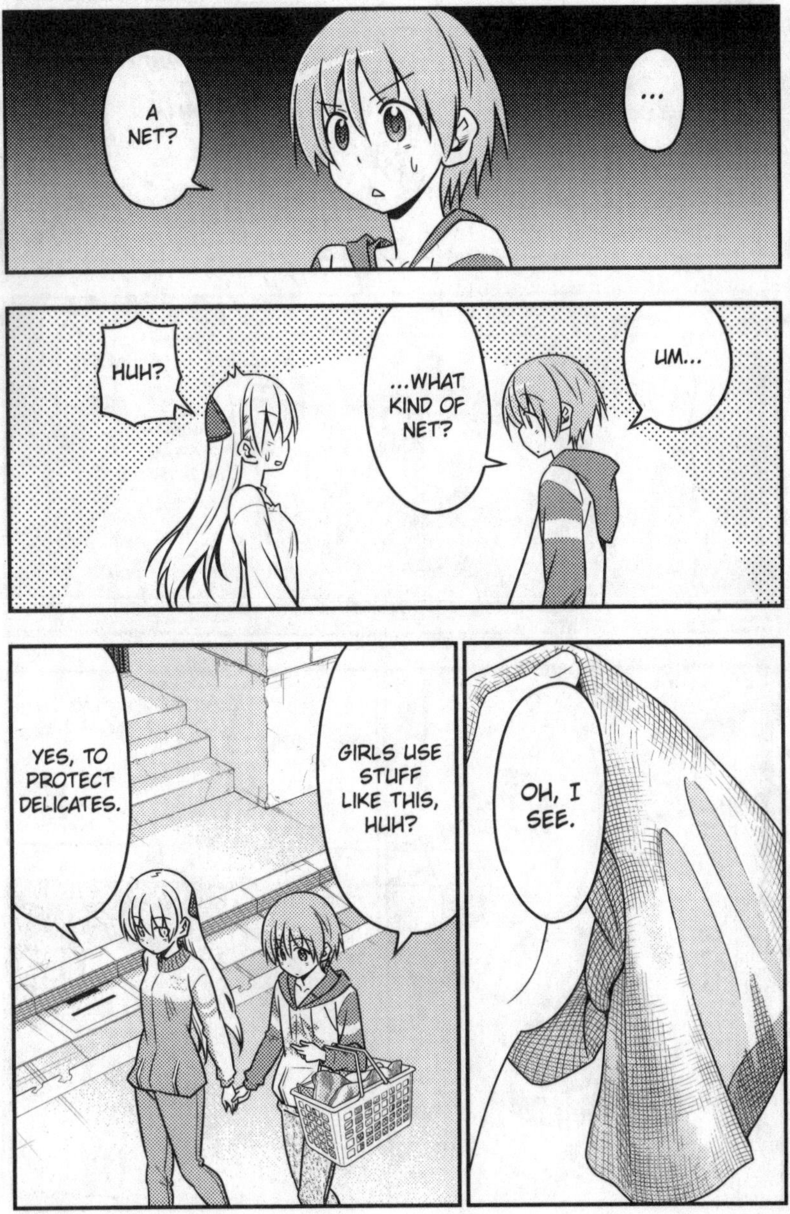
...
A NET?
UM...
...WHAT KIND OF NET?
HUH?
OH, I SEE.
GIRLS USE STUFF LIKE THIS, HUH?
YES, TO PROTECT DELICATES.

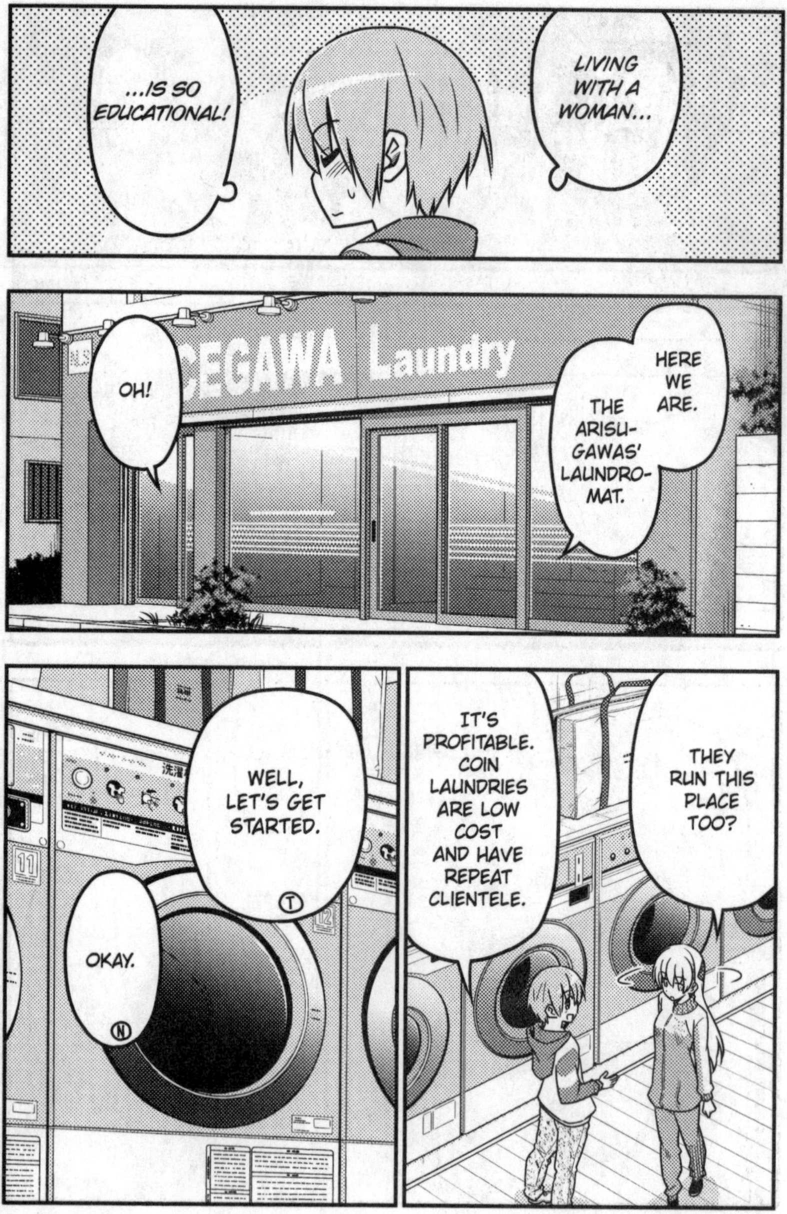
LIVING WITH A WOMAN...
...IS SO EDUCATIONAL!
HERE WE ARE.
THE ARISUGAWAS' LAUNDROMAT.
CEGAWA Laundry
OH!
THEY RUN THIS PLACE TOO?
IT'S PROFITABLE. COIN LAUNDRIES ARE LOW COST AND HAVE REPEAT CLIENTELE.
WELL, LET'S GET STARTED.
OKAY.

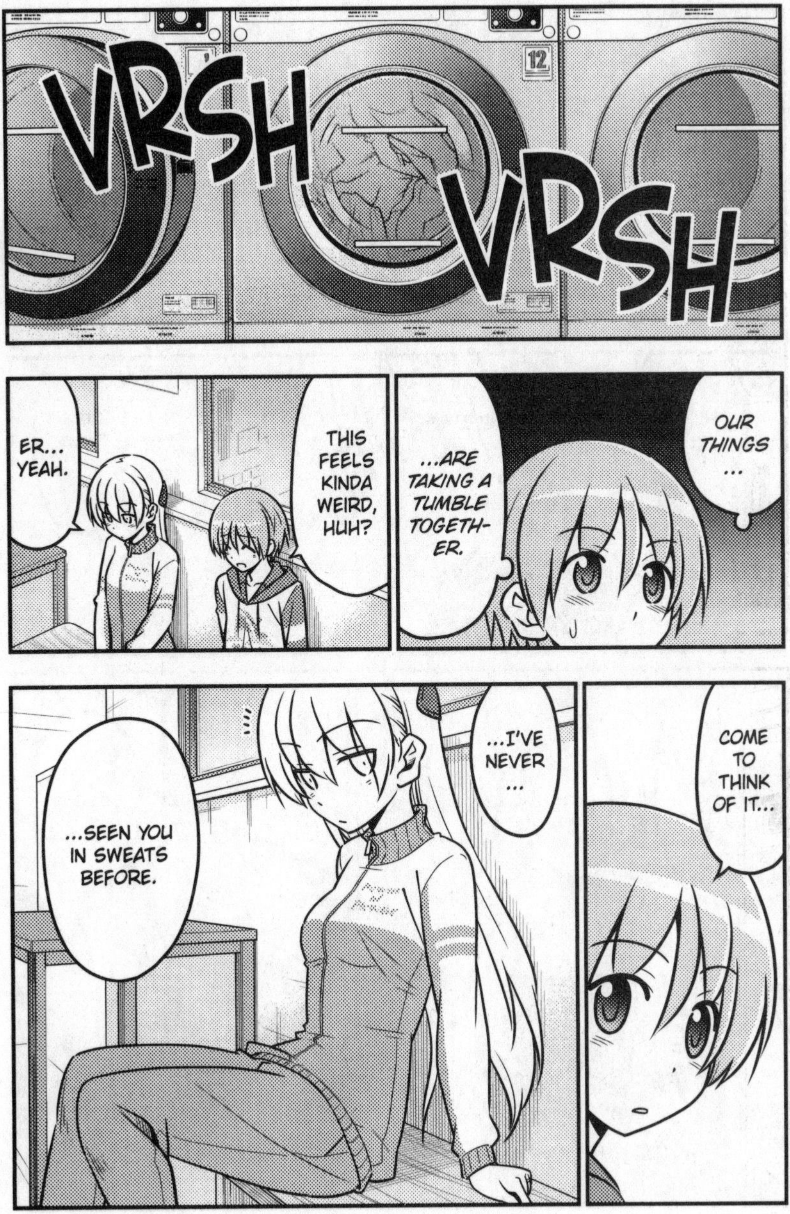
VRSH
VRSH
OUR THINGS...
...ARE TAKING A TUMBLE TOGETH-ER.
THIS FEELS KINDA WEIRD, HUH?
ER... YEAH.
COME TO THINK OF IT...
...I'VE NEVER...
...SEEN YOU IN SWEATS BEFORE.

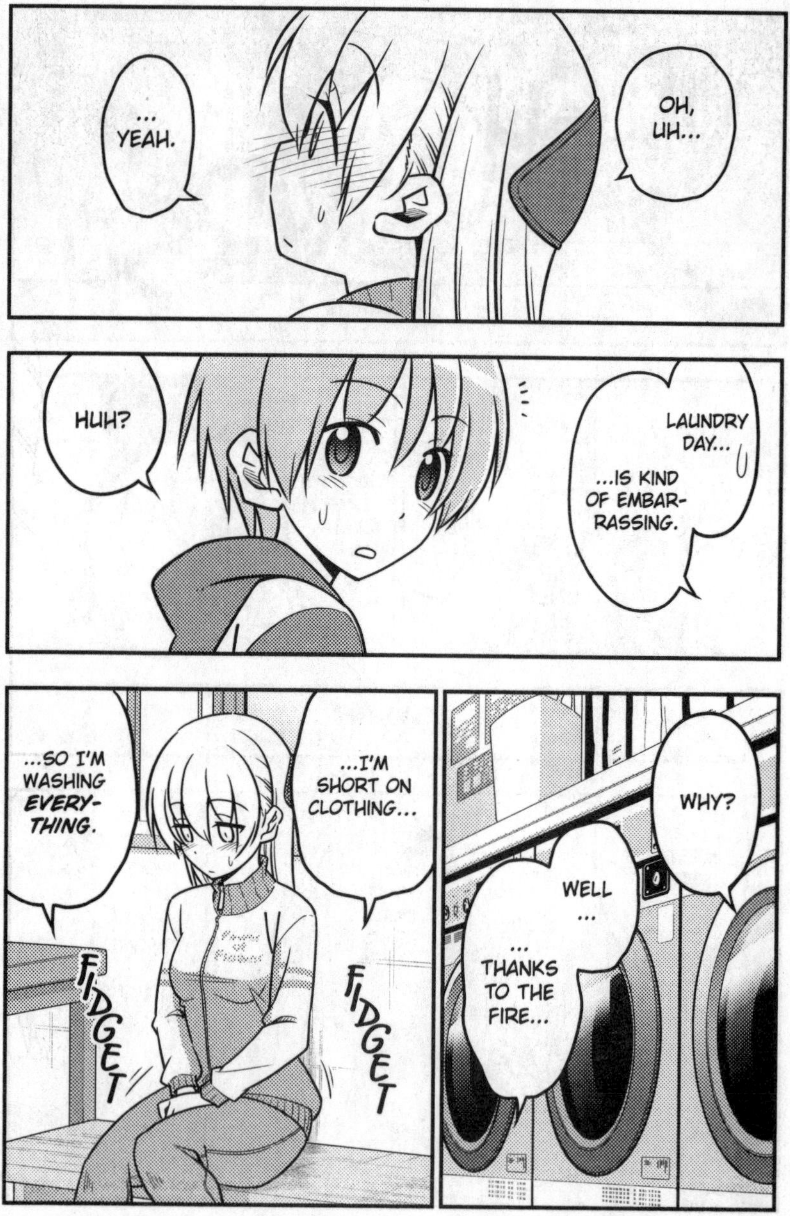
OH, UH...
...YEAH.
LAUNDRY DAY...
...IS KIND OF EMBARRASSING.
HUH?
WHY?
WELL...
...THANKS TO THE FIRE...
...I'M SHORT ON CLOTHING...
...SO I'M WASHING EVERYTHING.
FIDGET
FIDGET

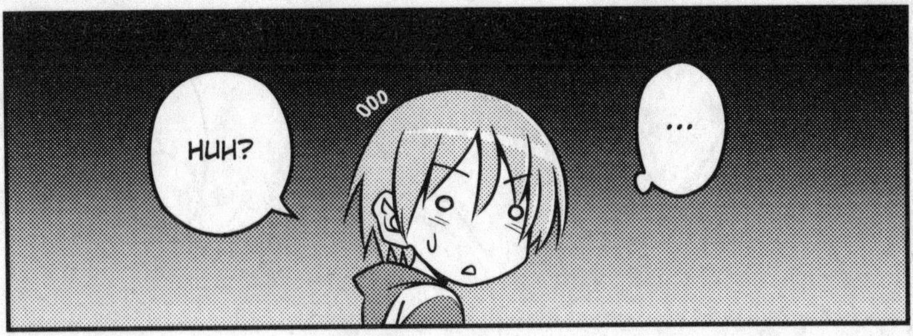
...
HUH?

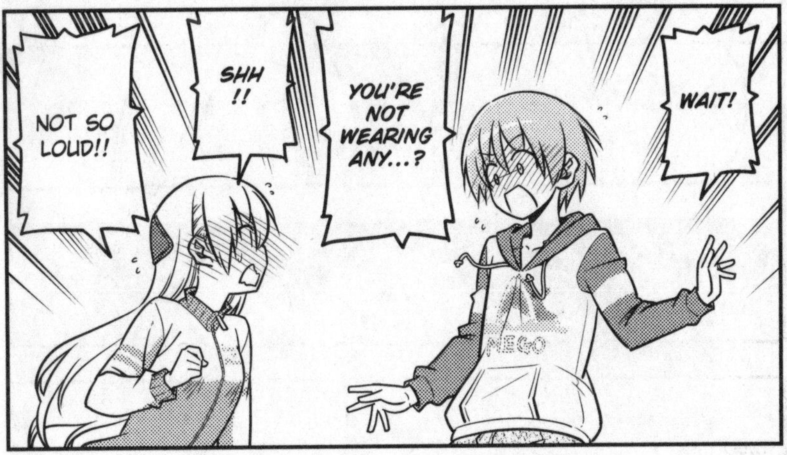
WAIT!
YOU'RE NOT WEARING ANY...?
SHH !!
NOT SO LOUD!!

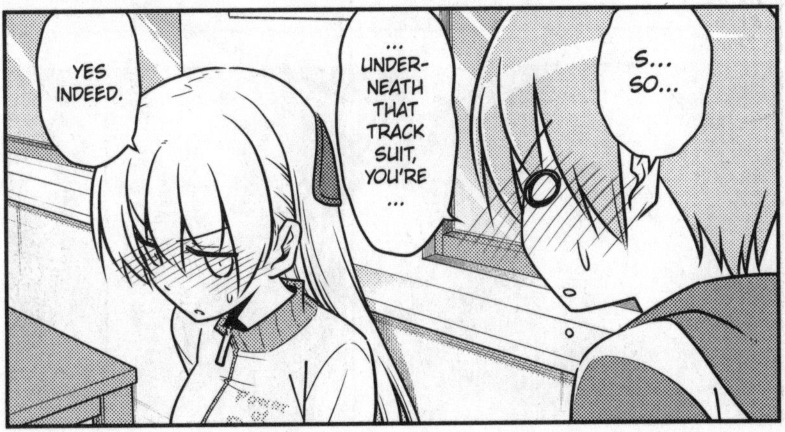
S... SO...
... UNDER-NEATH THAT TRACK SUIT, YOU'RE ...
YES INDEED.

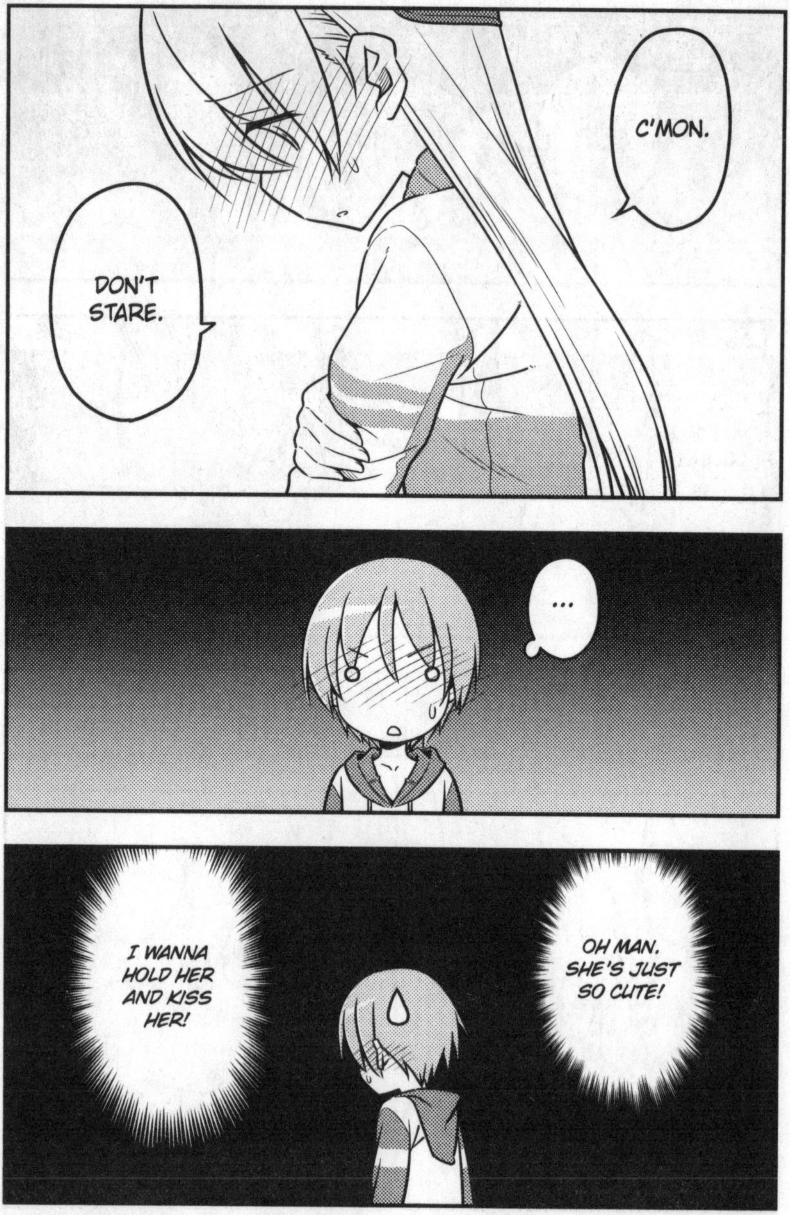
C'MON.
DON'T STARE.
...
OH MAN. SHE'S JUST SO CUTE!
I WANNA HOLD HER AND KISS HER!

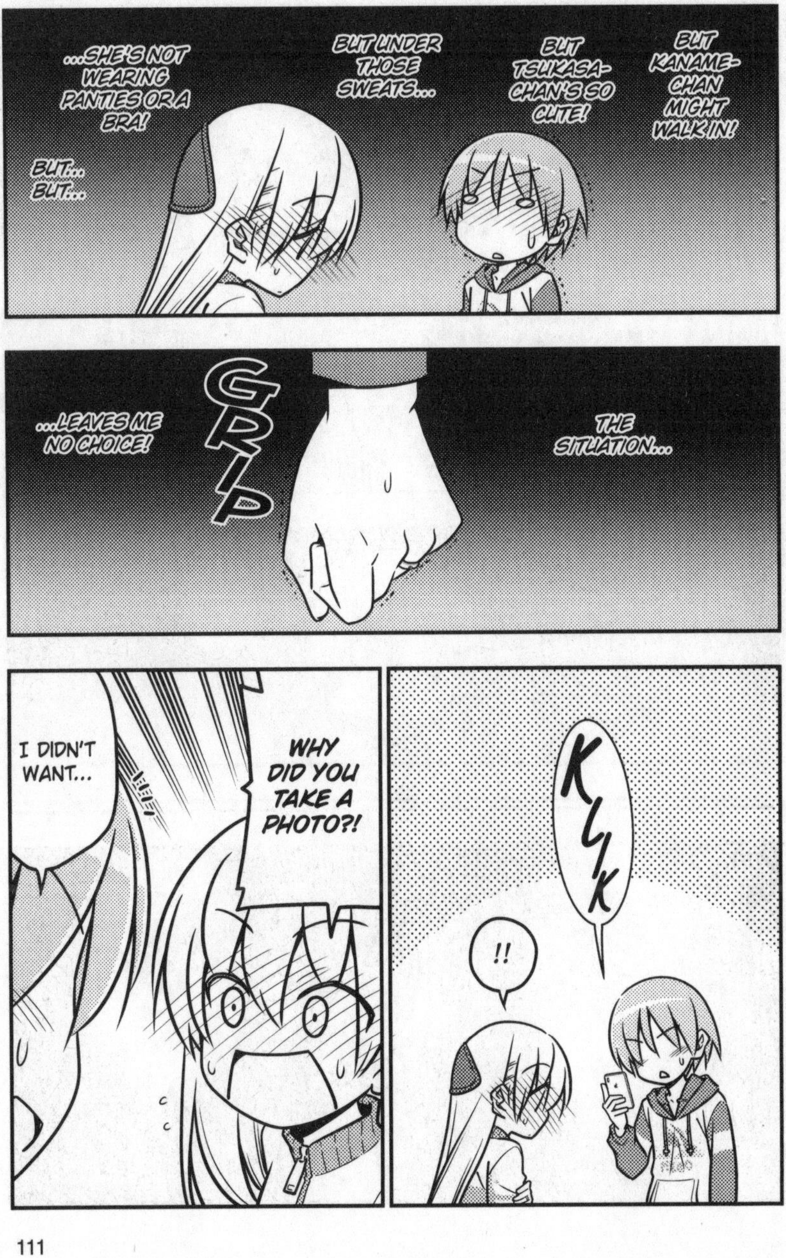
BUT KANAME-CHAN MIGHT WALK IN!
BUT TSUKASA-CHAN'S SO CUTE!
BUT UNDER THOSE SWEATS...
...SHE'S NOT WEARING PANTIES OR A BRA!
BUT... BUT...
THE SITUATION...
GRIP
...LEAVES ME NO CHOICE!
KLIK
!!
WHY DID YOU TAKE A PHOTO?!
I DIDN'T WANT...

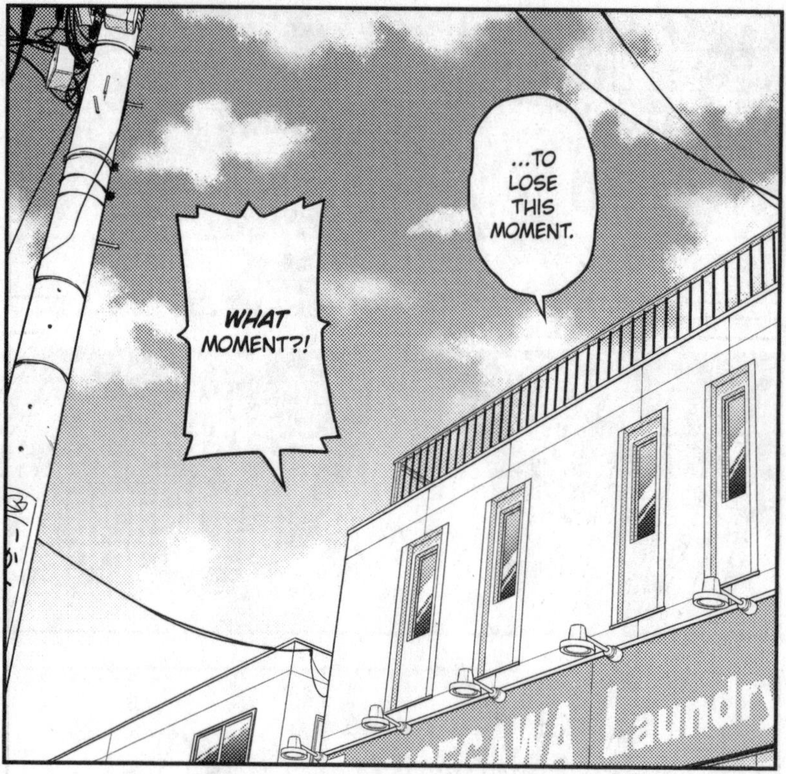
...TO LOSE THIS MOMENT.
WHAT MOMENT?!

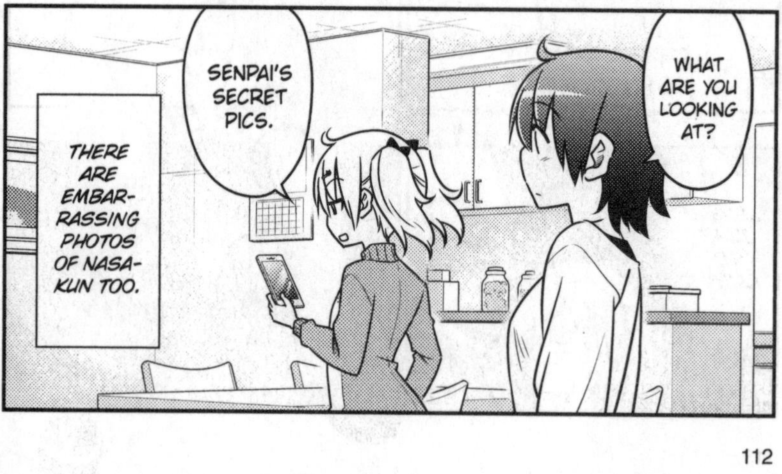
WHAT ARE YOU LOOKING AT?
SENPAI'S SECRET PICS.
THERE ARE EMBARRASSING PHOTOS OF NASA-KUN TOO.

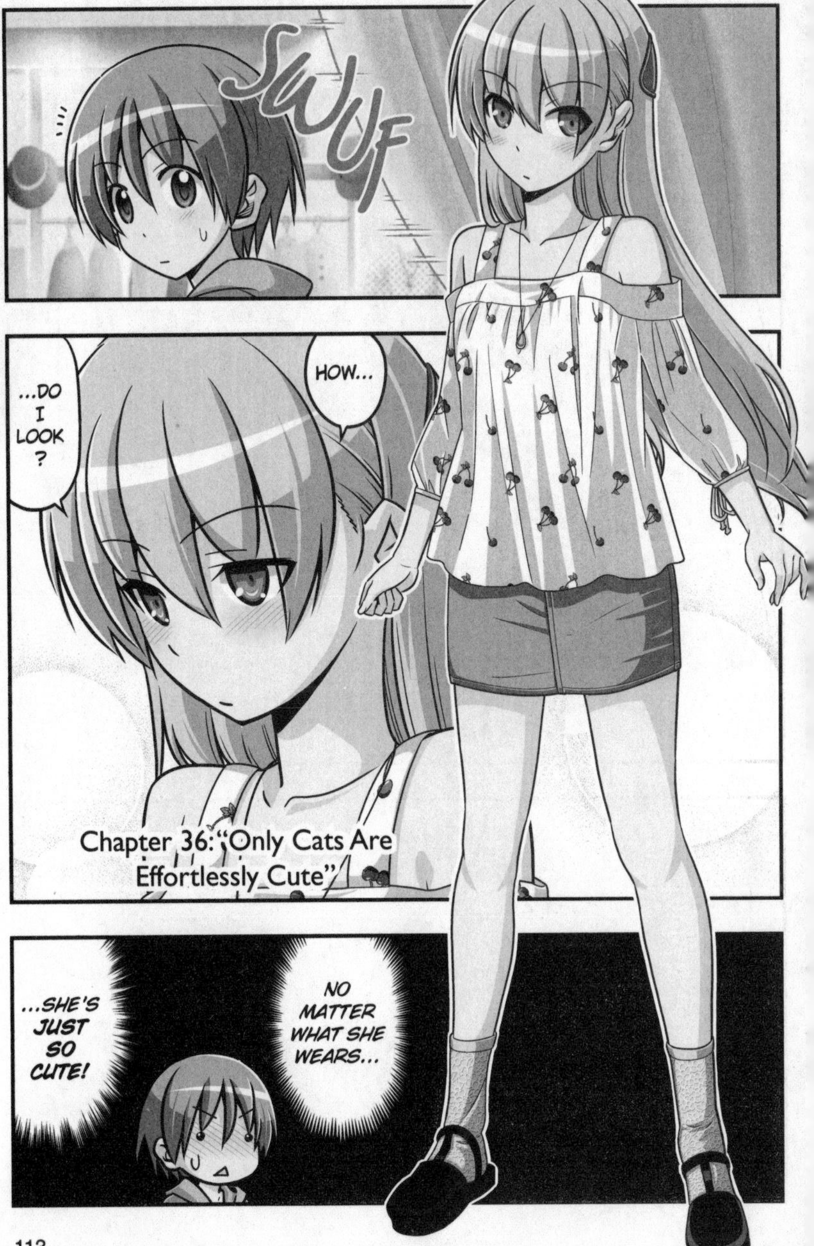
SWUF
HOW...
...DO I LOOK?
Chapter 36: "Only Cats Are Effortlessly Cute"
NO MATTER WHAT SHE WEARS...
...SHE'S JUST SO CUTE!

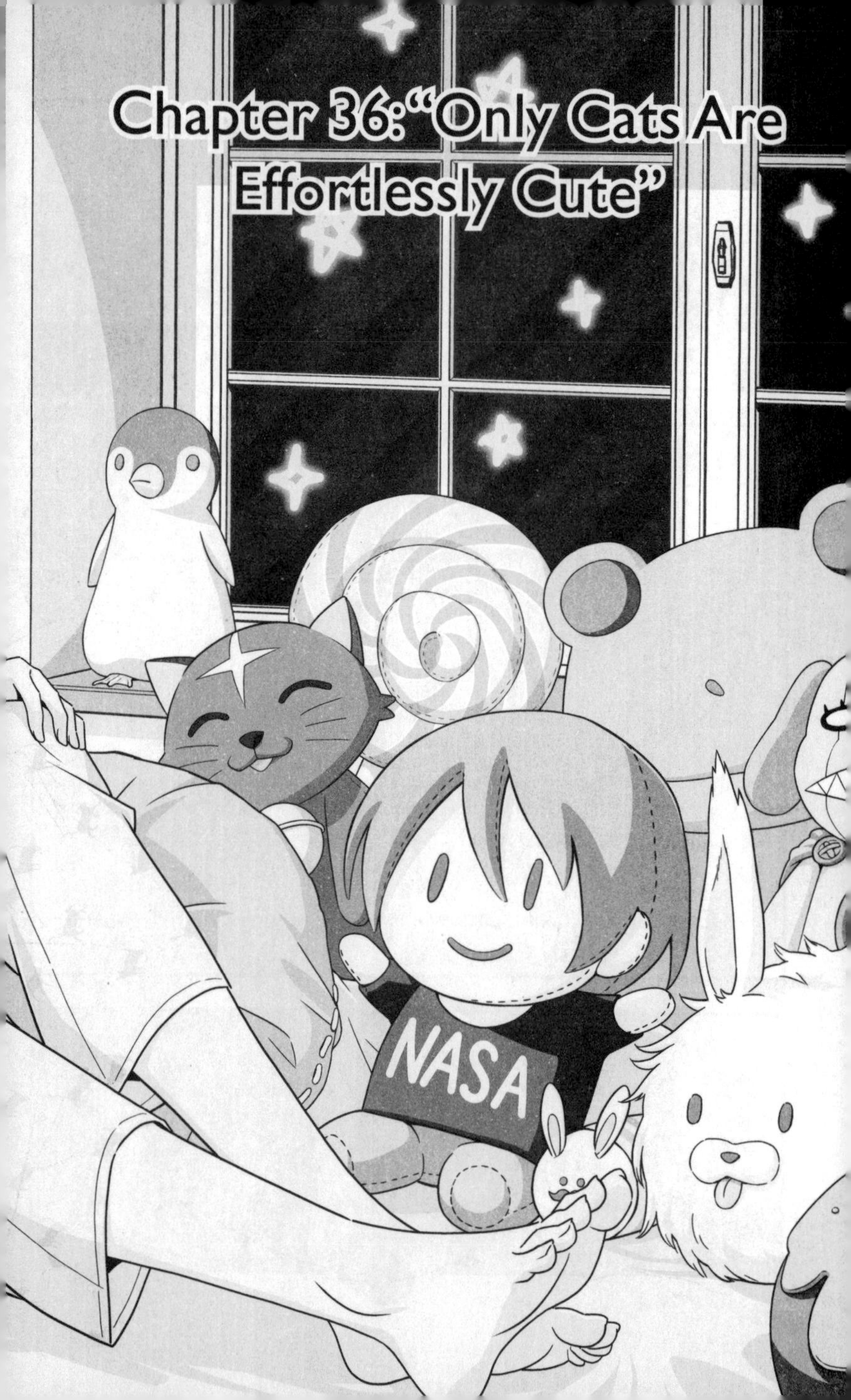
Chapter 36: "Only Cats Are Effortlessly Cute"
NASA

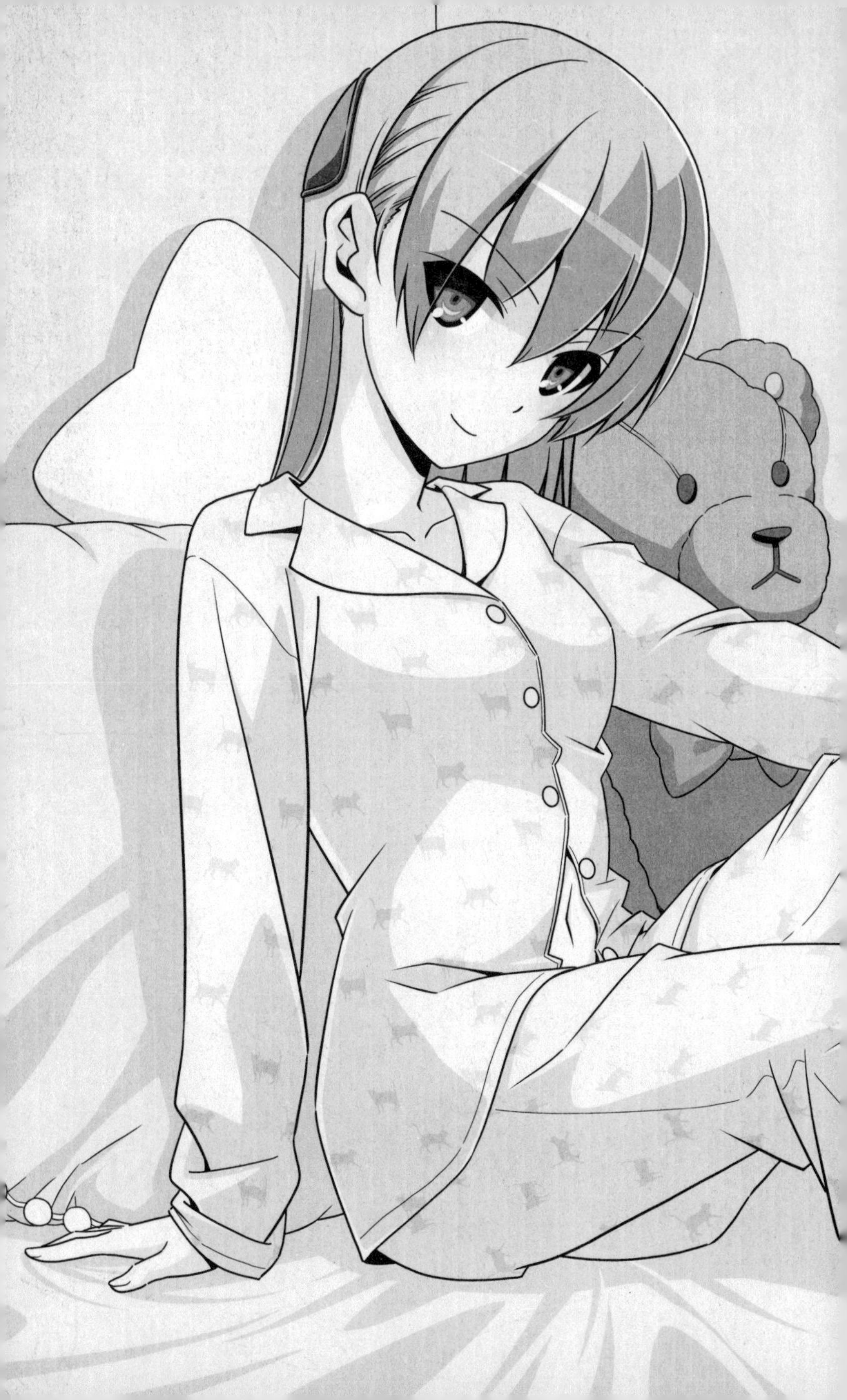

FLY ME <sup>TO</sup><sub>THE</sub> MOON

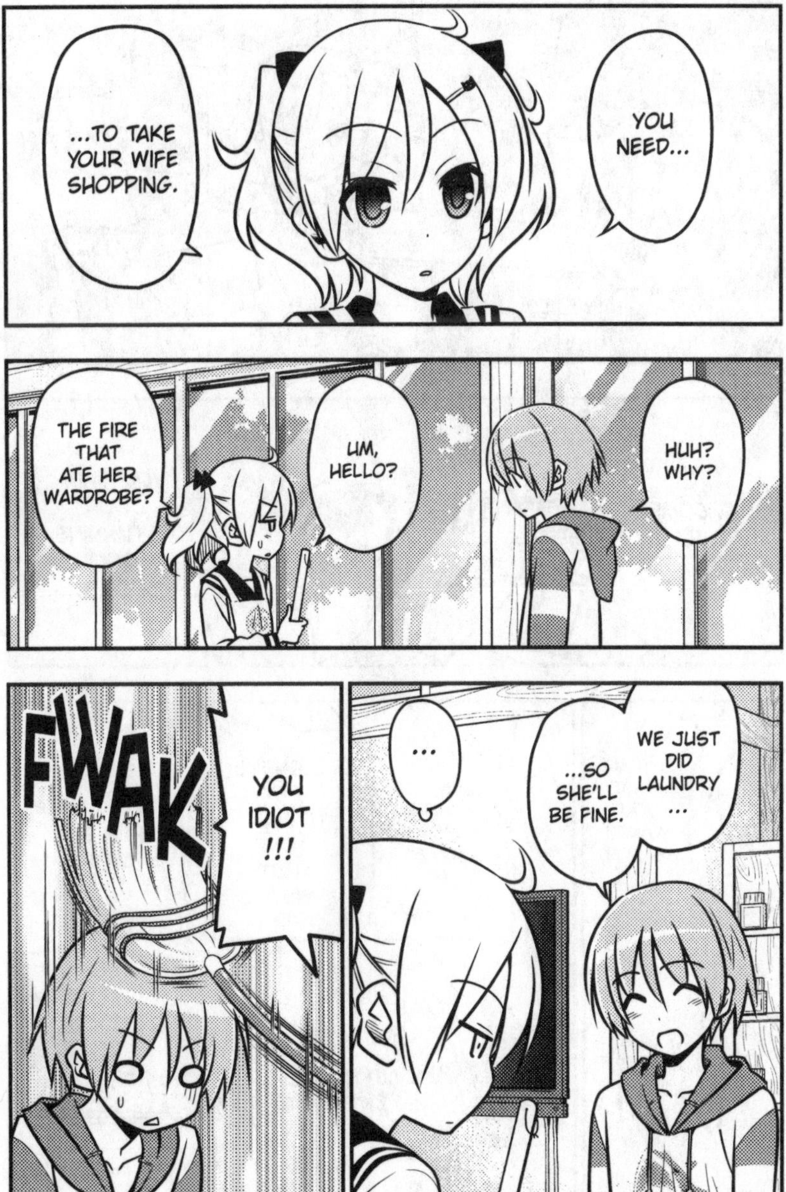
YOU NEED...
...TO TAKE YOUR WIFE SHOPPING.
HUH? WHY?
UM, HELLO?
THE FIRE THAT ATE HER WARDROBE?
WE JUST DID LAUNDRY ...
...SO SHE'LL BE FINE.
...
YOU IDIOT !!!
FWAK

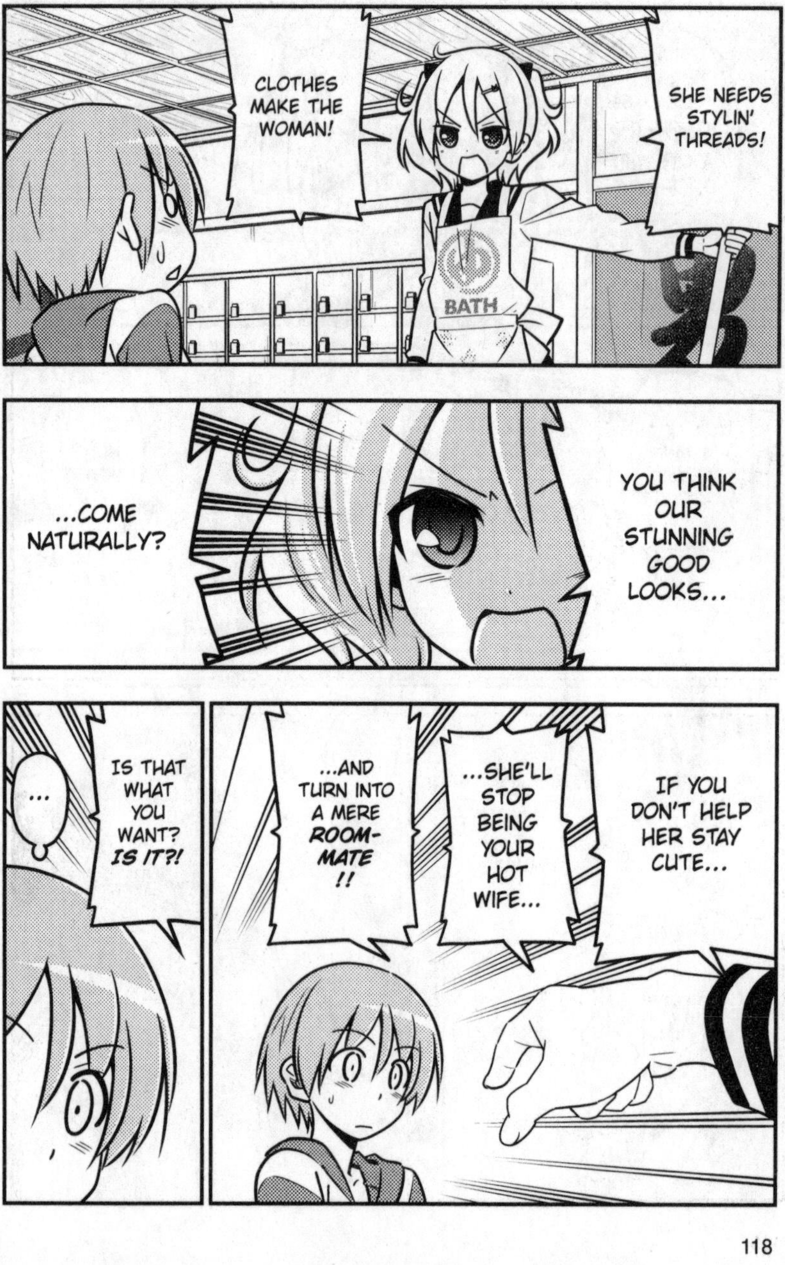
SHE NEEDS STYLIN' THREADS!
CLOTHES MAKE THE WOMAN!
YOU THINK OUR STUNNING GOOD LOOKS...
...COME NATURALLY?
IF YOU DON'T HELP HER STAY CUTE...
...SHE'LL STOP BEING YOUR HOT WIFE...
...AND TURN INTO A MERE ROOM-MATE!!
IS THAT WHAT YOU WANT? IS IT?!
...

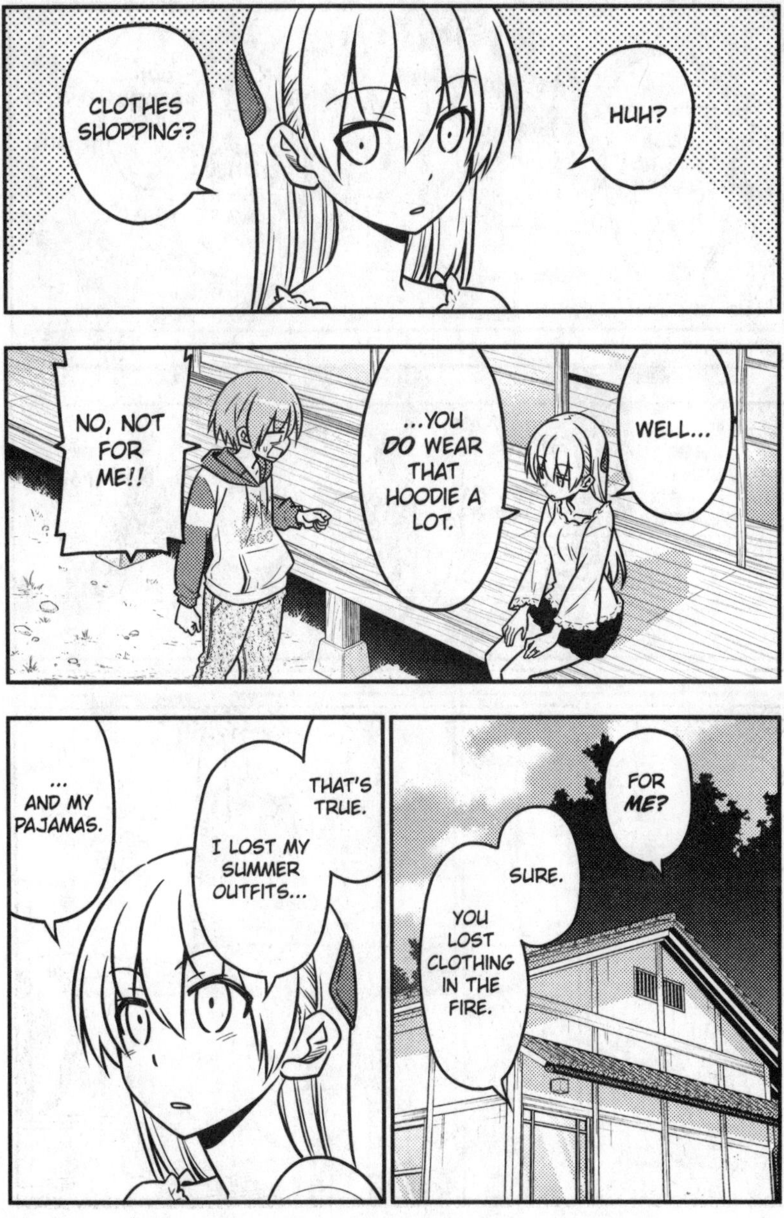
HUH?
CLOTHES SHOPPING?
WELL...
...YOU DO WEAR THAT HOODIE A LOT.
NO, NOT FOR ME!!
FOR ME?
SURE.
YOU LOST CLOTHING IN THE FIRE.
THAT'S TRUE.
I LOST MY SUMMER OUTFITS...
... AND MY PAJAMAS.

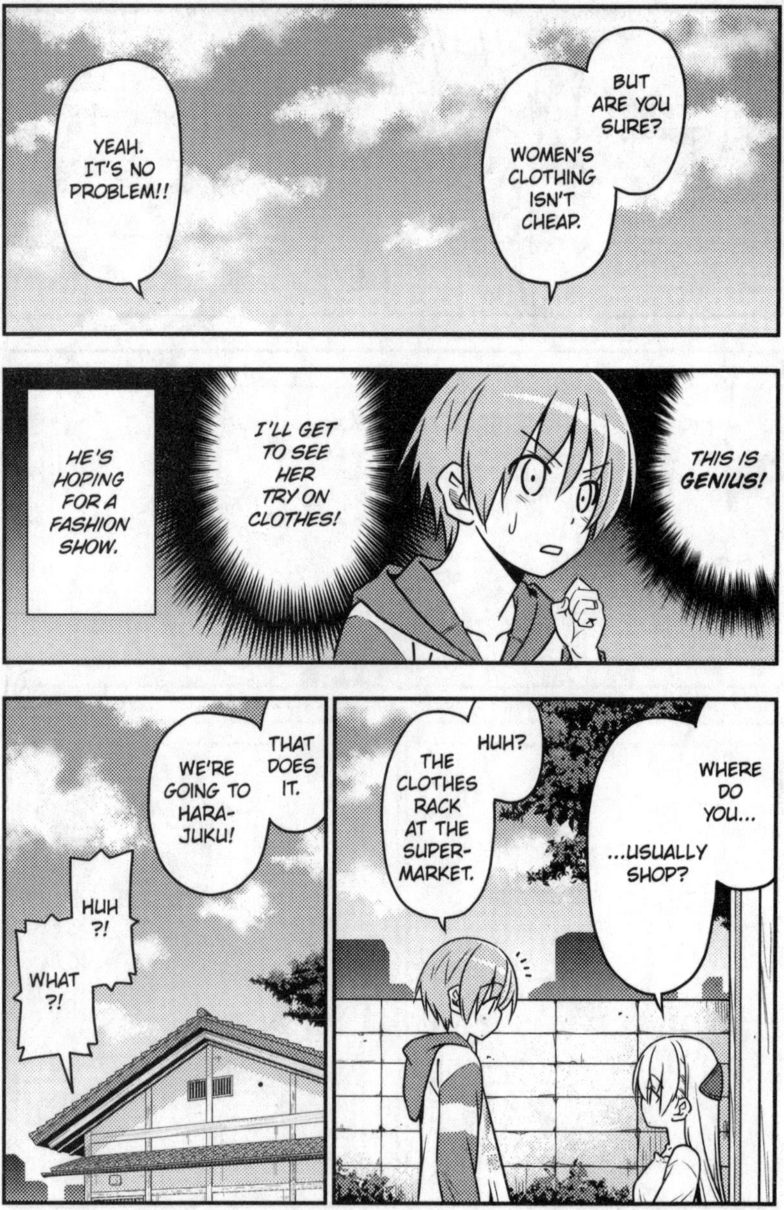
BUT ARE YOU SURE?
WOMEN'S CLOTHING ISN'T CHEAP.
YEAH. IT'S NO PROBLEM!!
THIS IS GENIUS!
I'LL GET TO SEE HER TRY ON CLOTHES!
HE'S HOPING FOR A FASHION SHOW.
WHERE DO YOU...
...USUALLY SHOP?
HUH?
THE CLOTHES RACK AT THE SUPER-MARKET.
THAT DOES IT.
WE'RE GOING TO HARA-JUKU!
HUH?!
WHAT?!

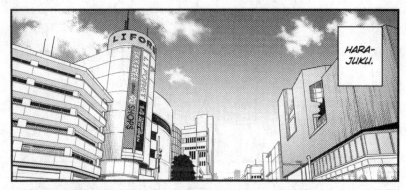

HARA-JUKU.
FASHION CENTER OF TOKYO.
SO MANY CLOTHES ...
YUP, THIS IS THE PLACE!
I'LL TRY ON A FEW OUTFITS.
WANNA WATCH?

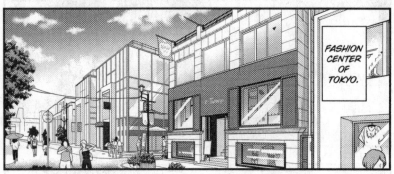

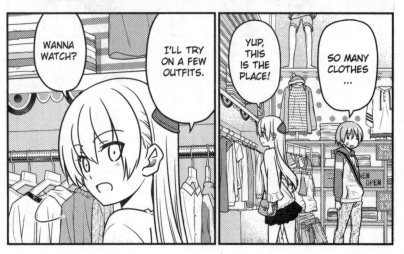

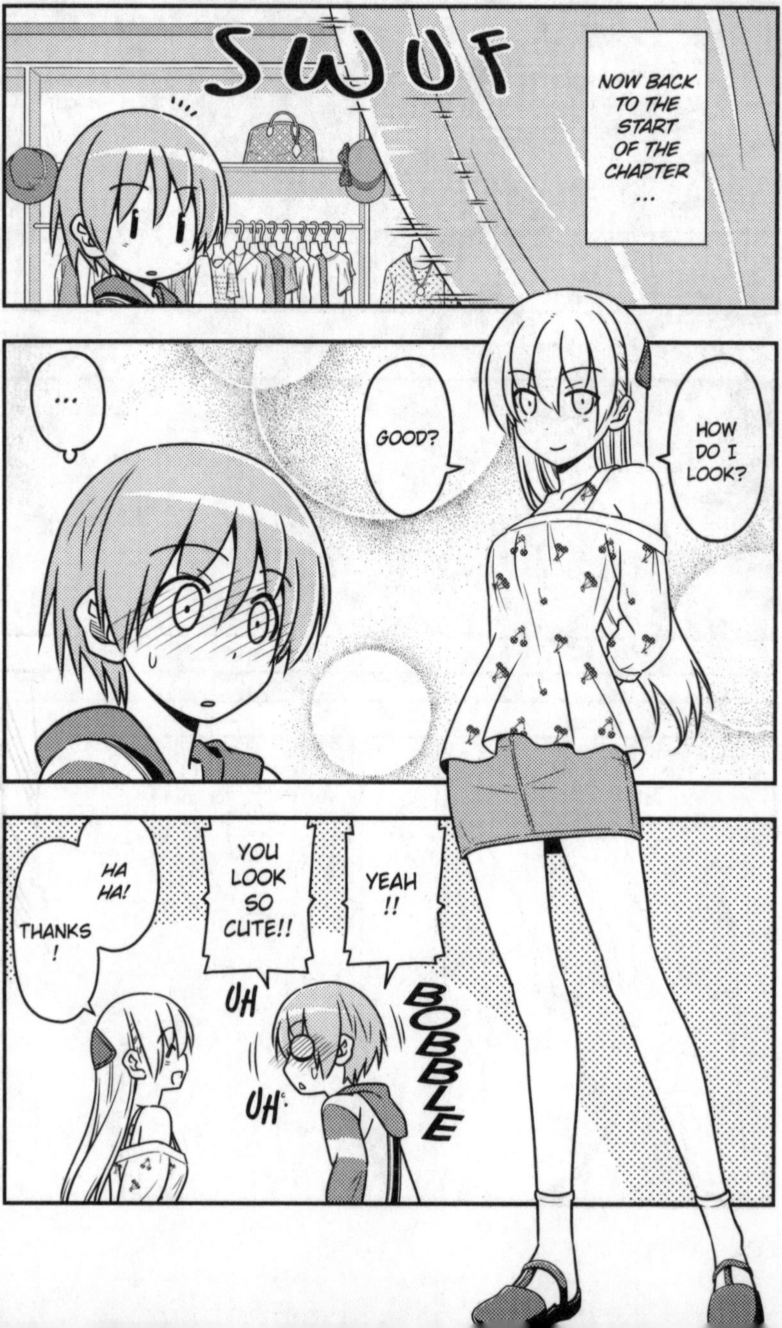

NOW BACK TO THE START OF THE CHAPTER ...
SWUF
HOW DO I LOOK?
GOOD?
...
YEAH !!
YOU LOOK SO CUTE!!
HA HA! THANKS !
BOBBLE
UH
UH

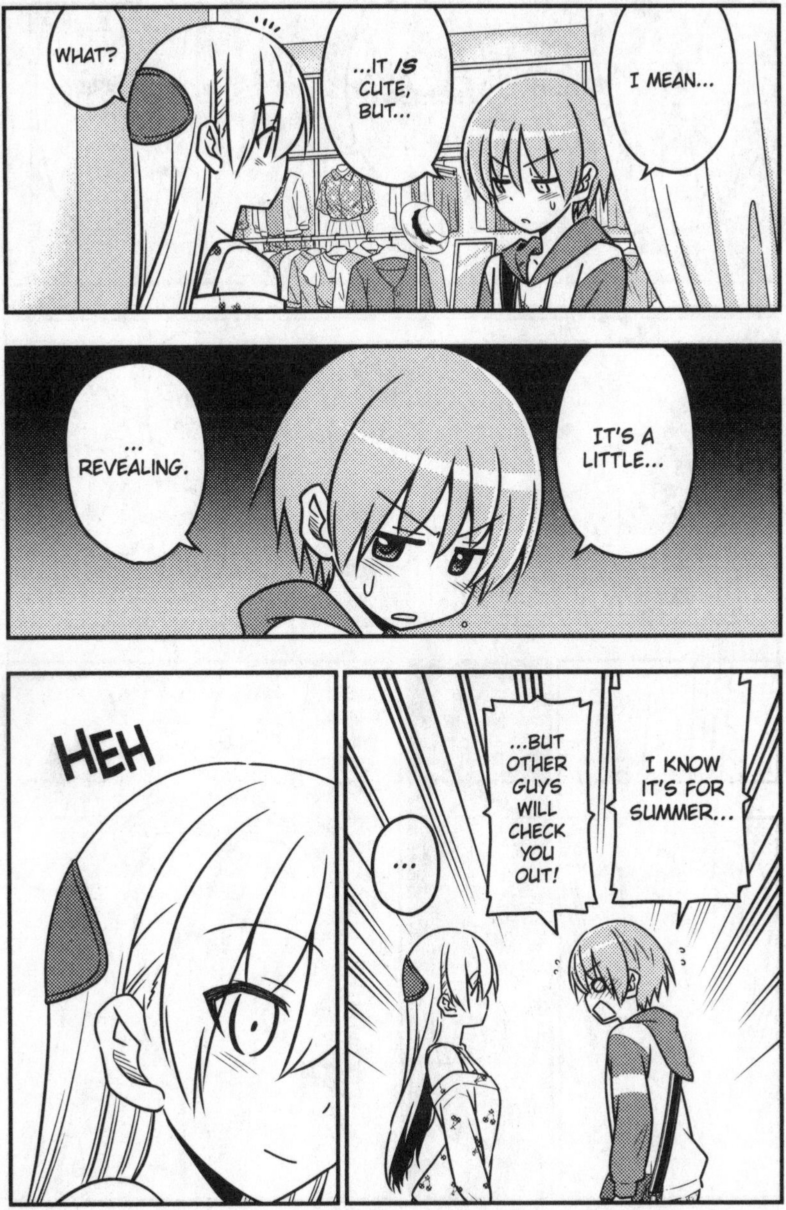
I MEAN...
...IT *IS* CUTE, BUT...
WHAT?
IT'S A LITTLE...
...REVEALING.
I KNOW IT'S FOR SUMMER...
...BUT OTHER GUYS WILL CHECK YOU OUT!
...
HEH

ARE YOU...
...FEELING POSSESSIVE?
?
IN THAT CASE ...
...MAYBE YOU CAN DRESS ME.
HUH?
PICK OUT SOME-THING ...
...YOU THINK WILL LOOK GOOD.
HEH
...
UM... OKAY!!
I'LL GIVE IT A TRY!!

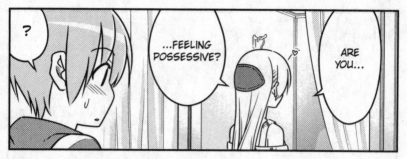

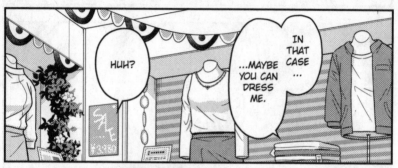

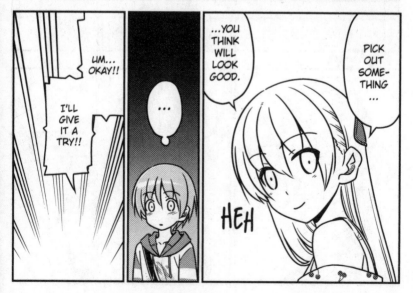

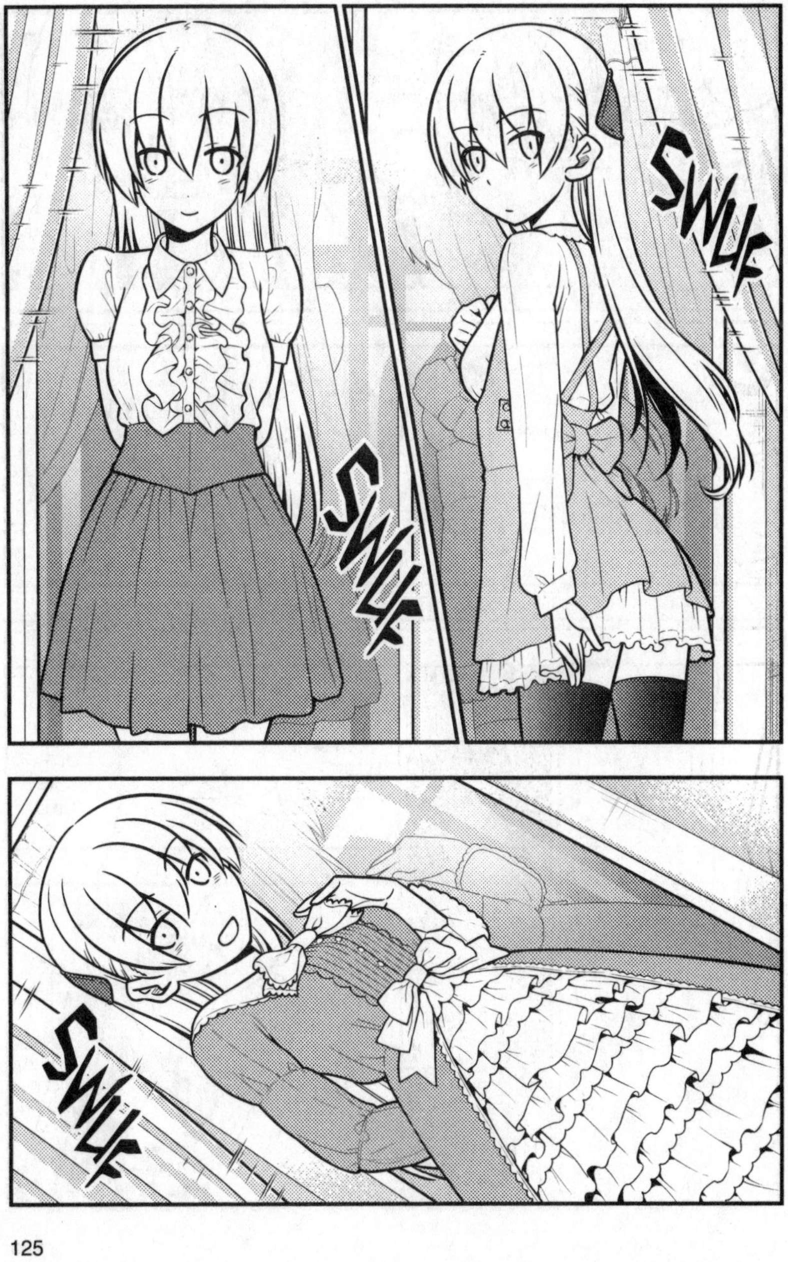
SWUF
SWUF
SWUF

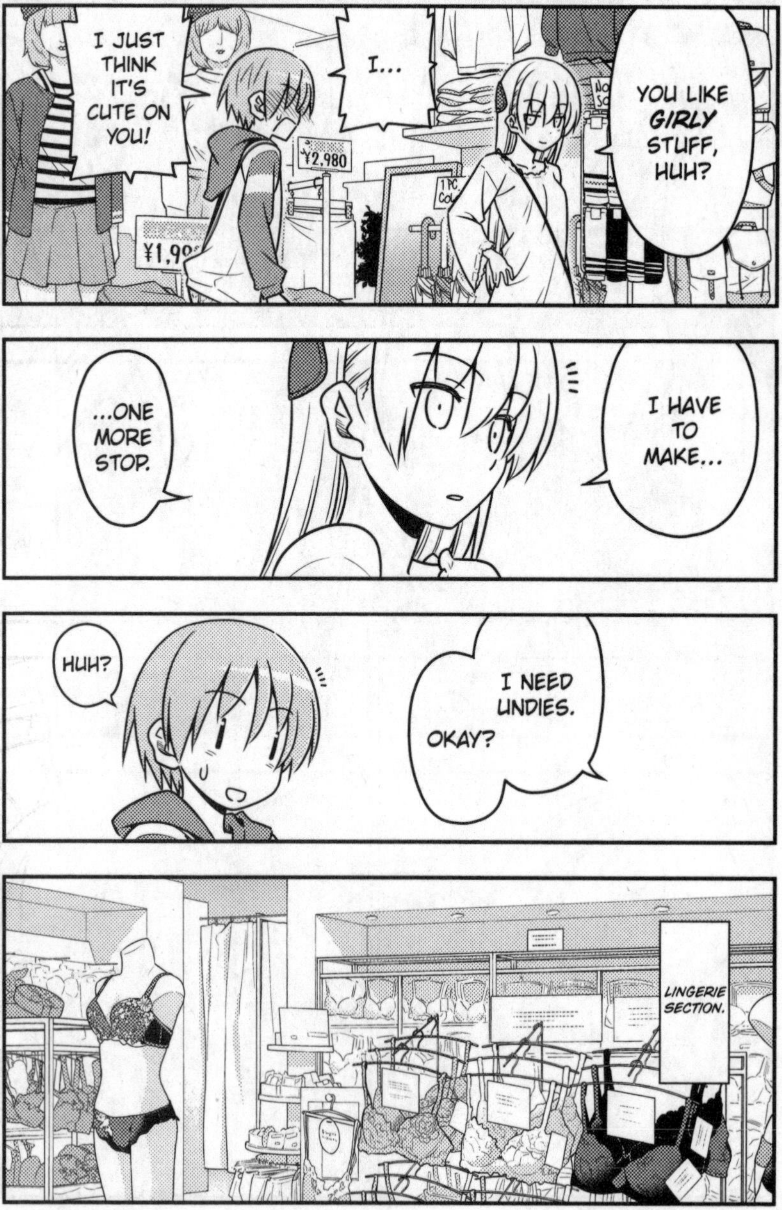
YOU LIKE GIRLY STUFF, HUH?
I...
I JUST THINK IT'S CUTE ON YOU!
¥2,980
I HAVE TO MAKE...
...ONE MORE STOP.
I NEED UNDIES.
OKAY?
HUH?
LINGERIE SECTION.

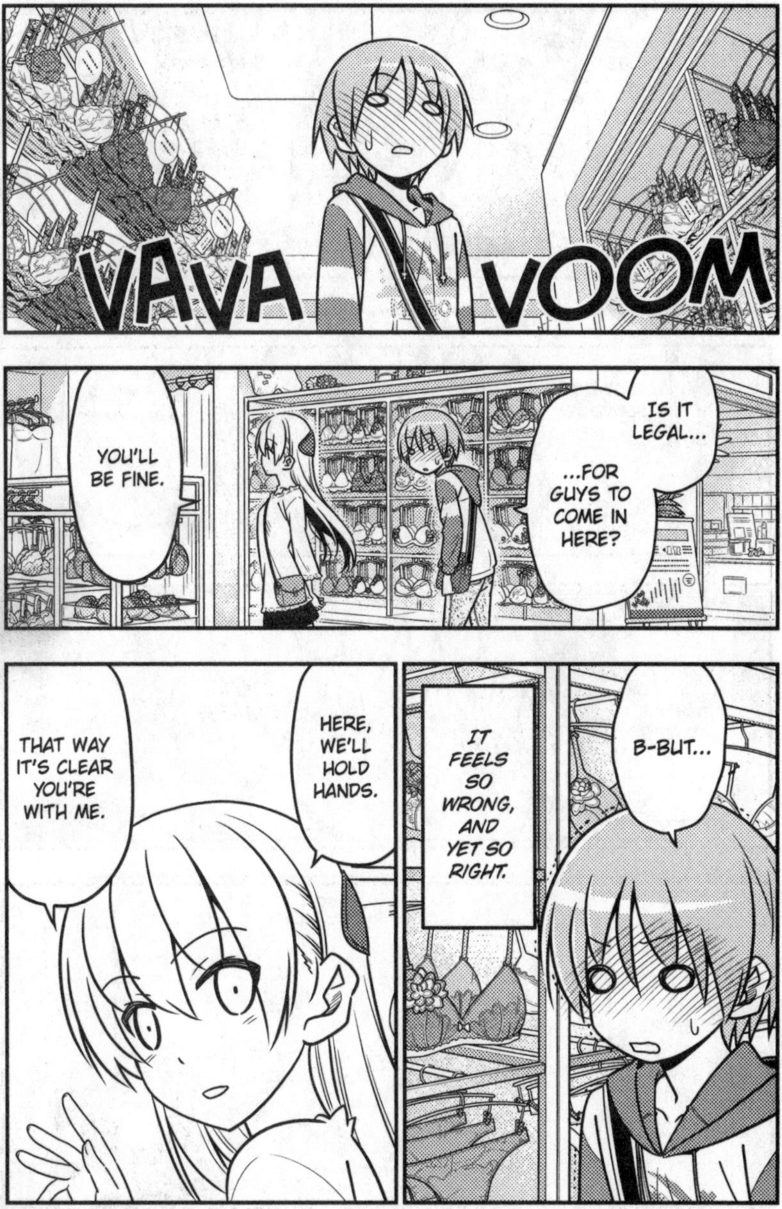
VAVA VOOM
IS IT LEGAL...
...FOR GUYS TO COME IN HERE?
YOU'LL BE FINE.
B-BUT...
IT FEELS SO WRONG, AND YET SO RIGHT.
HERE, WE'LL HOLD HANDS.
THAT WAY IT'S CLEAR YOU'RE WITH ME.

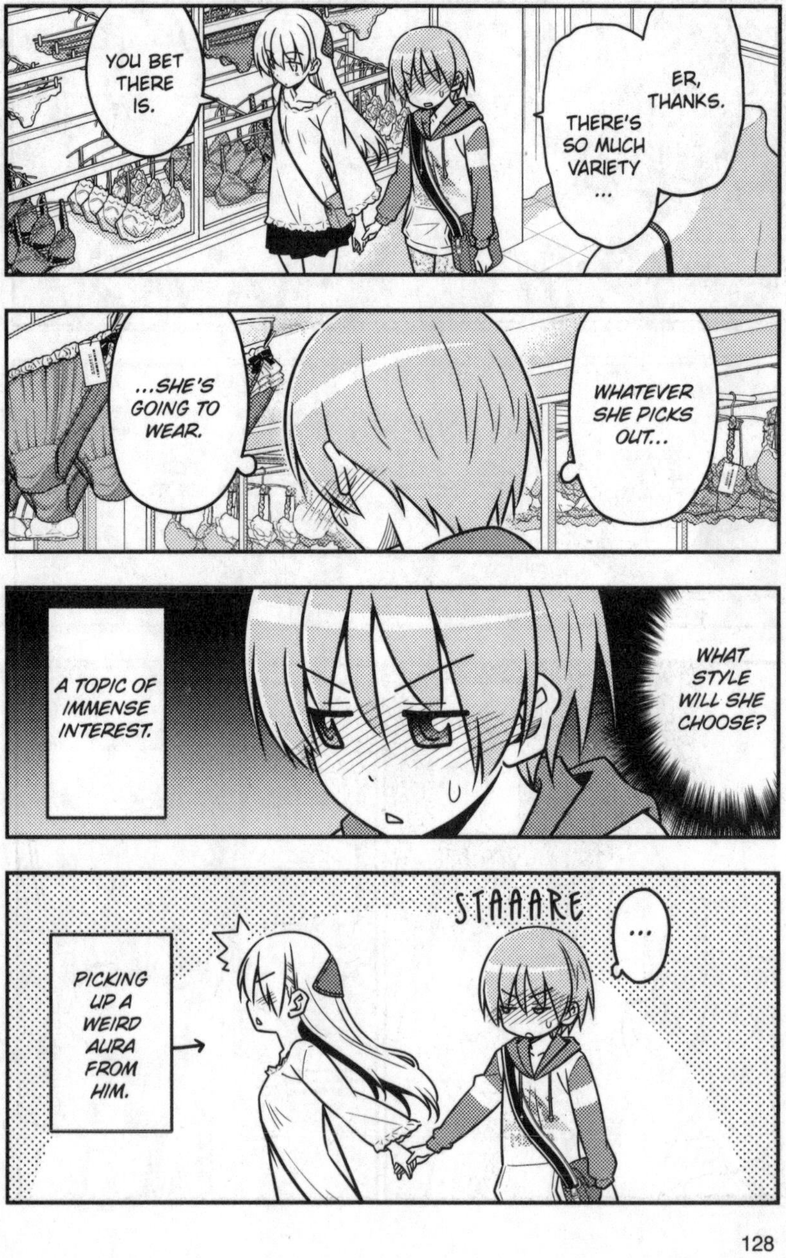
ER, THANKS.
THERE'S SO MUCH VARIETY ...
YOU BET THERE IS.
WHATEVER SHE PICKS OUT...
...SHE'S GOING TO WEAR.
WHAT STYLE WILL SHE CHOOSE?
A TOPIC OF IMMENSE INTEREST.
STAAARE
...
PICKING UP A WEIRD AURA FROM HIM.

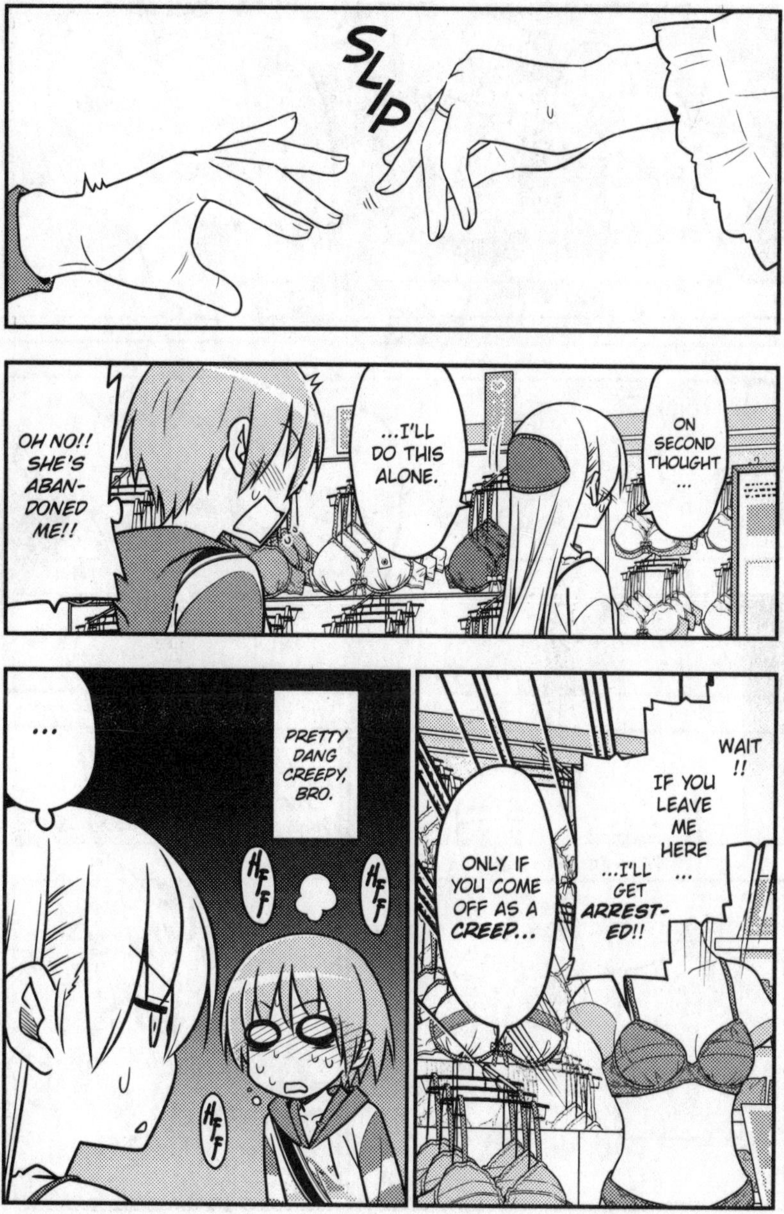
SLIP
ON SECOND THOUGHT ...
...I'LL DO THIS ALONE.
OH NO!! SHE'S ABAN-DONED ME!!
WAIT !!
IF YOU LEAVE ME HERE ...
...I'LL GET ARREST-ED!!
ONLY IF YOU COME OFF AS A CREEP...
...
PRETTY DANG CREEPY, BRO.
HFF
HFF
HFF

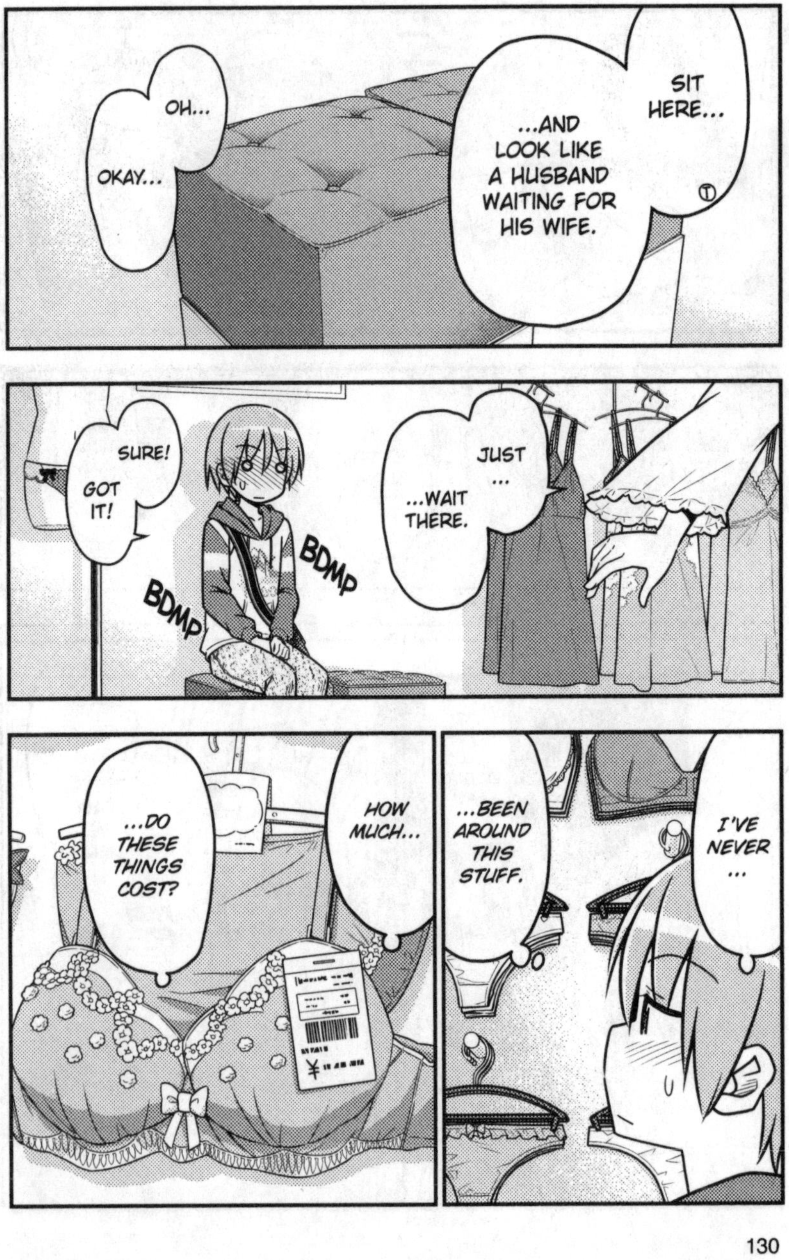
SIT HERE...
...AND LOOK LIKE A HUSBAND WAITING FOR HIS WIFE.
OH... OKAY...
JUST ...
...WAIT THERE.
BDMP
BDMP
SURE! GOT IT!
I'VE NEVER ...
...BEEN AROUND THIS STUFF.
HOW MUCH...
...DO THESE THINGS COST?

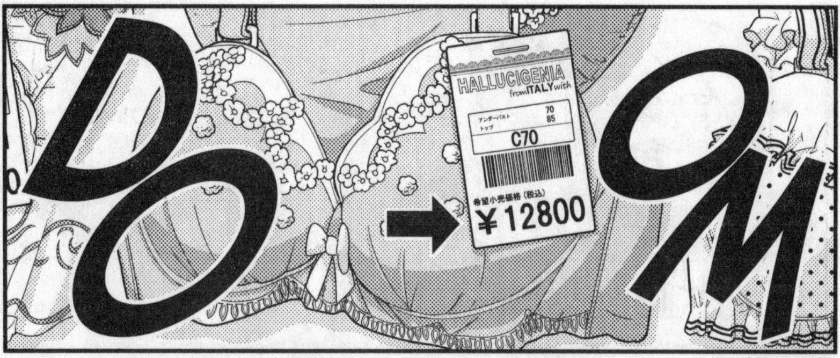
DOOM
HALLUCIGENIA
fromITALY with
アンダーバスト 70
トップ 85
C70
希望小売価格(税込)
¥12800
*About $128

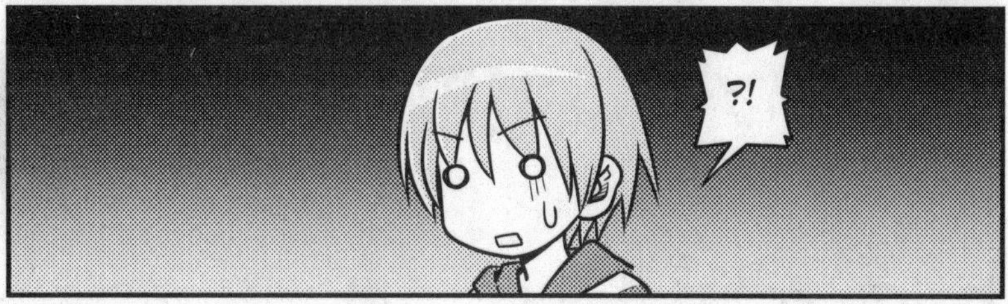
?!

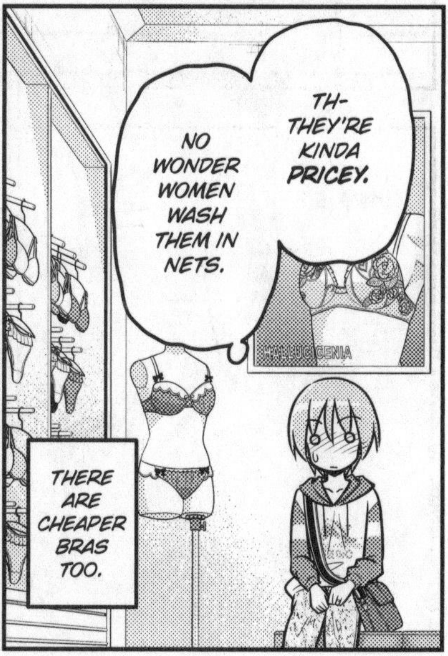
TH-THEY'RE KINDA PRICEY.
NO WONDER WOMEN WASH THEM IN NETS.
THERE ARE CHEAPER BRAS TOO.
HALLUCIGENIA

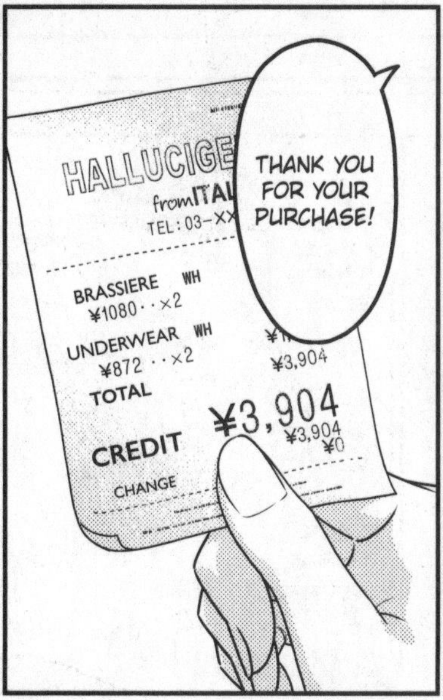
THANK YOU FOR YOUR PURCHASE!
HALLUCIGE
fromITAL
TEL: 03-XX
BRASSIERE WH
¥1080 · · ×2
UNDERWEAR WH
¥872 · · ×2
¥3,904
TOTAL
¥3,904
CREDIT
¥3,904
CHANGE
¥0
*About $39.04

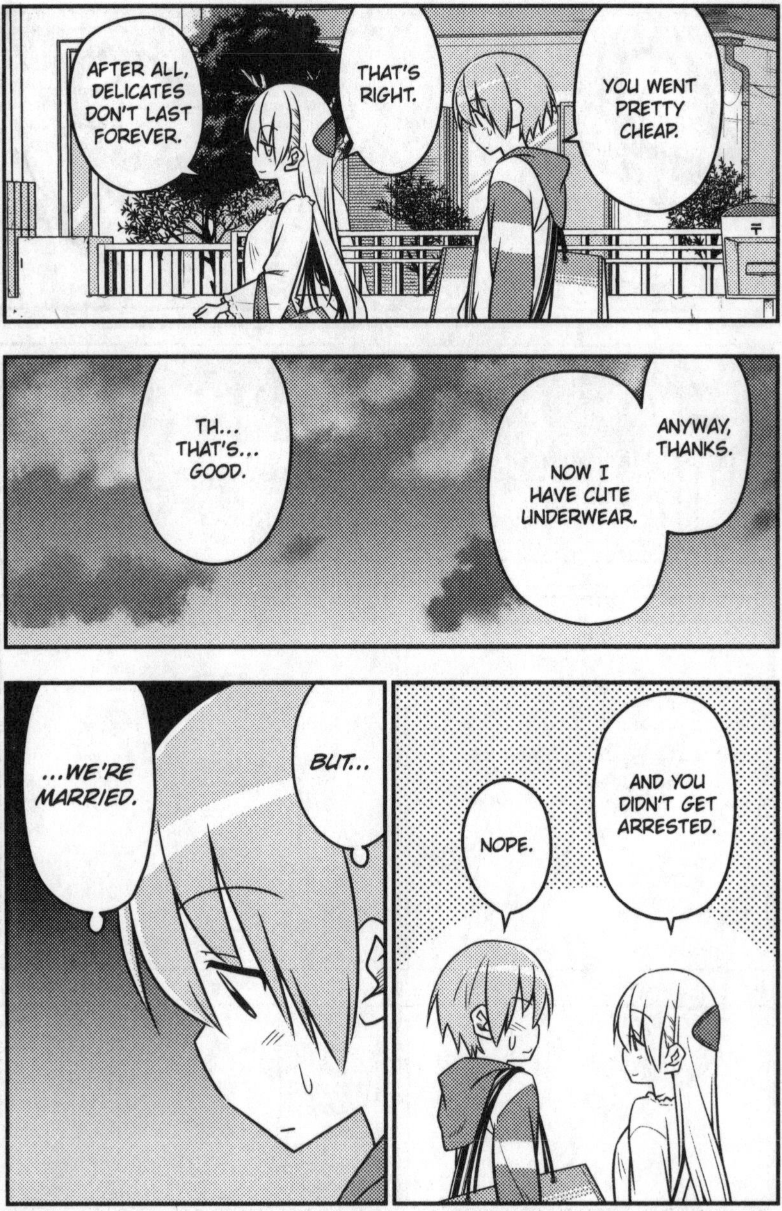
YOU WENT PRETTY CHEAP.
THAT'S RIGHT.
AFTER ALL, DELICATES DON'T LAST FOREVER.
ANYWAY, THANKS.
NOW I HAVE CUTE UNDERWEAR.
TH... THAT'S... GOOD.
AND YOU DIDN'T GET ARRESTED.
NOPE.
BUT...
...WE'RE MARRIED.

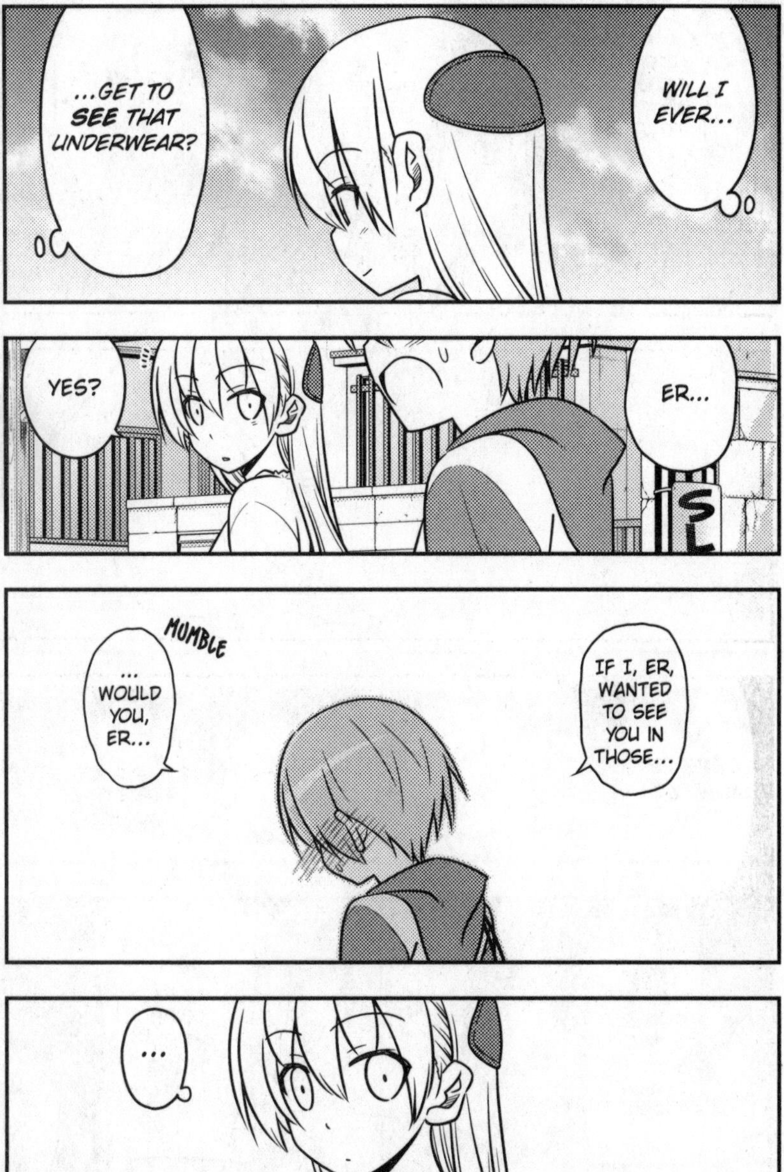
WILL I EVER...
...GET TO SEE THAT UNDERWEAR?
ER...
YES?
IF I, ER, WANTED TO SEE YOU IN THOSE...
MUMBLE
... WOULD YOU, ER...
...

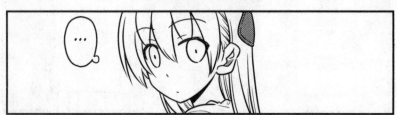

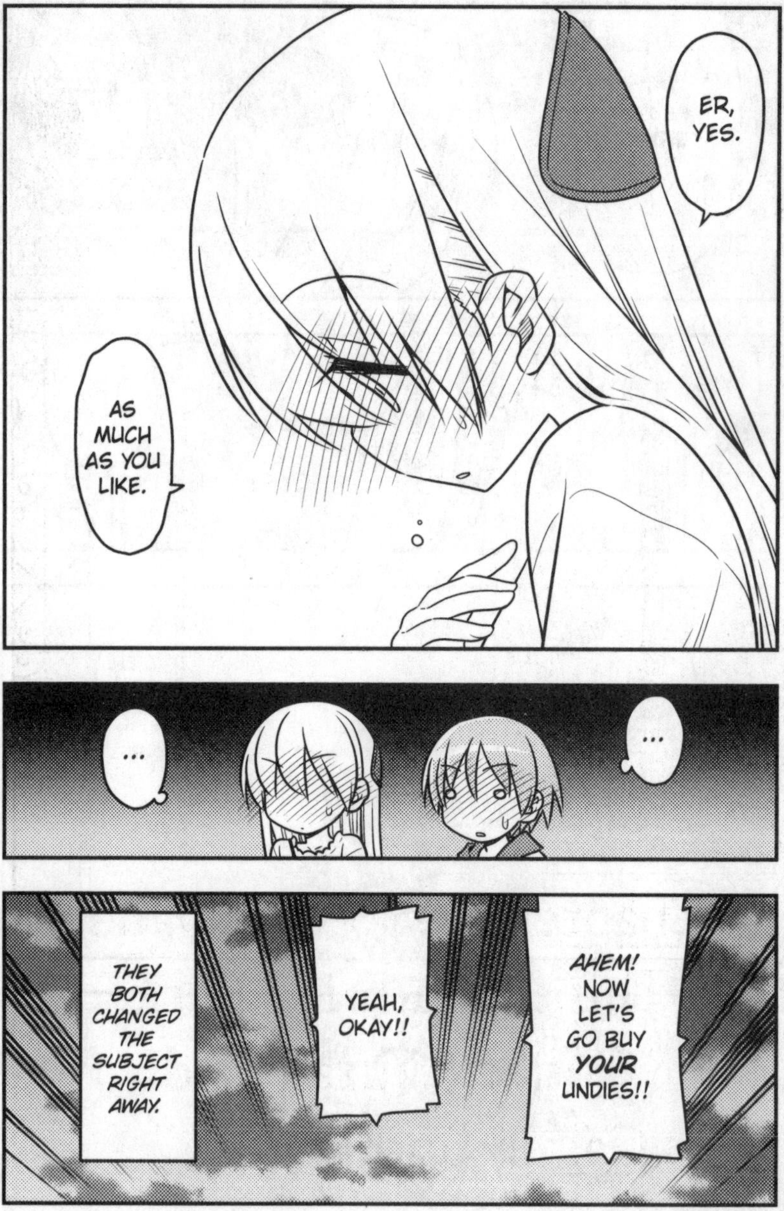
ER, YES.
AS MUCH AS YOU LIKE.
...
...
AHEM! NOW LET'S GO BUY YOUR UNDIES!!
YEAH, OKAY!!
THEY BOTH CHANGED THE SUBJECT RIGHT AWAY.

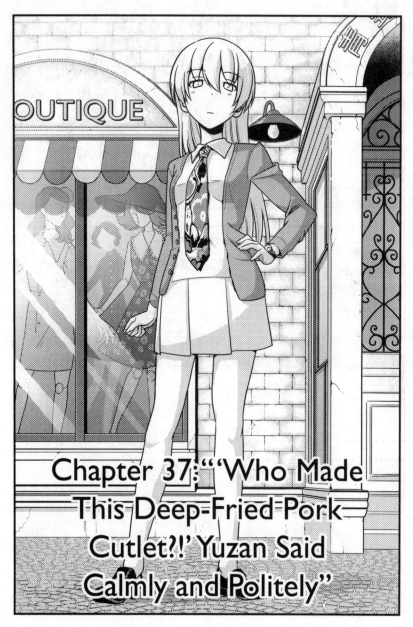

Chapter 37: "'Who Made This Deep-Fried Pork Cutlet?!' Yuzan Said Calmly and Politely"

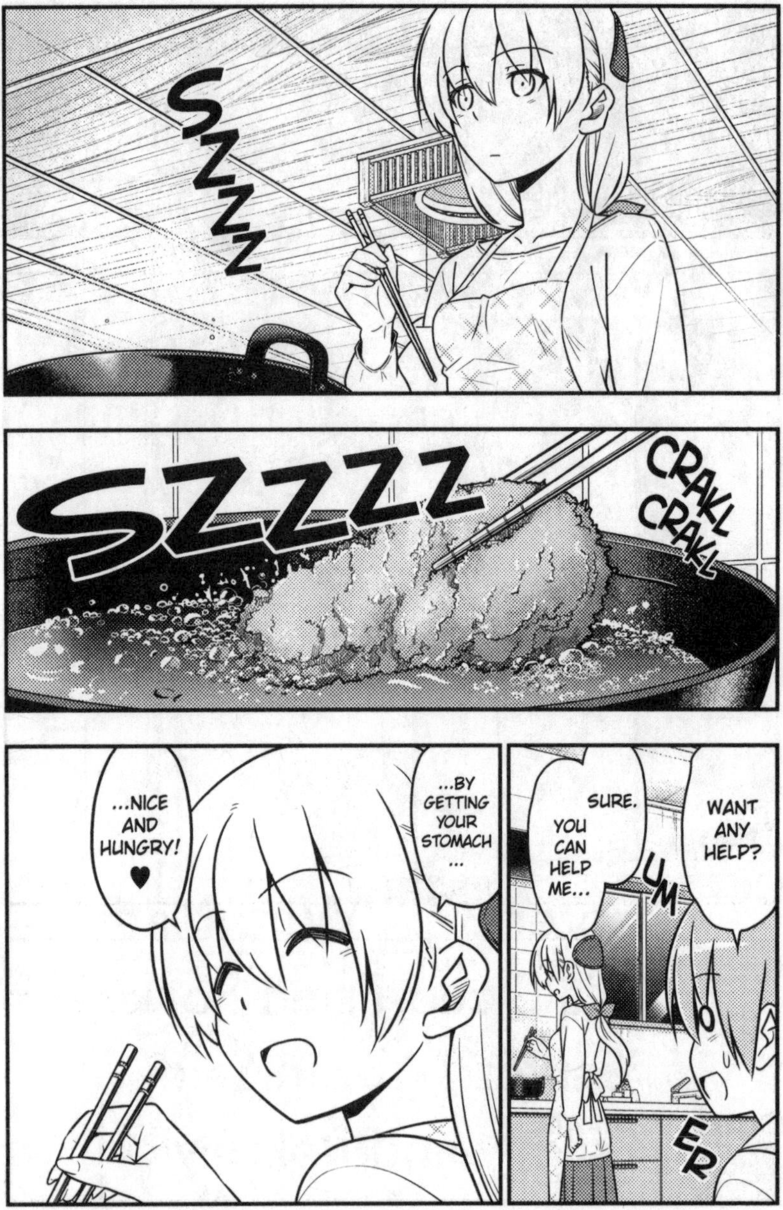
SZZZZ
CRAKL CRAKL
SZZZZZ
WANT ANY HELP?
UM
SURE. YOU CAN HELP ME...
ER
...BY GETTING YOUR STOMACH ...
...NICE AND HUNGRY! ♥

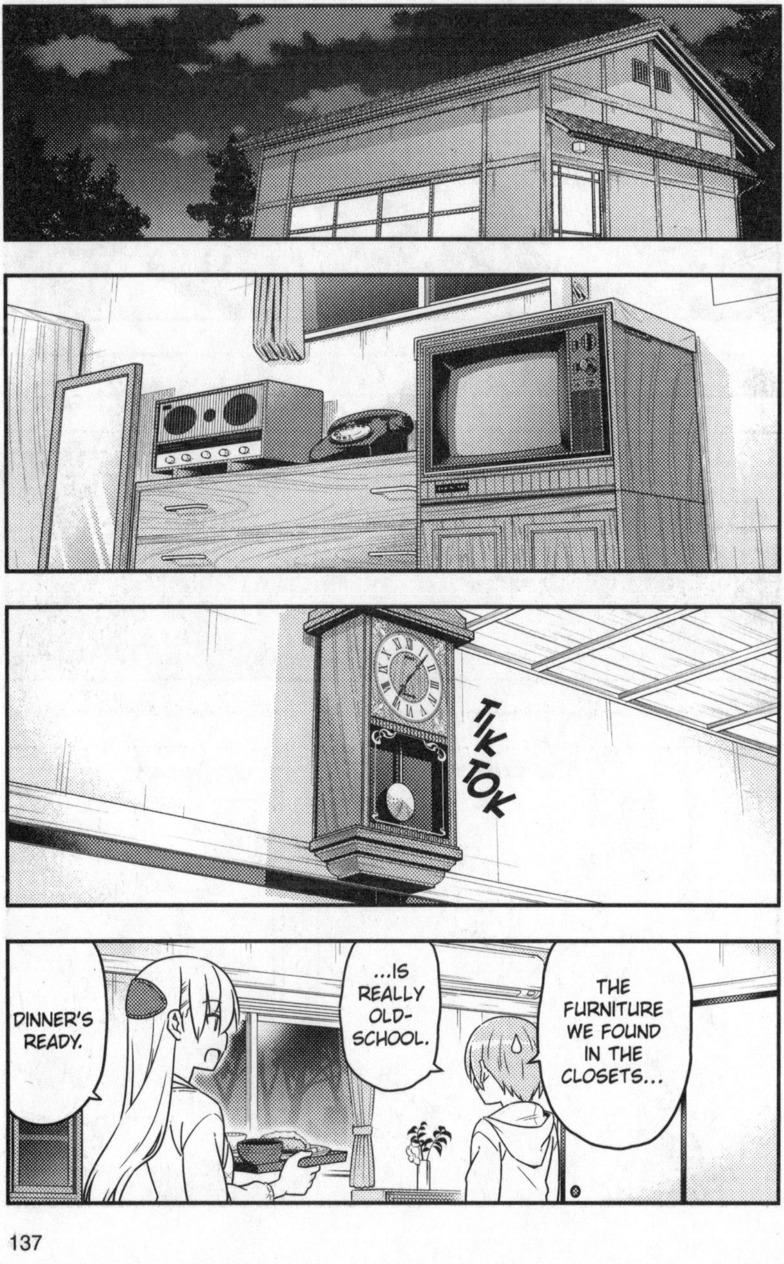
TIK TOK
THE FURNITURE WE FOUND IN THE CLOSETS...
...IS REALLY OLD-SCHOOL.
DINNER'S READY.

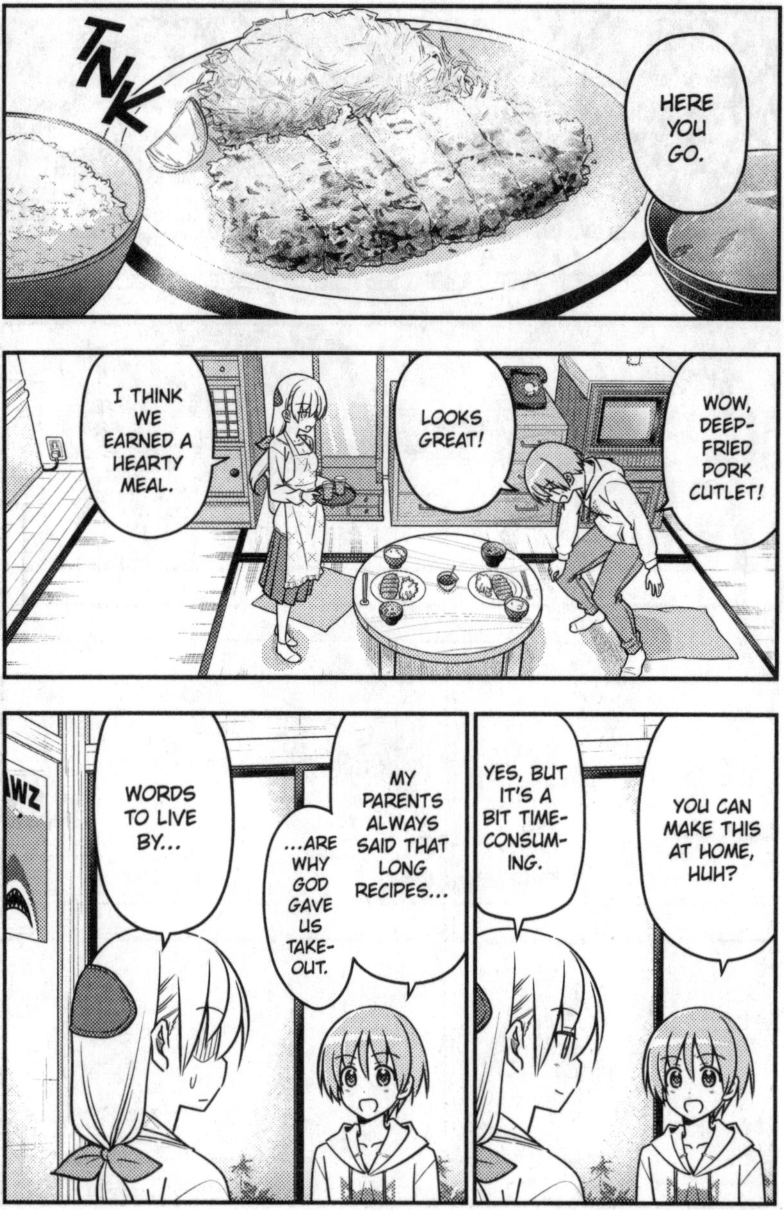
HERE YOU GO.
TNK
WOW, DEEP-FRIED PORK CUTLET!
LOOKS GREAT!
I THINK WE EARNED A HEARTY MEAL.
YOU CAN MAKE THIS AT HOME, HUH?
YES, BUT IT'S A BIT TIME-CONSUMING.
MY PARENTS ALWAYS SAID THAT LONG RECIPES...
...ARE WHY GOD GAVE US TAKE-OUT.
WORDS TO LIVE BY...

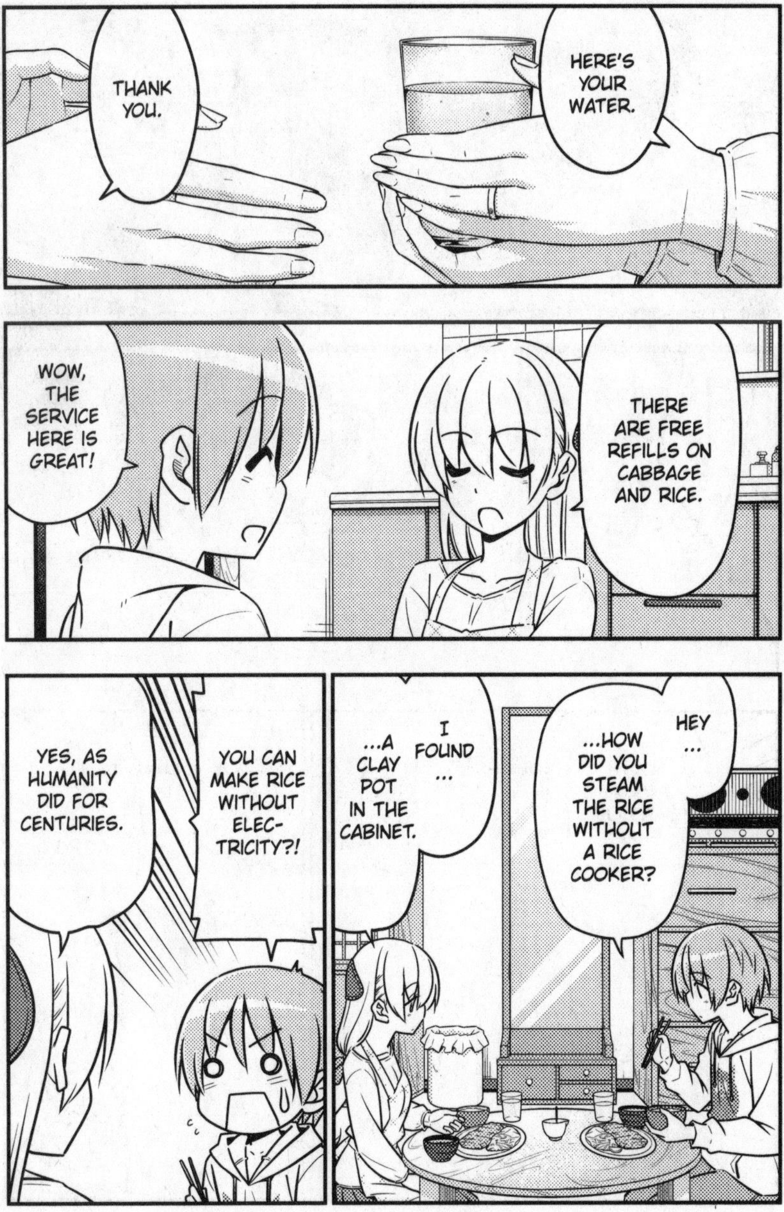
HERE'S YOUR WATER.
THANK YOU.
THERE ARE FREE REFILLS ON CABBAGE AND RICE.
WOW, THE SERVICE HERE IS GREAT!
HEY ...
...HOW DID YOU STEAM THE RICE WITHOUT A RICE COOKER?
I FOUND ...
...A CLAY POT IN THE CABINET.
YOU CAN MAKE RICE WITHOUT ELEC-TRICITY?!
YES, AS HUMANITY DID FOR CENTURIES.

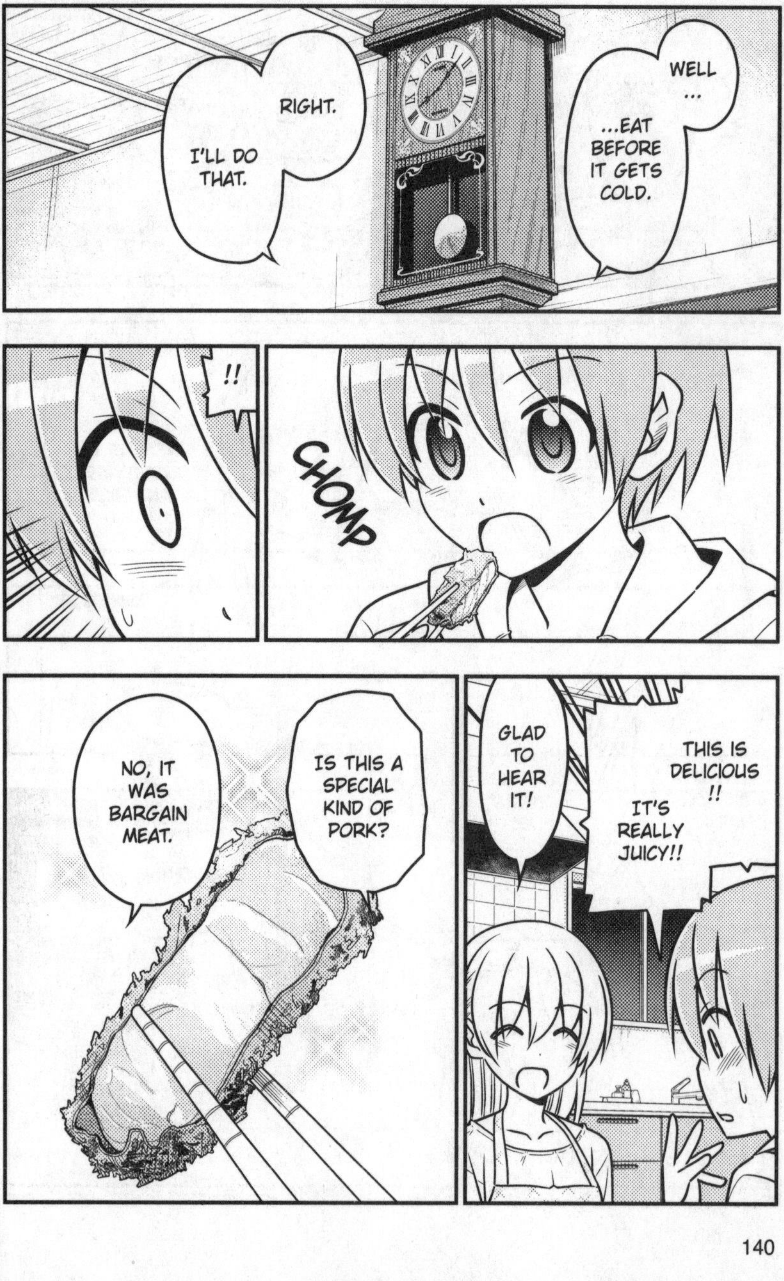
WELL ...
...EAT BEFORE IT GETS COLD.
RIGHT.
I'LL DO THAT.
CHOMP
!!
THIS IS DELICIOUS!!
IT'S REALLY JUICY!!
GLAD TO HEAR IT!
IS THIS A SPECIAL KIND OF PORK?
NO, IT WAS BARGAIN MEAT.

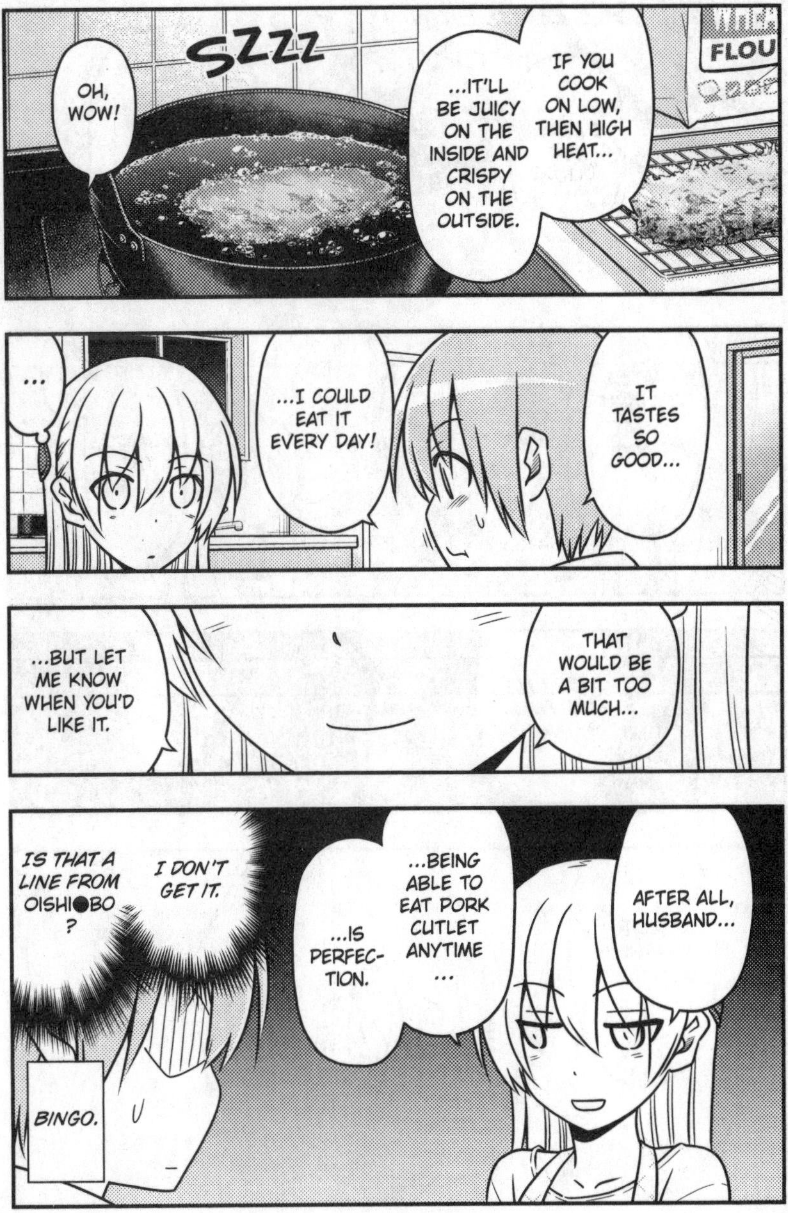
IF YOU COOK ON LOW, THEN HIGH HEAT...
...IT'LL BE JUICY ON THE INSIDE AND CRISPY ON THE OUTSIDE.
SZZZ
OH, WOW!
IT TASTES SO GOOD...
...I COULD EAT IT EVERY DAY!
...
THAT WOULD BE A BIT TOO MUCH...
...BUT LET ME KNOW WHEN YOU'D LIKE IT.
AFTER ALL, HUSBAND...
...BEING ABLE TO EAT PORK CUTLET ANYTIME...
...IS PERFECTION.
I DON'T GET IT.
IS THAT A LINE FROM OISHI●BO?
BINGO.

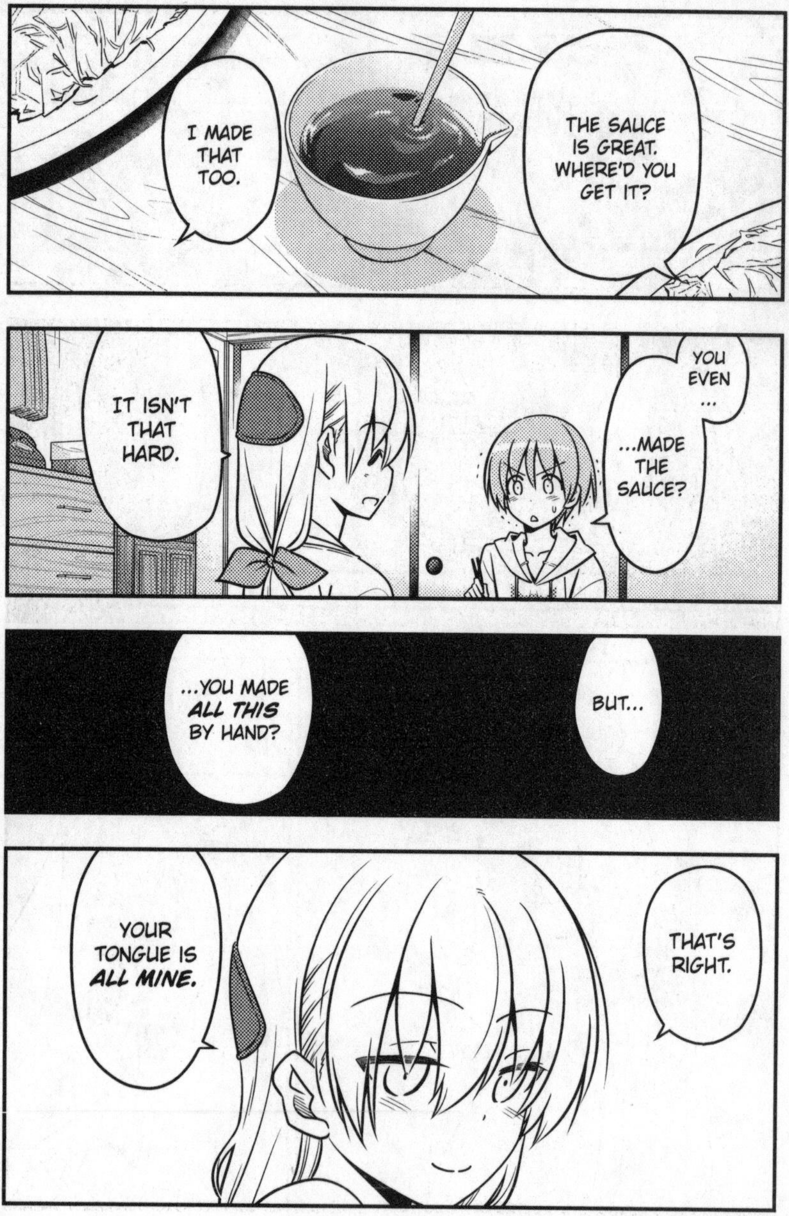
THE SAUCE IS GREAT. WHERE'D YOU GET IT?
I MADE THAT TOO.
YOU EVEN ...
...MADE THE SAUCE?
IT ISN'T THAT HARD.
BUT...
...YOU MADE ALL THIS BY HAND?
THAT'S RIGHT.
YOUR TONGUE IS ALL MINE.

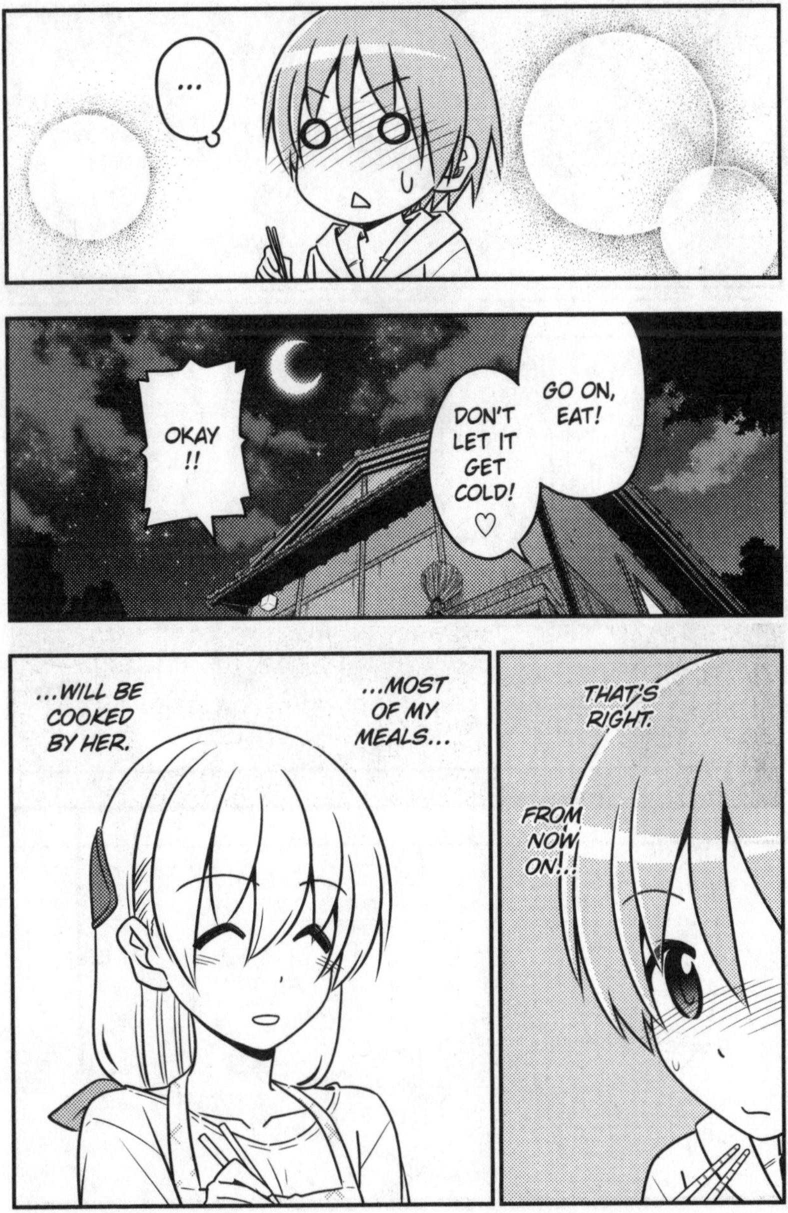
...
GO ON, EAT!
DON'T LET IT GET COLD! ♡
OKAY!!
THAT'S RIGHT.
FROM NOW ON...
...MOST OF MY MEALS...
...WILL BE COOKED BY HER.

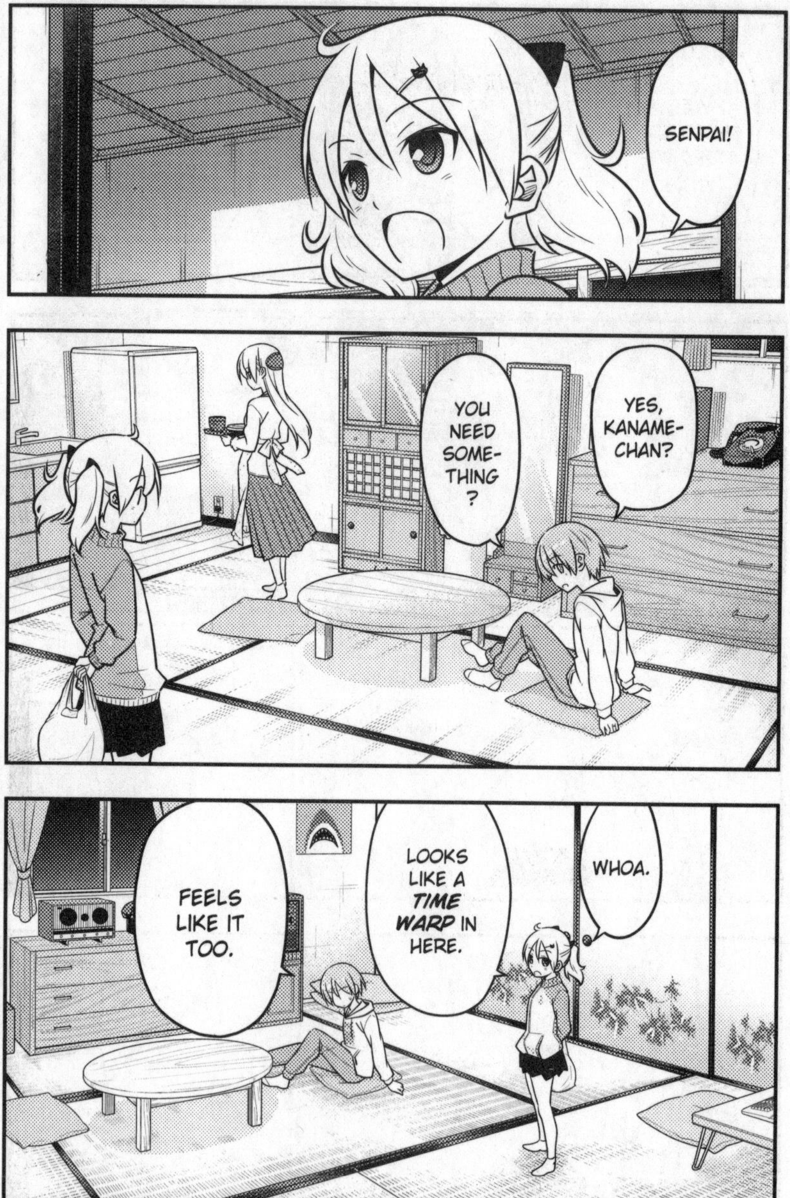
SENPAI!
YES, KANAME-CHAN?
YOU NEED SOME-THING?
WHOA.
LOOKS LIKE A TIME WARP IN HERE.
FEELS LIKE IT TOO.

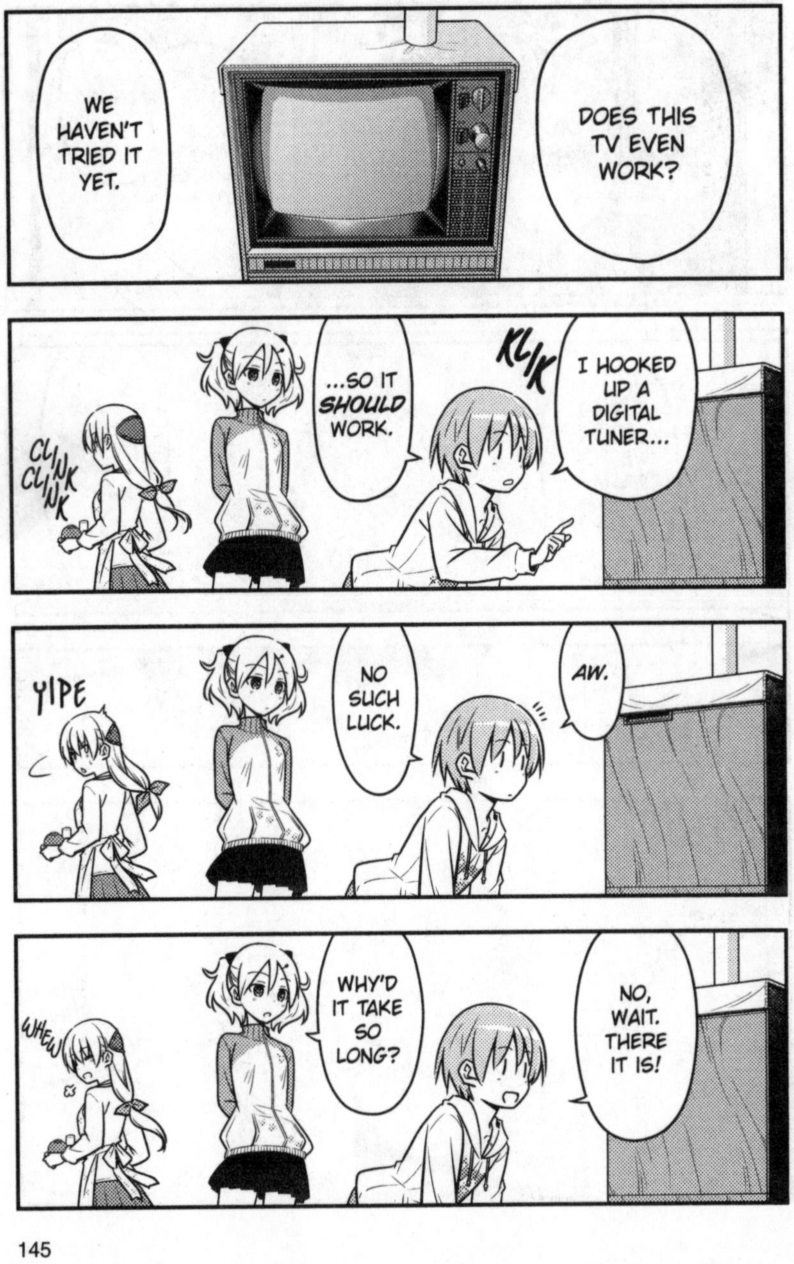
DOES THIS TV EVEN WORK?
WE HAVEN'T TRIED IT YET.
I HOOKED UP A DIGITAL TUNER...
KLIK
...SO IT SHOULD WORK.
CLINK CLINK
AW.
NO SUCH LUCK.
YIPE
NO, WAIT. THERE IT IS!
WHY'D IT TAKE SO LONG?
WHEW

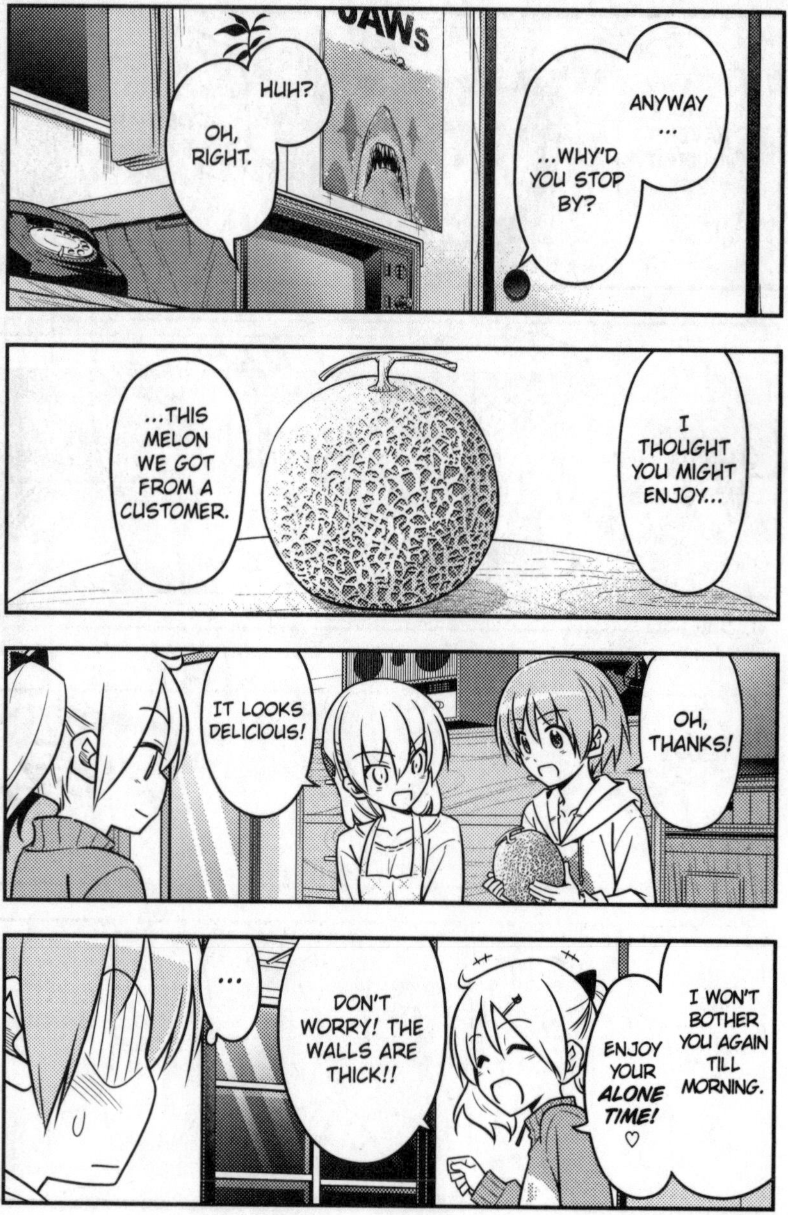
ANYWAY ...
...WHY'D YOU STOP BY?
HUH?
OH, RIGHT.
I THOUGHT YOU MIGHT ENJOY...
...THIS MELON WE GOT FROM A CUSTOMER.
OH, THANKS!
IT LOOKS DELICIOUS!
I WON'T BOTHER YOU AGAIN TILL MORNING.
ENJOY YOUR ALONE TIME! ♡
DON'T WORRY! THE WALLS ARE THICK!!
...

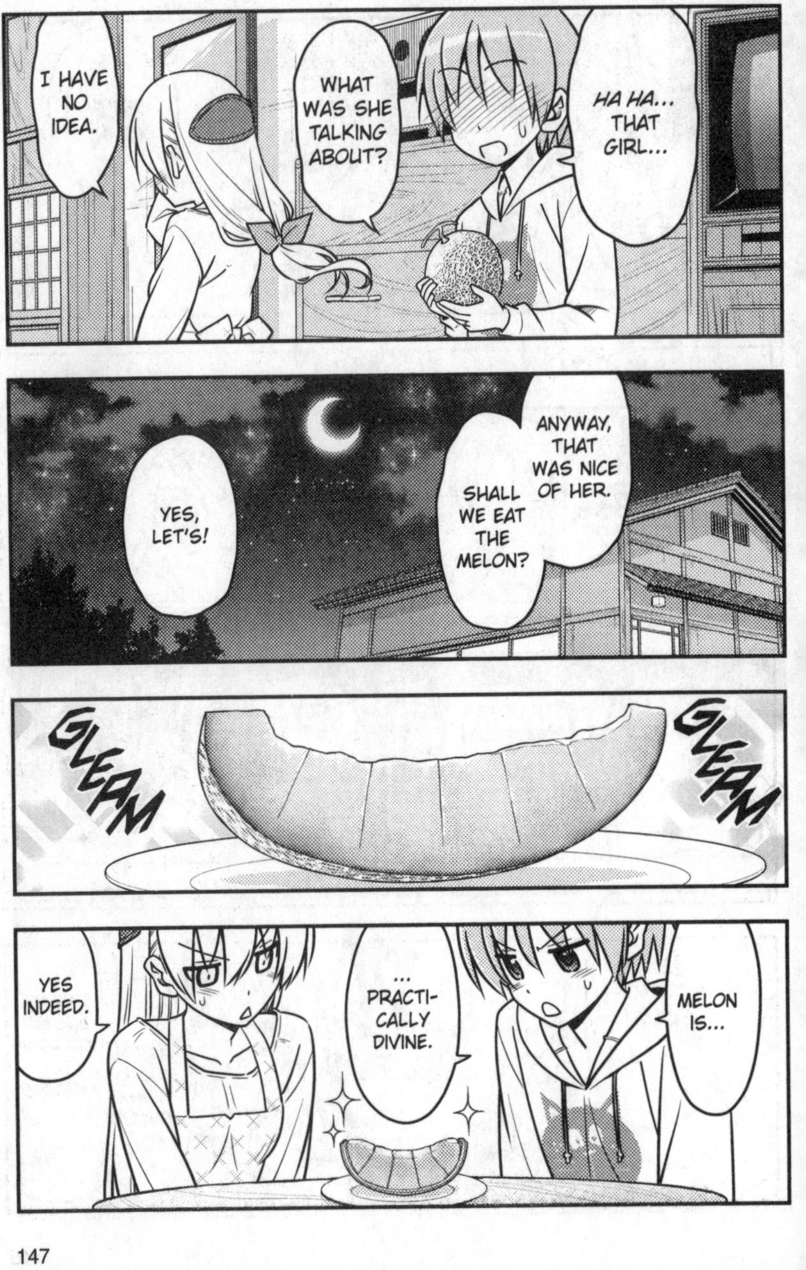
HA HA... THAT GIRL...
WHAT WAS SHE TALKING ABOUT?
I HAVE NO IDEA.
ANYWAY, THAT WAS NICE OF HER.
SHALL WE EAT THE MELON?
YES, LET'S!
GLEAM
GLEAM
MELON IS...
... PRACTI-CALLY DIVINE.
YES INDEED.

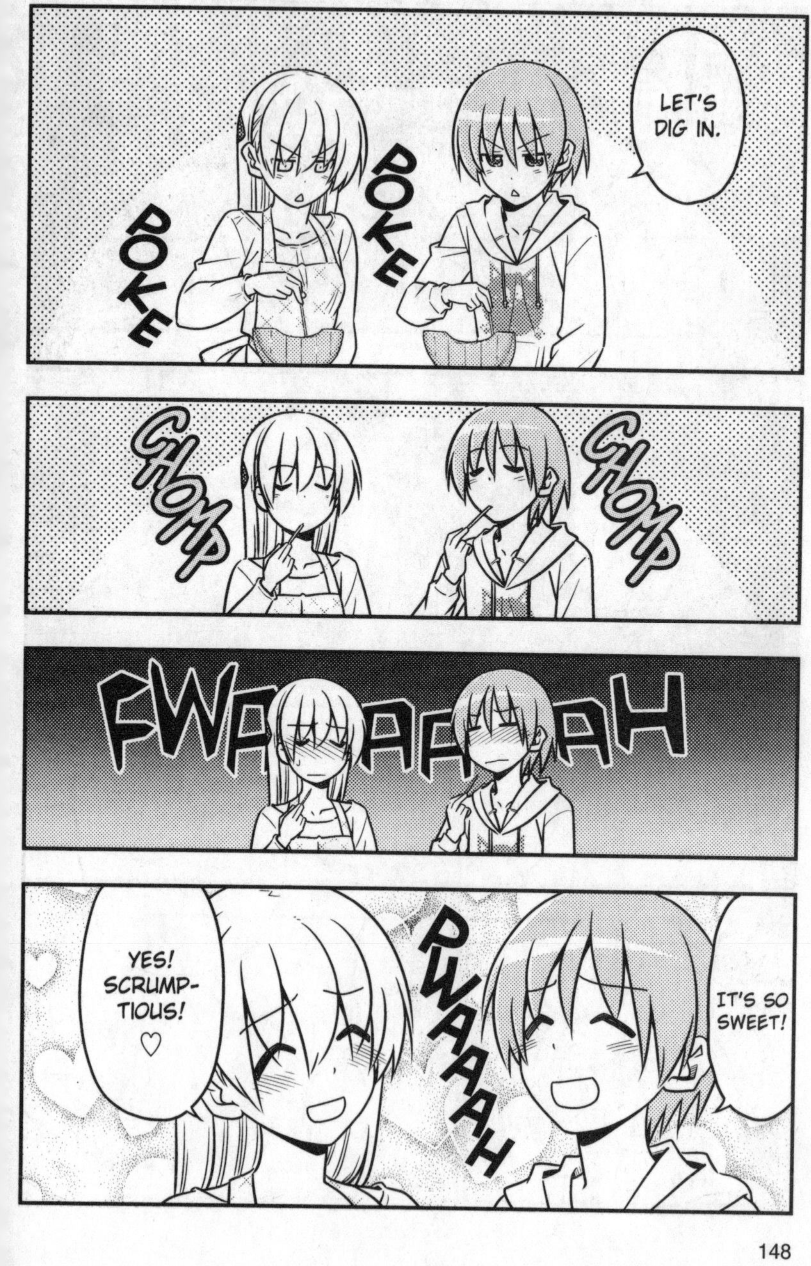

LET'S DIG IN.
POKE
POKE
CHOMP
CHOMP
FWAAAAAH
IT'S SO SWEET!
PWAAAAH
YES! SCRUMP-TIOUS! ♡

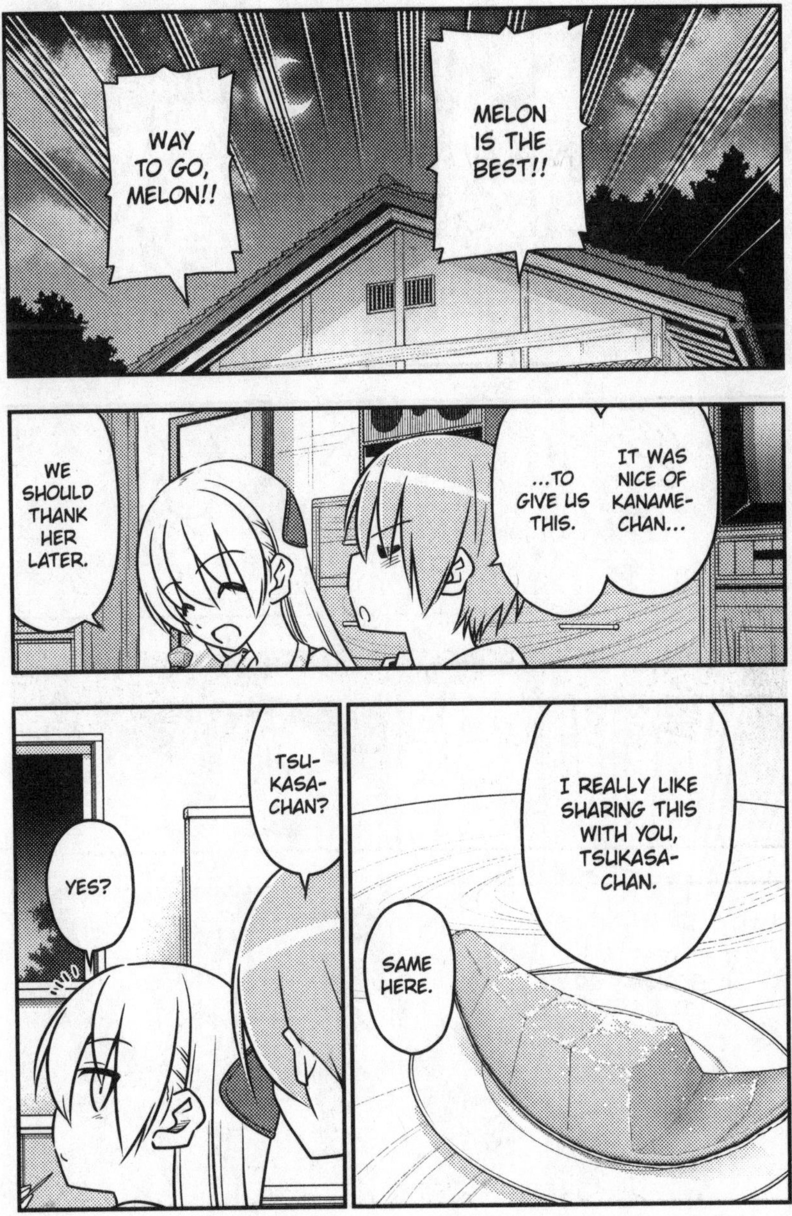
MELON IS THE BEST!!
WAY TO GO, MELON!!
IT WAS NICE OF KANAME-CHAN...
...TO GIVE US THIS.
WE SHOULD THANK HER LATER.
I REALLY LIKE SHARING THIS WITH YOU, TSUKASA-CHAN.
SAME HERE.
TSU-KASA-CHAN?
YES?

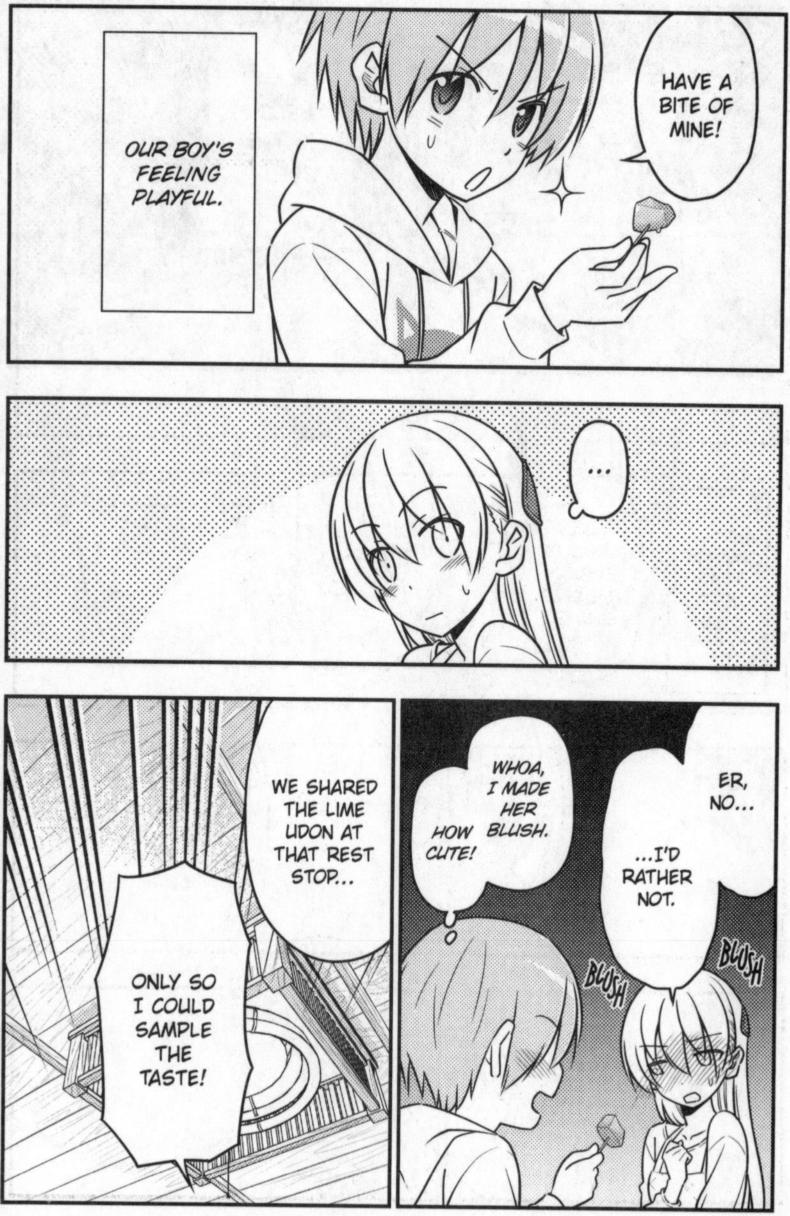
HAVE A BITE OF MINE!
OUR BOY'S FEELING PLAYFUL.
...
ER, NO...
...I'D RATHER NOT.
BLUSH
BLUSH
WHOA, I MADE HER BLUSH.
HOW CUTE!
WE SHARED THE LIME UDON AT THAT REST STOP...
ONLY SO I COULD SAMPLE THE TASTE!

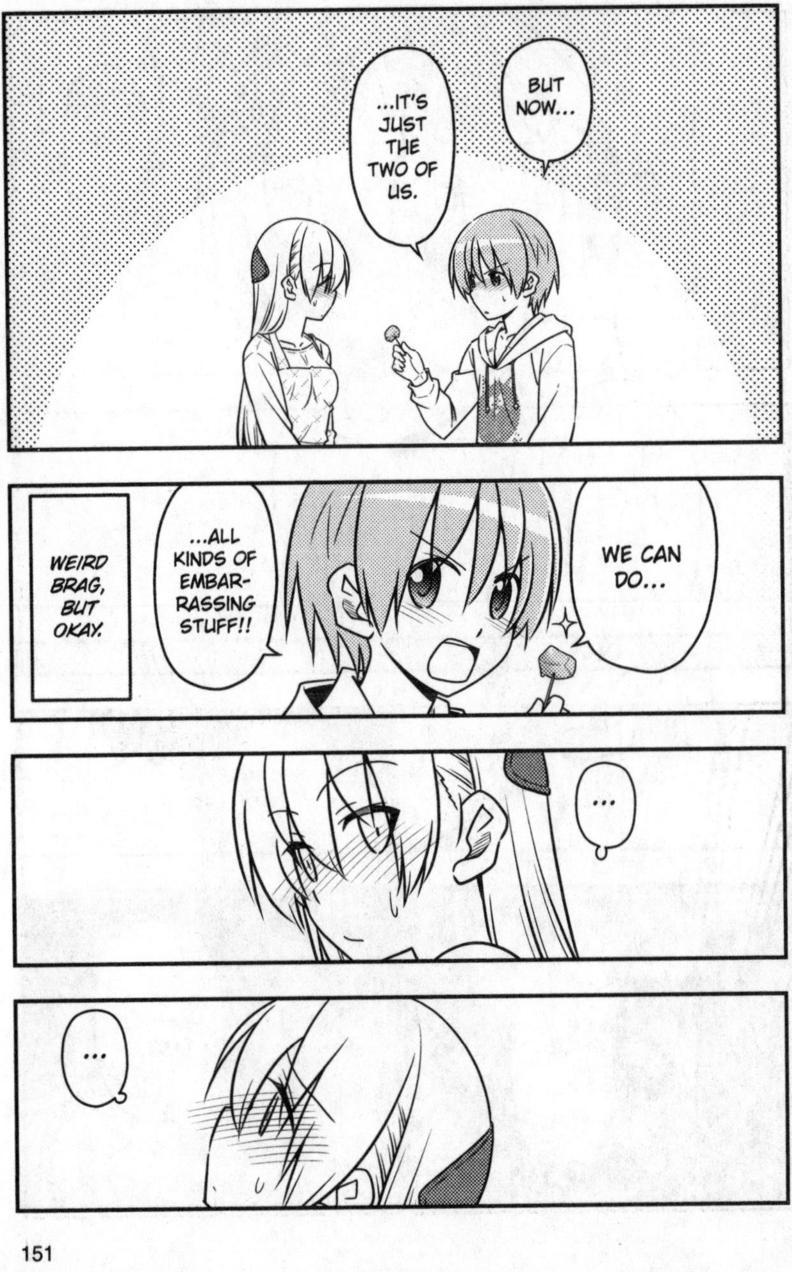
BUT NOW...
...IT'S JUST THE TWO OF US.
WE CAN DO...
...ALL KINDS OF EMBAR-RASSING STUFF!!
WEIRD BRAG, BUT OKAY.
...
...

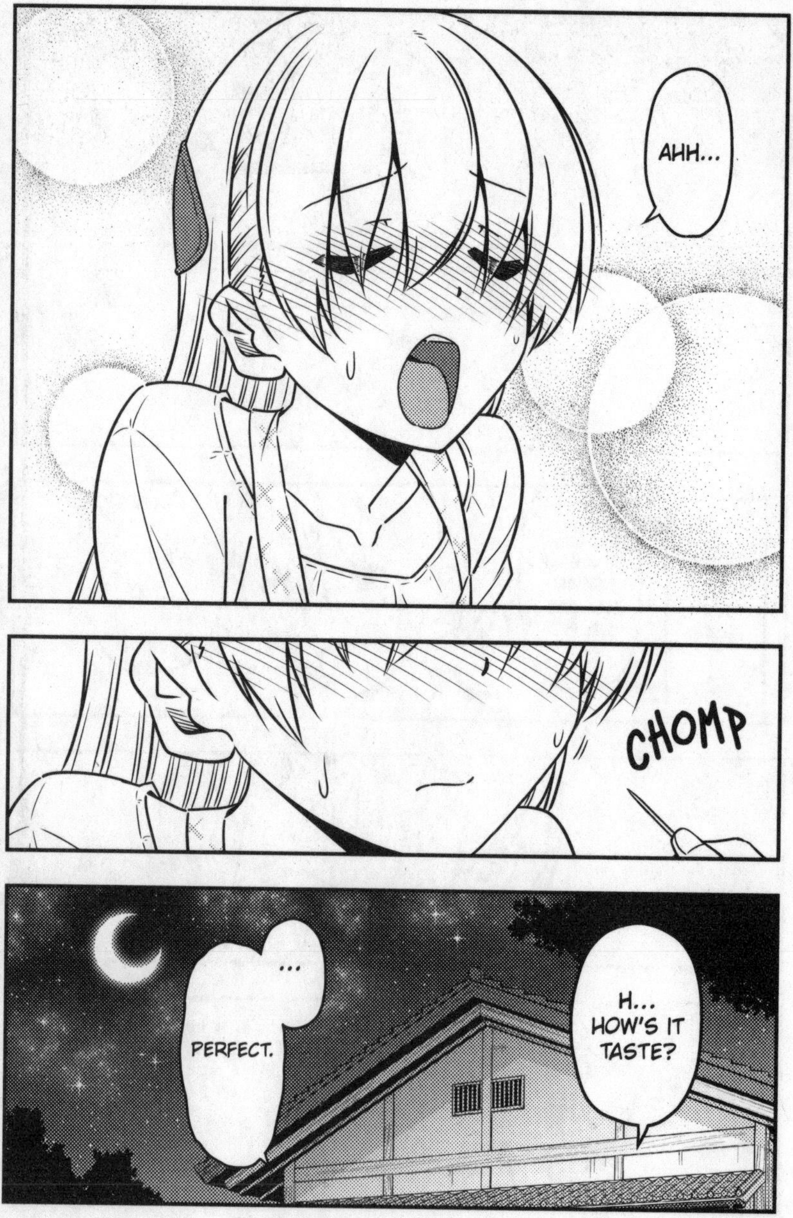
AHH...
CHOMP
H... HOW'S IT TASTE?
... PERFECT.

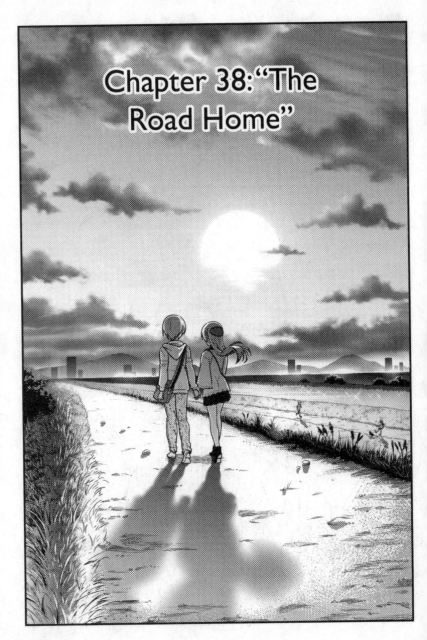

Chapter 38:"The Road Home"

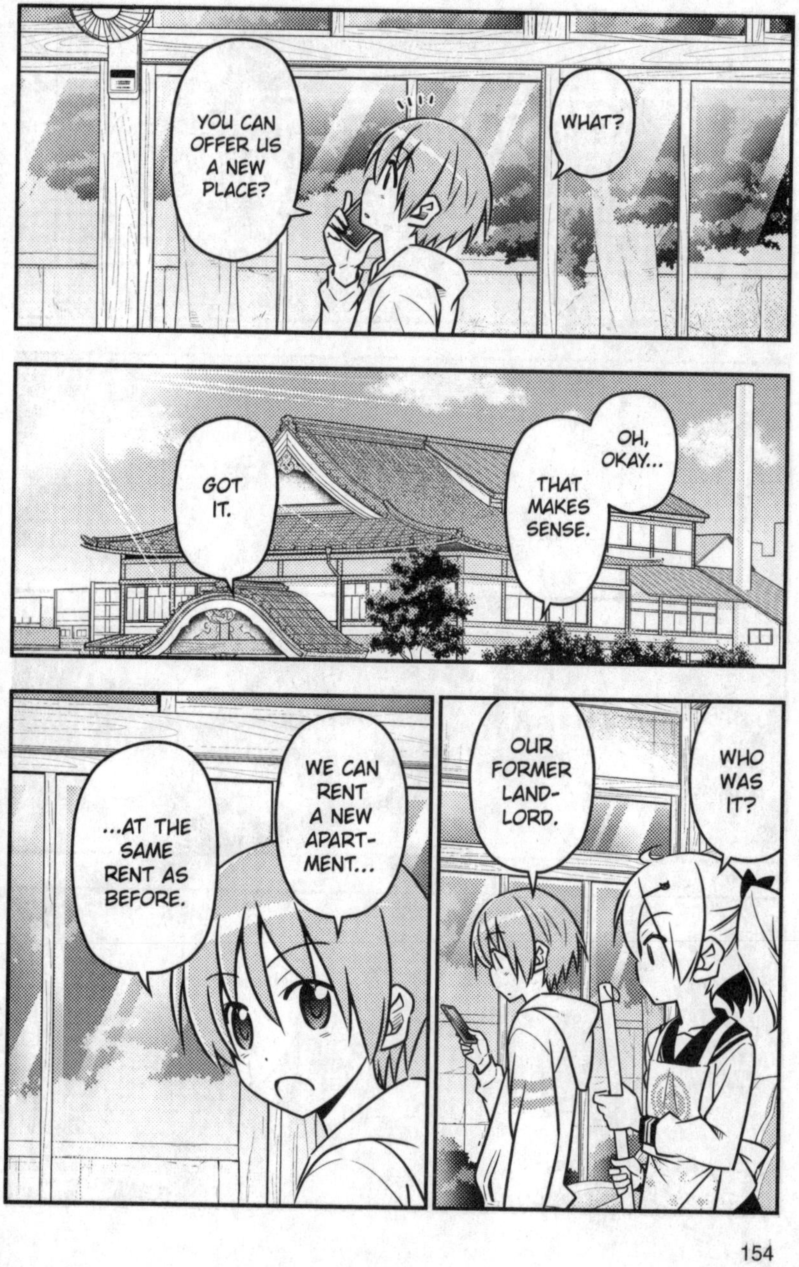
WHAT?
YOU CAN OFFER US A NEW PLACE?
OH, OKAY... THAT MAKES SENSE.
GOT IT.
WHO WAS IT?
OUR FORMER LAND-LORD.
WE CAN RENT A NEW APART-MENT...
...AT THE SAME RENT AS BEFORE.

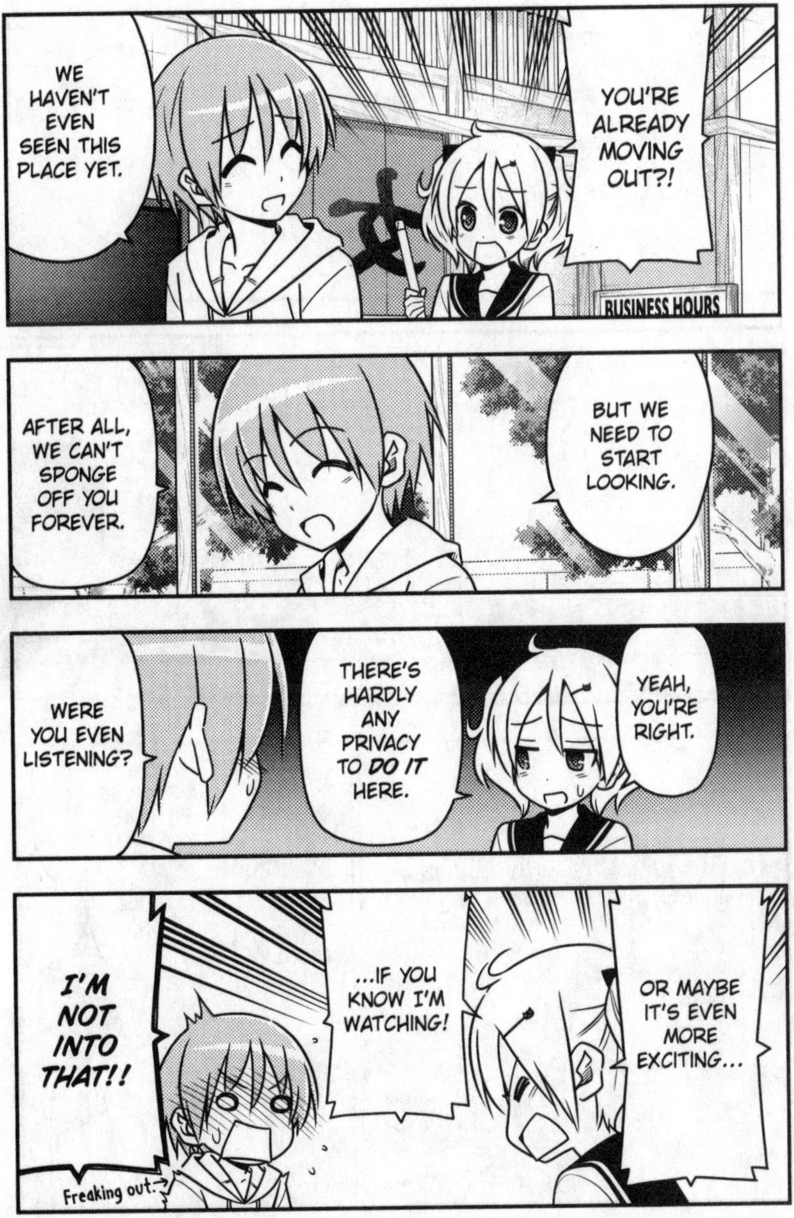
YOU'RE ALREADY MOVING OUT?!
WE HAVEN'T EVEN SEEN THIS PLACE YET.
BUSINESS HOURS
BUT WE NEED TO START LOOKING.
AFTER ALL, WE CAN'T SPONGE OFF YOU FOREVER.
YEAH, YOU'RE RIGHT.
THERE'S HARDLY ANY PRIVACY TO *DO IT* HERE.
WERE YOU EVEN LISTENING?
OR MAYBE IT'S EVEN MORE EXCITING...
...IF YOU KNOW I'M WATCHING!
*I'M NOT INTO THAT!!*
Freaking out.

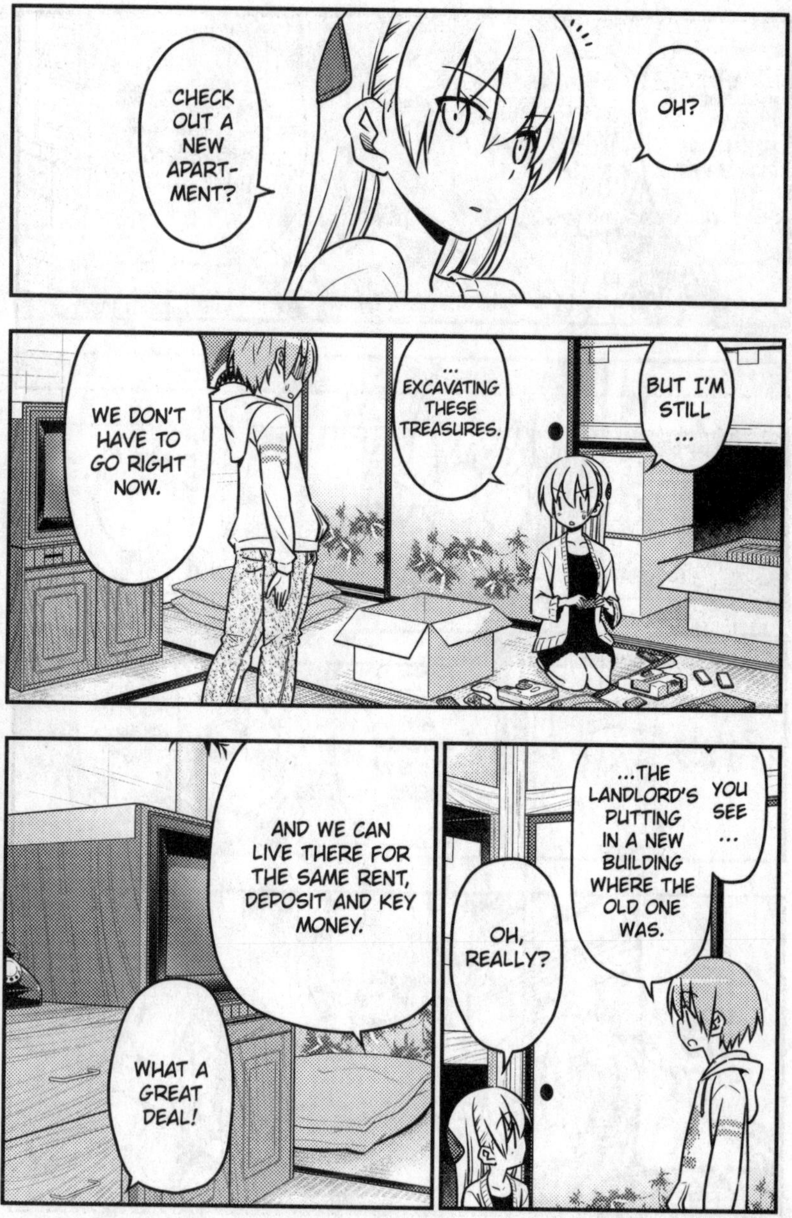
OH?
CHECK OUT A NEW APART-MENT?
BUT I'M STILL ...
... EXCAVATING THESE TREASURES.
WE DON'T HAVE TO GO RIGHT NOW.
YOU SEE ...
...THE LANDLORD'S PUTTING IN A NEW BUILDING WHERE THE OLD ONE WAS.
OH, REALLY?
AND WE CAN LIVE THERE FOR THE SAME RENT, DEPOSIT AND KEY MONEY.
WHAT A GREAT DEAL!

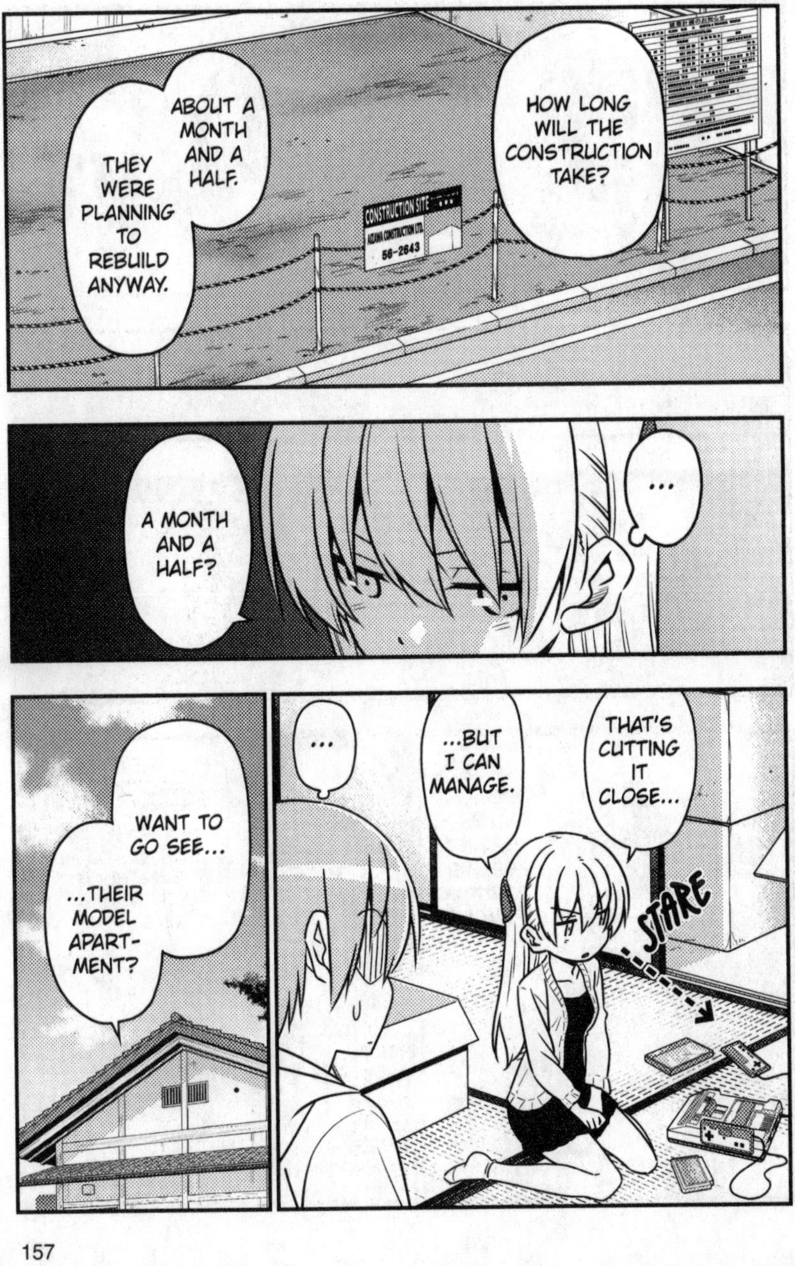
HOW LONG WILL THE CONSTRUCTION TAKE?
CONSTRUCTION SITE
56-2643
ABOUT A MONTH AND A HALF.
THEY WERE PLANNING TO REBUILD ANYWAY.
...
A MONTH AND A HALF?
THAT'S CUTTING IT CLOSE...
...BUT I CAN MANAGE.
...
STARE
WANT TO GO SEE...
...THEIR MODEL APARTMENT?

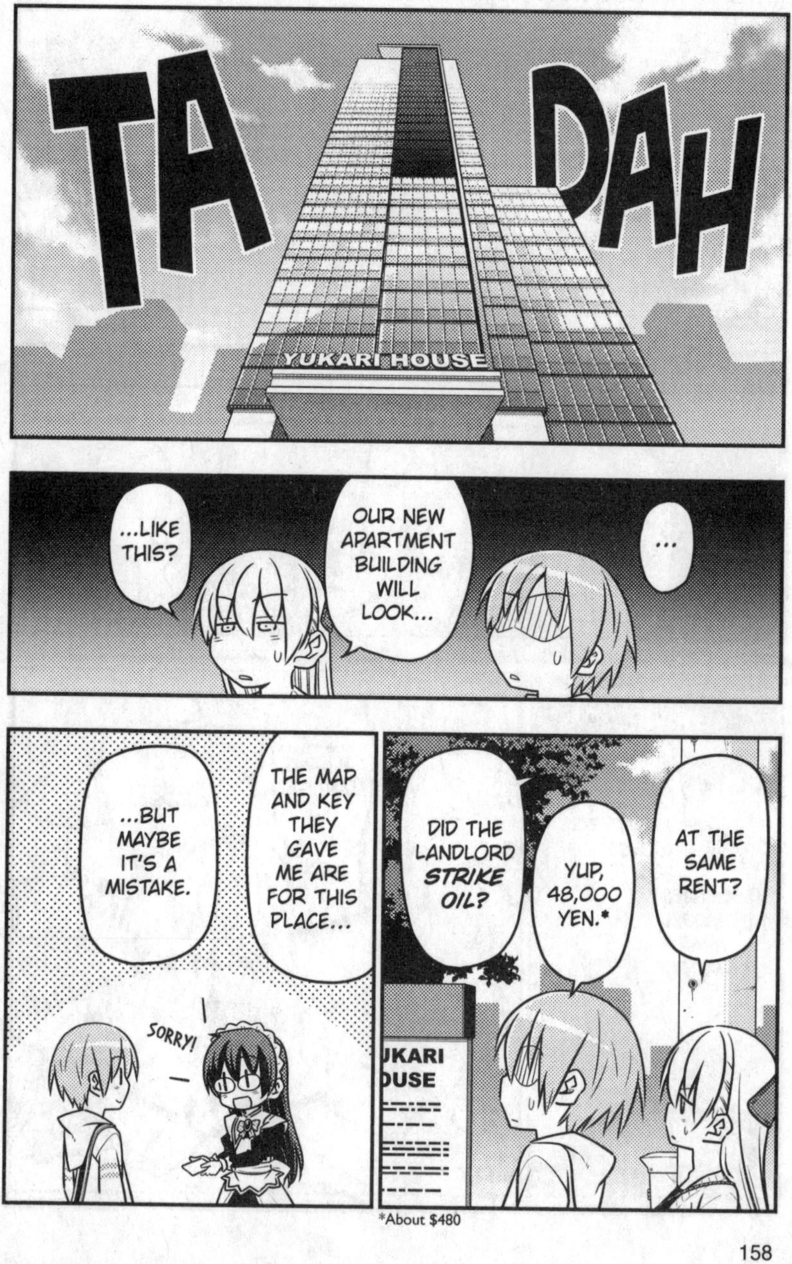
TA DAH
YUKARI HOUSE
...
OUR NEW APARTMENT BUILDING WILL LOOK...
...LIKE THIS?
AT THE SAME RENT?
YUP, 48,000 YEN.*
DID THE LANDLORD *STRIKE OIL?*
THE MAP AND KEY THEY GAVE ME ARE FOR THIS PLACE...
...BUT MAYBE IT'S A MISTAKE.
SORRY!

*About $480

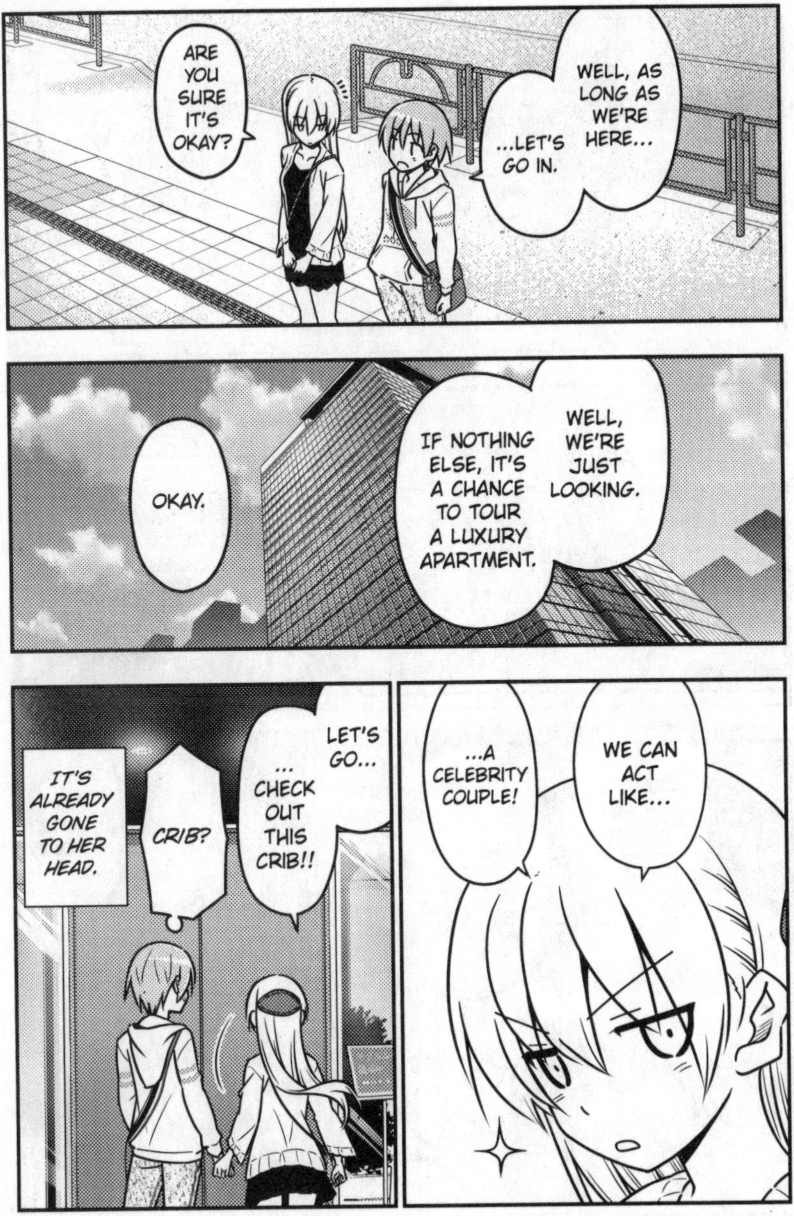
WELL, AS LONG AS WE'RE HERE...
...LET'S GO IN.
ARE YOU SURE IT'S OKAY?
WELL, WE'RE JUST LOOKING.
IF NOTHING ELSE, IT'S A CHANCE TO TOUR A LUXURY APARTMENT.
OKAY.
WE CAN ACT LIKE...
...A CELEBRITY COUPLE!
LET'S GO...
...CHECK OUT THIS CRIB!!
CRIB?
IT'S ALREADY GONE TO HER HEAD.

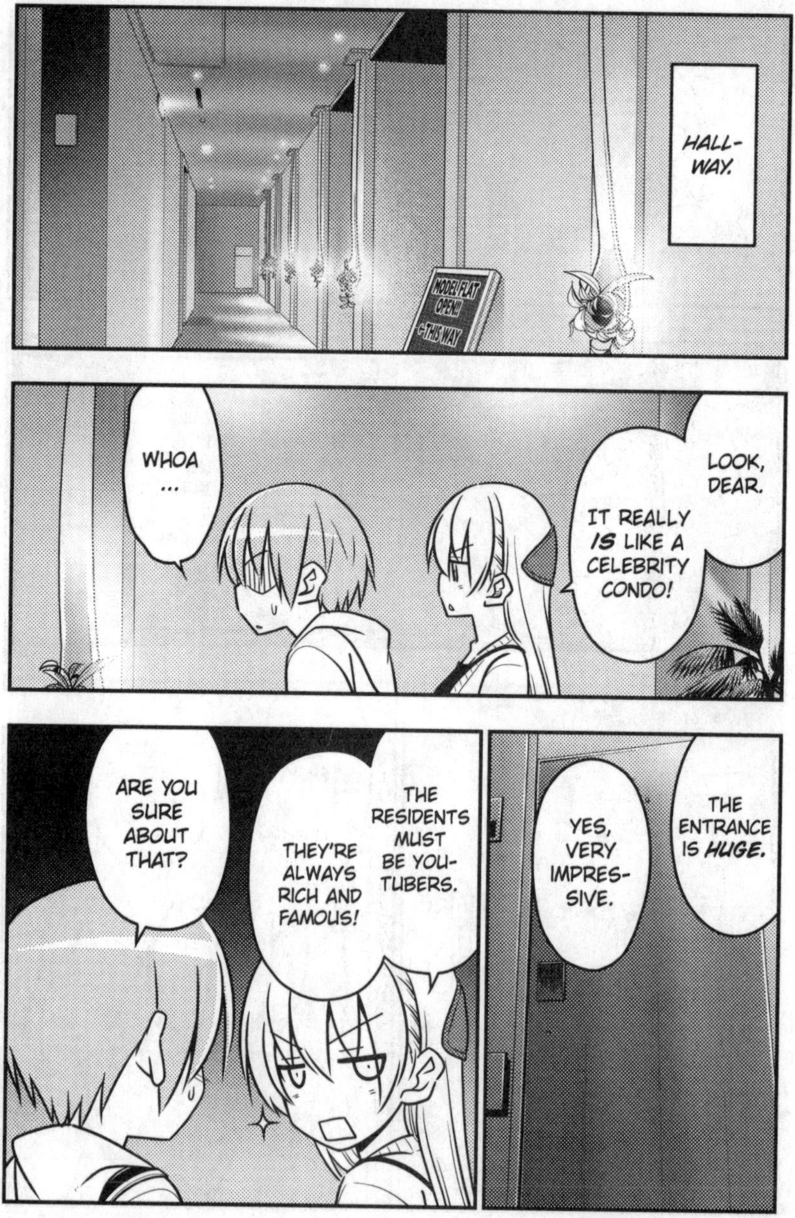
HALL-WAY.
MODEL FLAT OPEN!! ←THIS WAY
LOOK, DEAR.
IT REALLY *IS* LIKE A CELEBRITY CONDO!
WHOA ...
THE ENTRANCE IS *HUGE.*
YES, VERY IMPRES-SIVE.
THE RESIDENTS MUST BE YOU-TUBERS.
THEY'RE ALWAYS RICH AND FAMOUS!
ARE YOU SURE ABOUT THAT?

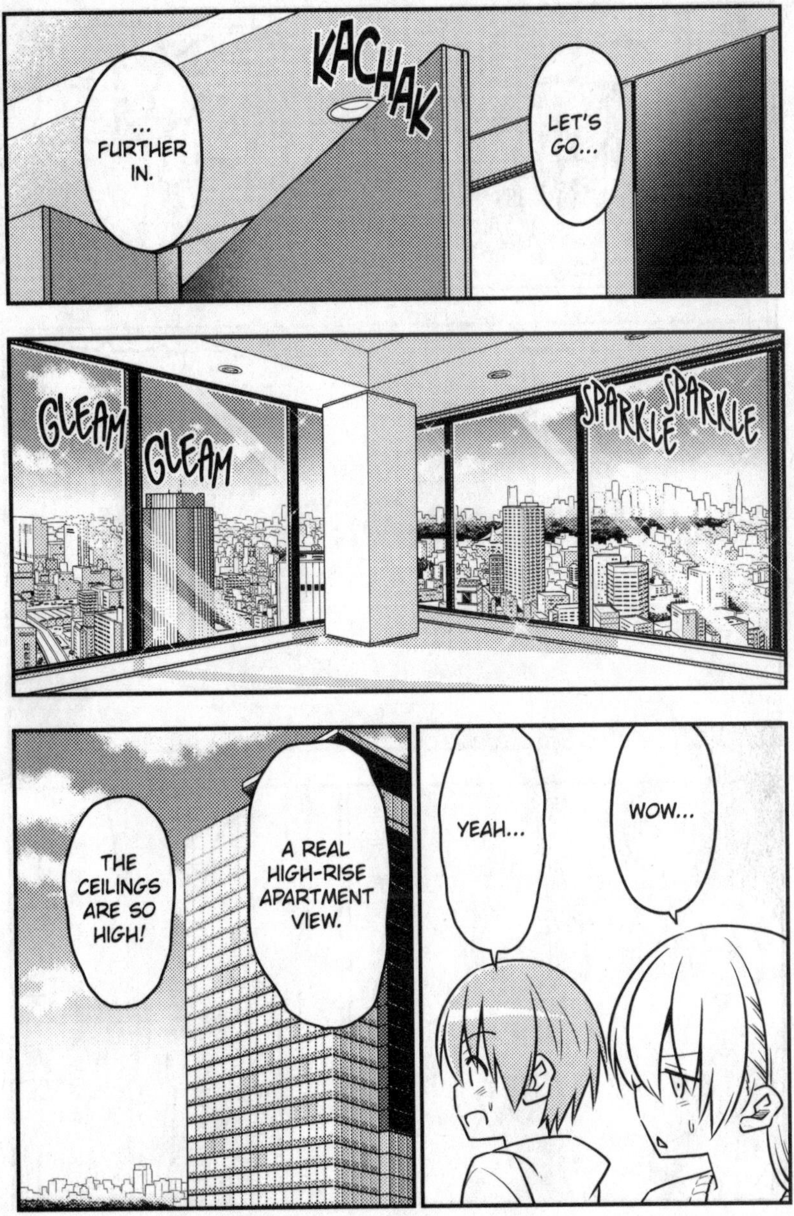
LET'S GO...
KACHAK
... FURTHER IN.
SPARKLE SPARKLE
GLEAM GLEAM
WOW...
YEAH...
A REAL HIGH-RISE APARTMENT VIEW.
THE CEILINGS ARE SO HIGH!

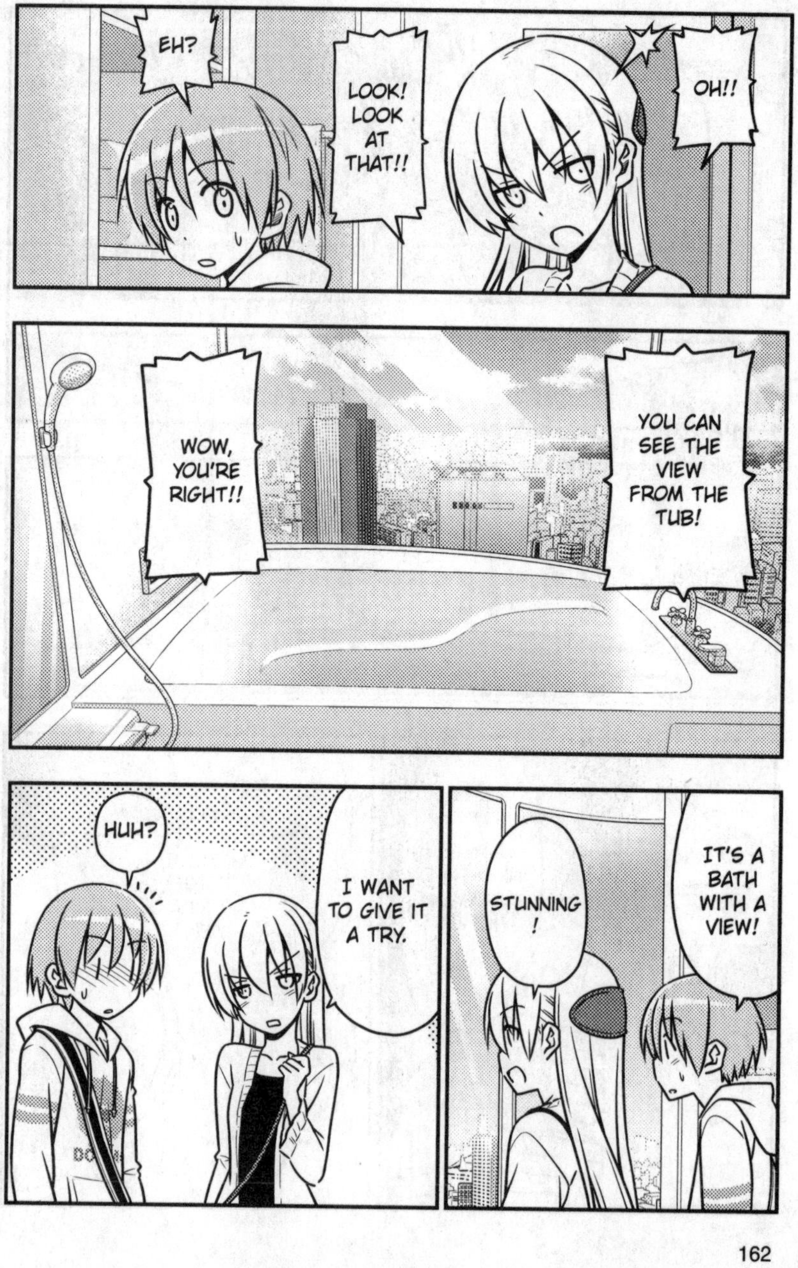
OH!!
LOOK! LOOK AT THAT!!
EH?
YOU CAN SEE THE VIEW FROM THE TUB!
WOW, YOU'RE RIGHT!!
IT'S A BATH WITH A VIEW!
STUNNING!
I WANT TO GIVE IT A TRY.
HUH?

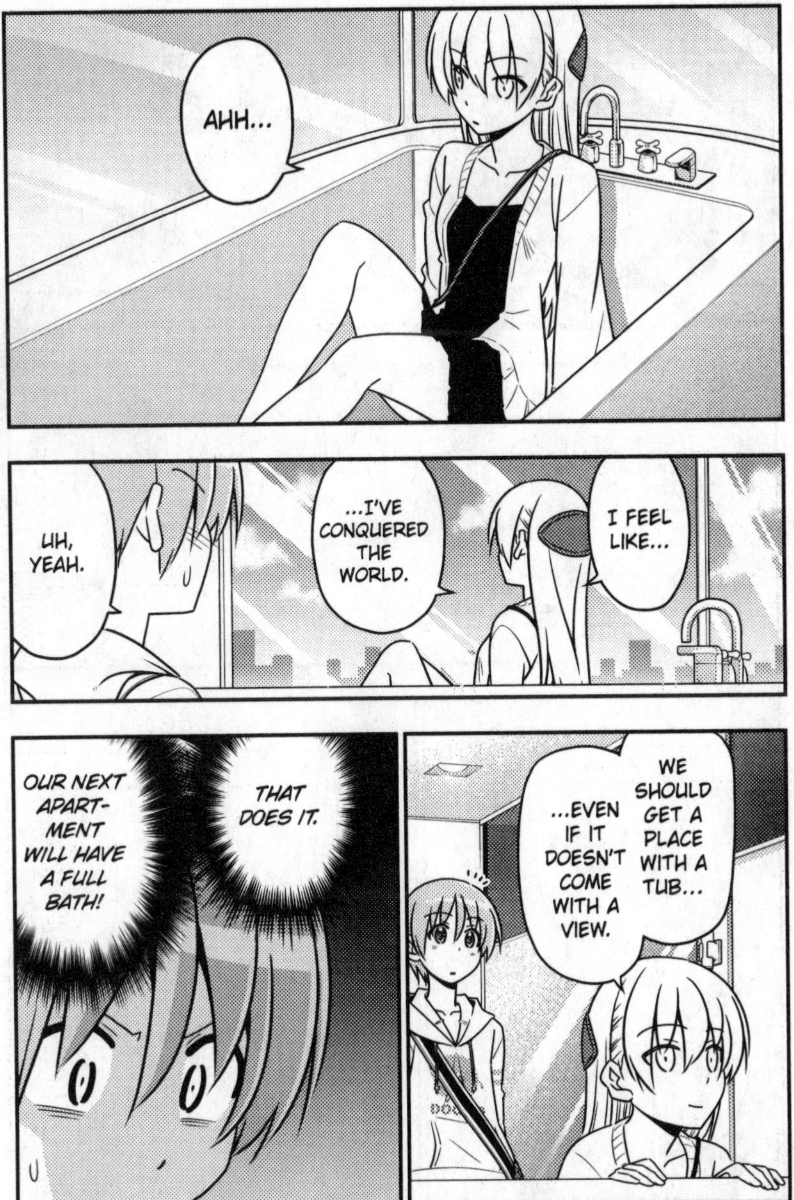
AHH...
I FEEL LIKE...
...I'VE CONQUERED THE WORLD.
UH, YEAH.
WE SHOULD GET A PLACE WITH A TUB...
...EVEN IF IT DOESN'T COME WITH A VIEW.
THAT DOES IT.
OUR NEXT APART-MENT WILL HAVE A FULL BATH!

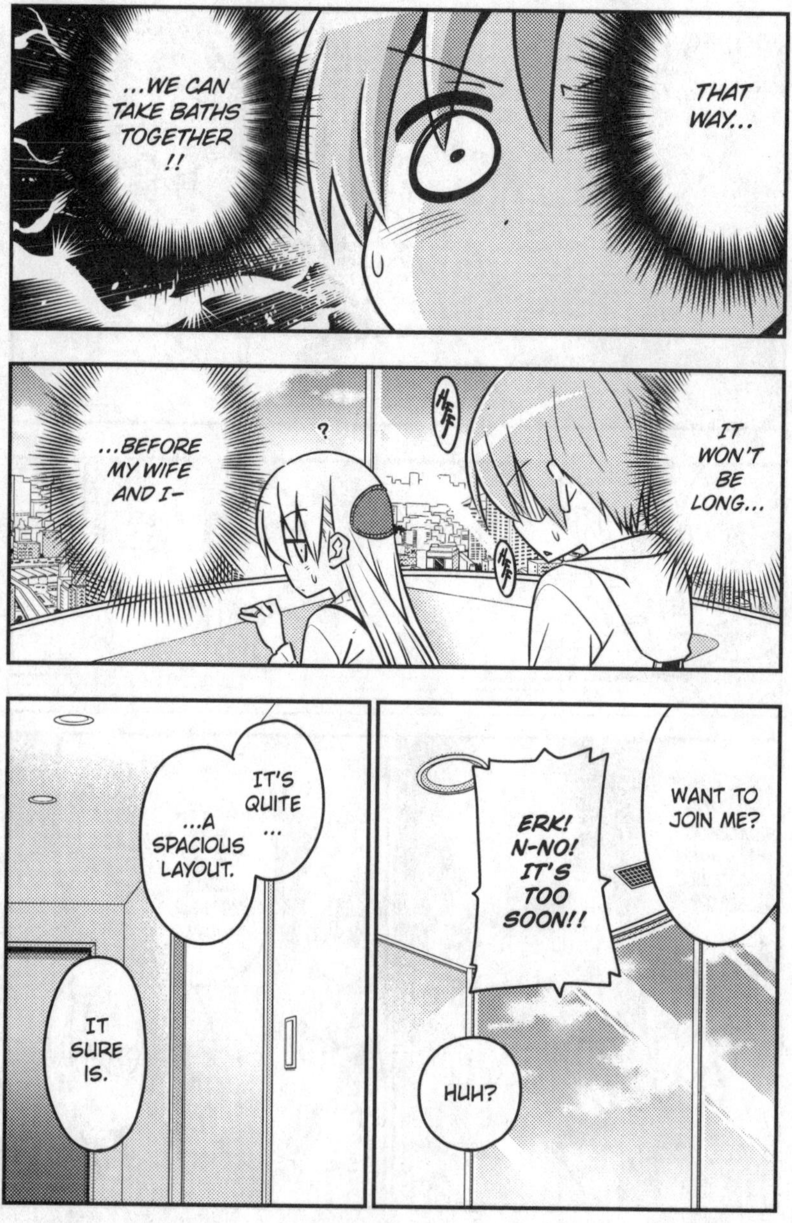
THAT WAY...
...WE CAN TAKE BATHS TOGETHER !!
IT WON'T BE LONG...
...BEFORE MY WIFE AND I-
?
WANT TO JOIN ME?
ERK! N-NO! IT'S TOO SOON!!
HUH?
IT'S QUITE ...
...A SPACIOUS LAYOUT.
IT SURE IS.

THIS MUST BE...
...THE BED-ROOM.
THE BED'S HUGE!
IT'S QUEEN SIZE.
IT LOOKS REALLY COMFY.
A BIG HOME...
...HAS SPACE FOR A BIG BED.
THAT'S RIGHT.
UH...
...AFTER WE MOVE... UM...
YES?

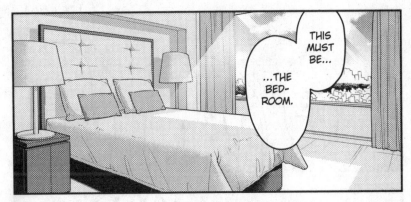

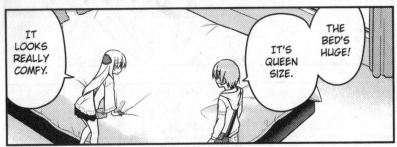

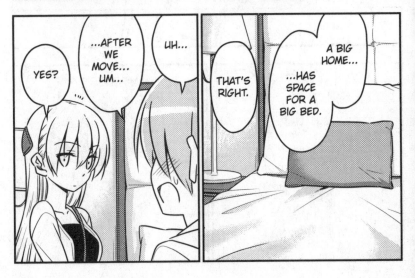

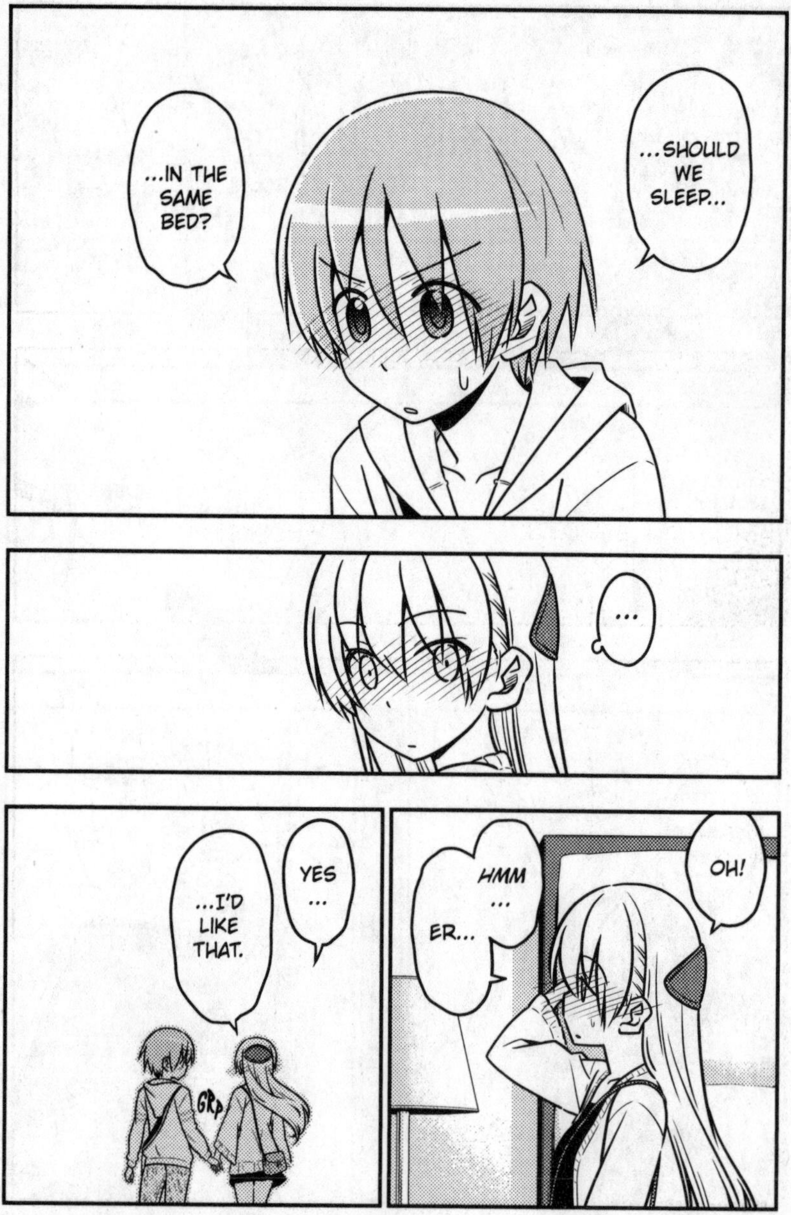
...SHOULD WE SLEEP...
...IN THE SAME BED?
...
OH!
HMM ... ER...
YES ...
...I'D LIKE THAT.
GRP

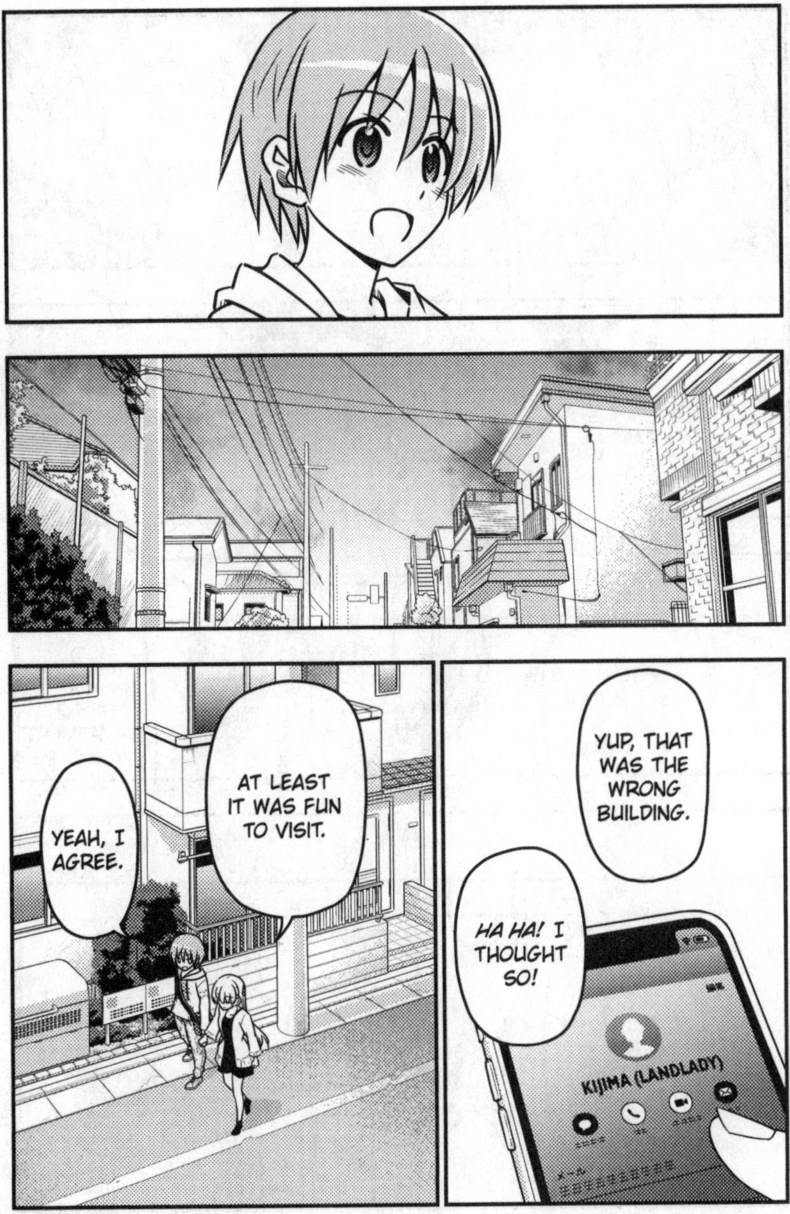
YUP, THAT WAS THE WRONG BUILDING.
HA HA! I THOUGHT SO!
KIJIMA (LANDLADY)
AT LEAST IT WAS FUN TO VISIT.
YEAH, I AGREE.

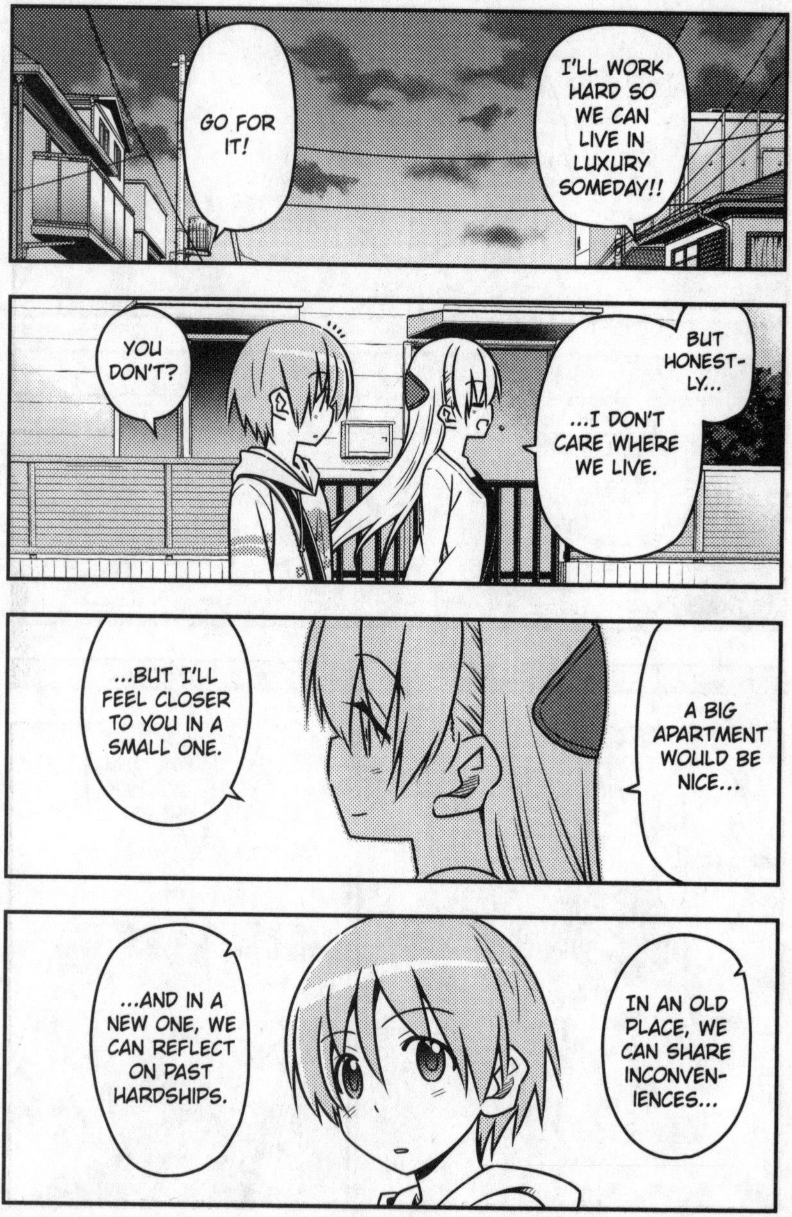
I'LL WORK HARD SO WE CAN LIVE IN LUXURY SOMEDAY!!
GO FOR IT!
BUT HONEST-LY...
...I DON'T CARE WHERE WE LIVE.
YOU DON'T?
A BIG APARTMENT WOULD BE NICE...
...BUT I'LL FEEL CLOSER TO YOU IN A SMALL ONE.
IN AN OLD PLACE, WE CAN SHARE INCONVEN-IENCES...
...AND IN A NEW ONE, WE CAN REFLECT ON PAST HARDSHIPS.

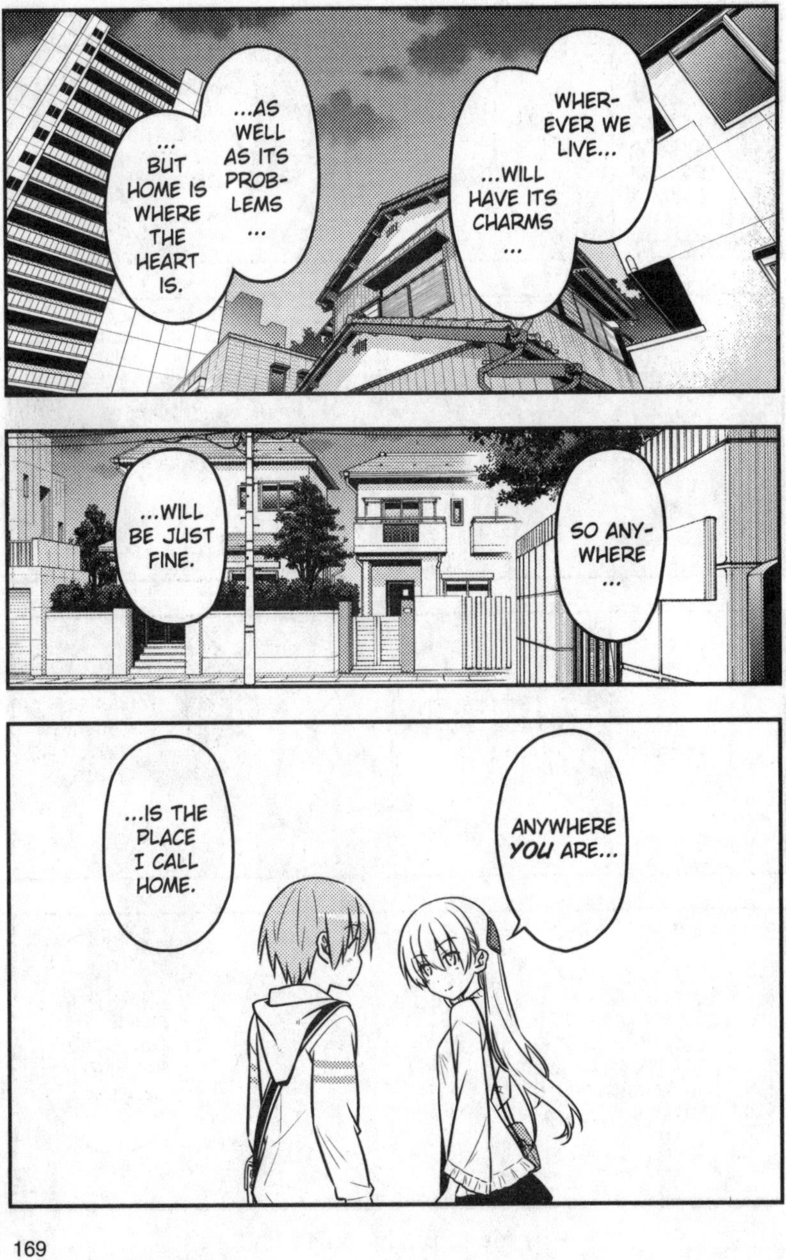
WHEREVER WE LIVE...
...WILL HAVE ITS CHARMS ...
...AS WELL AS ITS PROBLEMS ...
... BUT HOME IS WHERE THE HEART IS.
SO ANYWHERE ...
...WILL BE JUST FINE.
ANYWHERE *YOU* ARE...
...IS THE PLACE I CALL HOME.

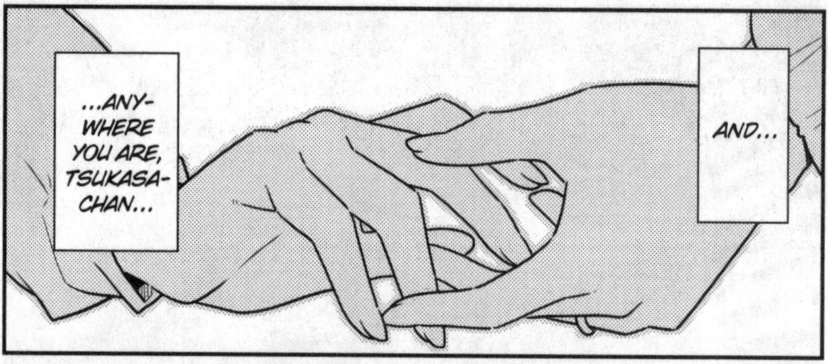
AND...
...ANY-WHERE YOU ARE, TSUKASA-CHAN...

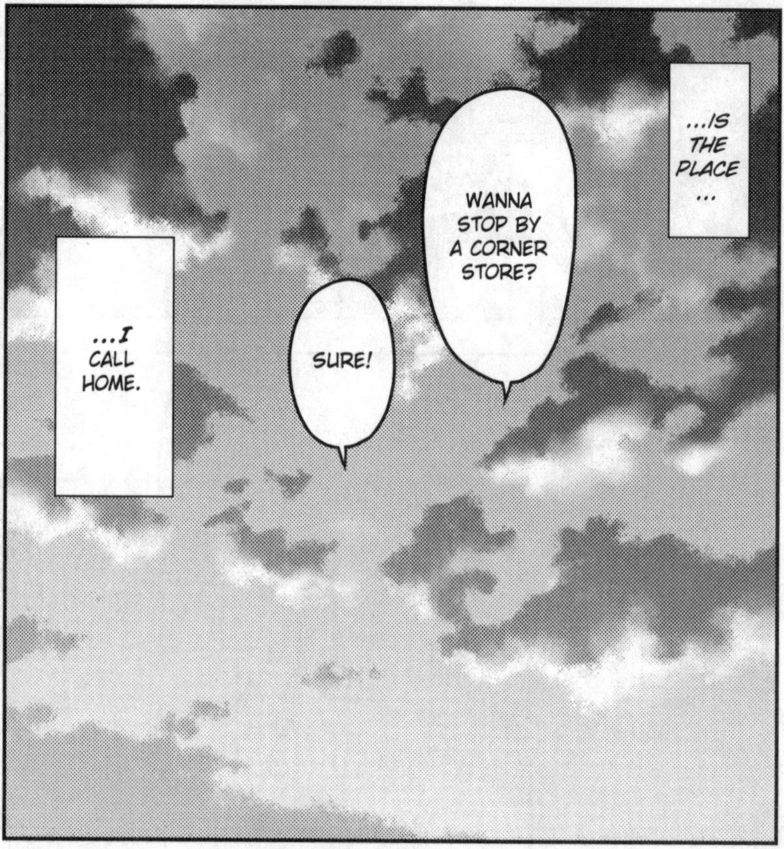
...IS THE PLACE ...
WANNA STOP BY A CORNER STORE?
SURE!
...I CALL HOME.

—Fly Me to the Moon 4 / End—

# Bonus Manga

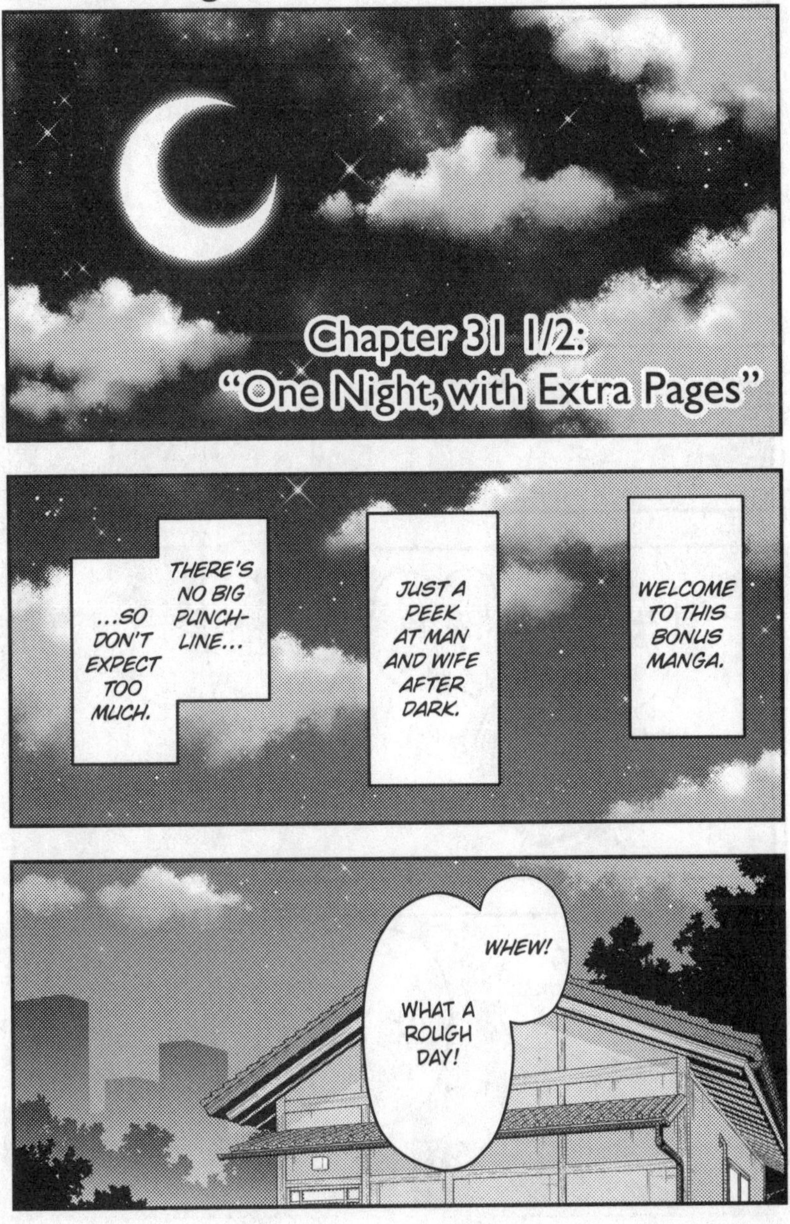

Chapter 31 1/2:
"One Night, with Extra Pages"
WELCOME TO THIS BONUS MANGA.
JUST A PEEK AT MAN AND WIFE AFTER DARK.
THERE'S NO BIG PUNCH-LINE...
...SO DON'T EXPECT TOO MUCH.
WHEW!
WHAT A ROUGH DAY!

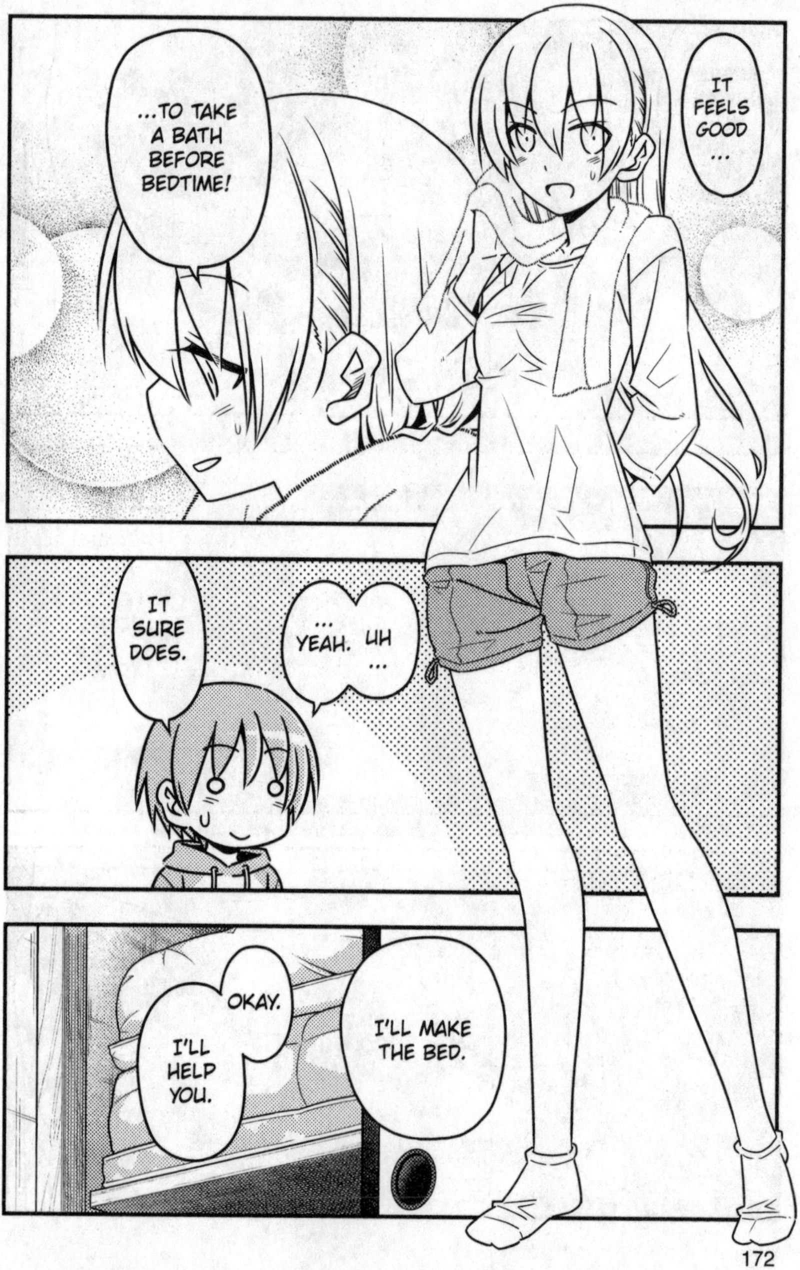
IT FEELS GOOD ...
...TO TAKE A BATH BEFORE BEDTIME!
... YEAH. UH ...
IT SURE DOES.
I'LL MAKE THE BED.
OKAY. I'LL HELP YOU.

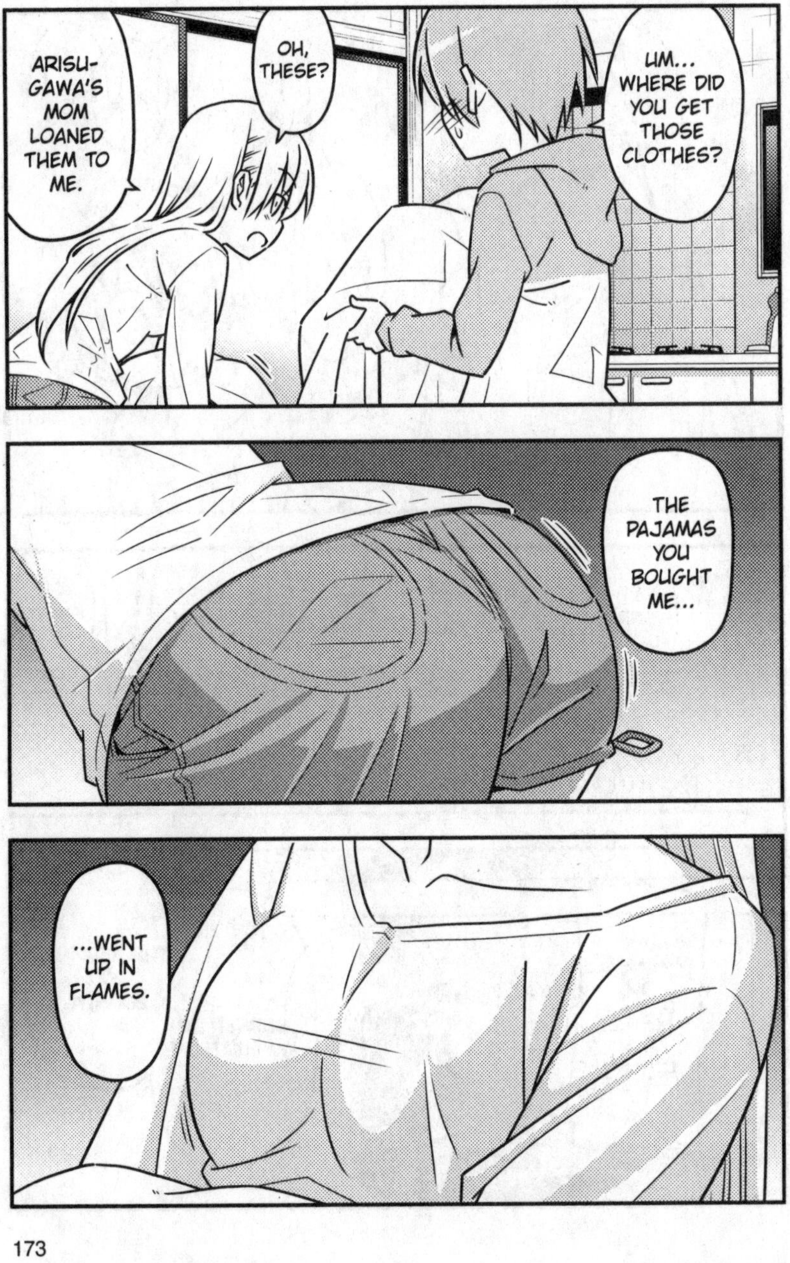
UM... WHERE DID YOU GET THOSE CLOTHES?
OH, THESE?
ARISU-GAWA'S MOM LOANED THEM TO ME.
THE PAJAMAS YOU BOUGHT ME...
...WENT UP IN FLAMES.

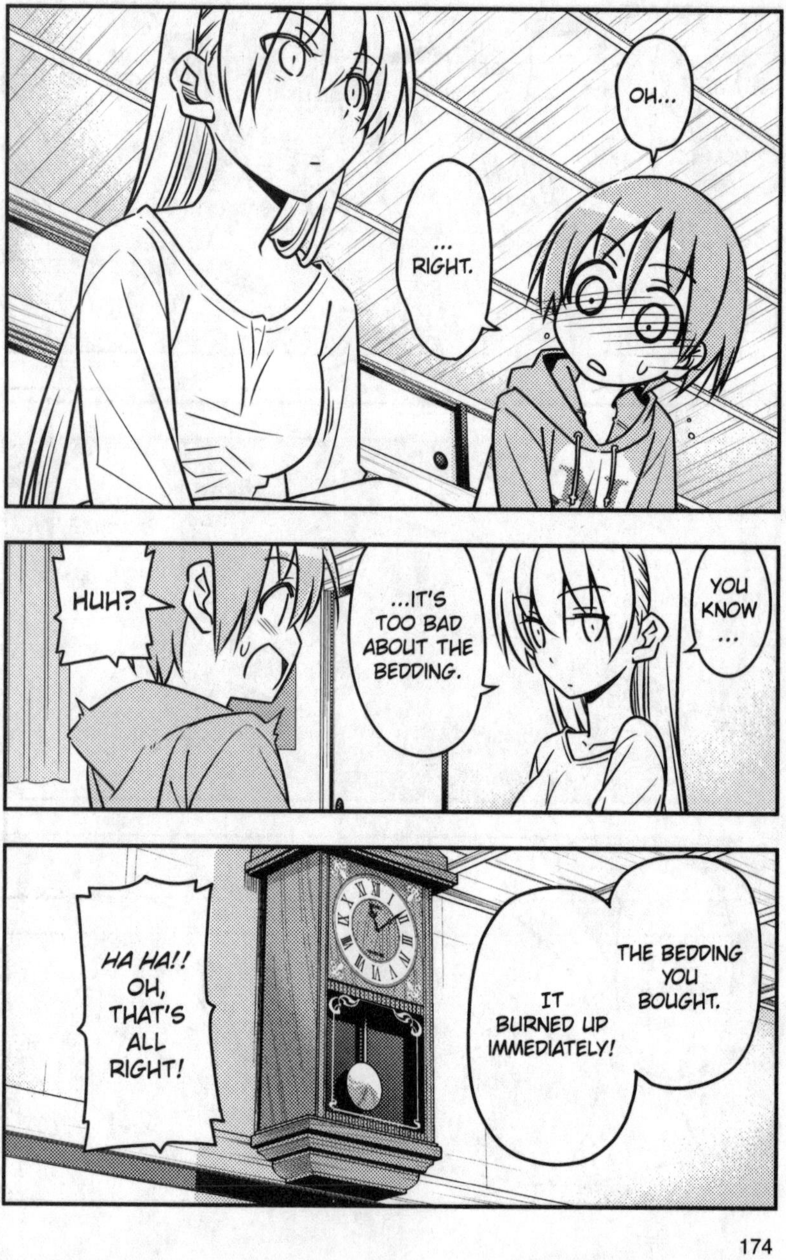
OH...
... RIGHT.
YOU KNOW ...
...IT'S TOO BAD ABOUT THE BEDDING.
HUH?
THE BEDDING YOU BOUGHT.
IT BURNED UP IMMEDIATELY!
HA HA!! OH, THAT'S ALL RIGHT!

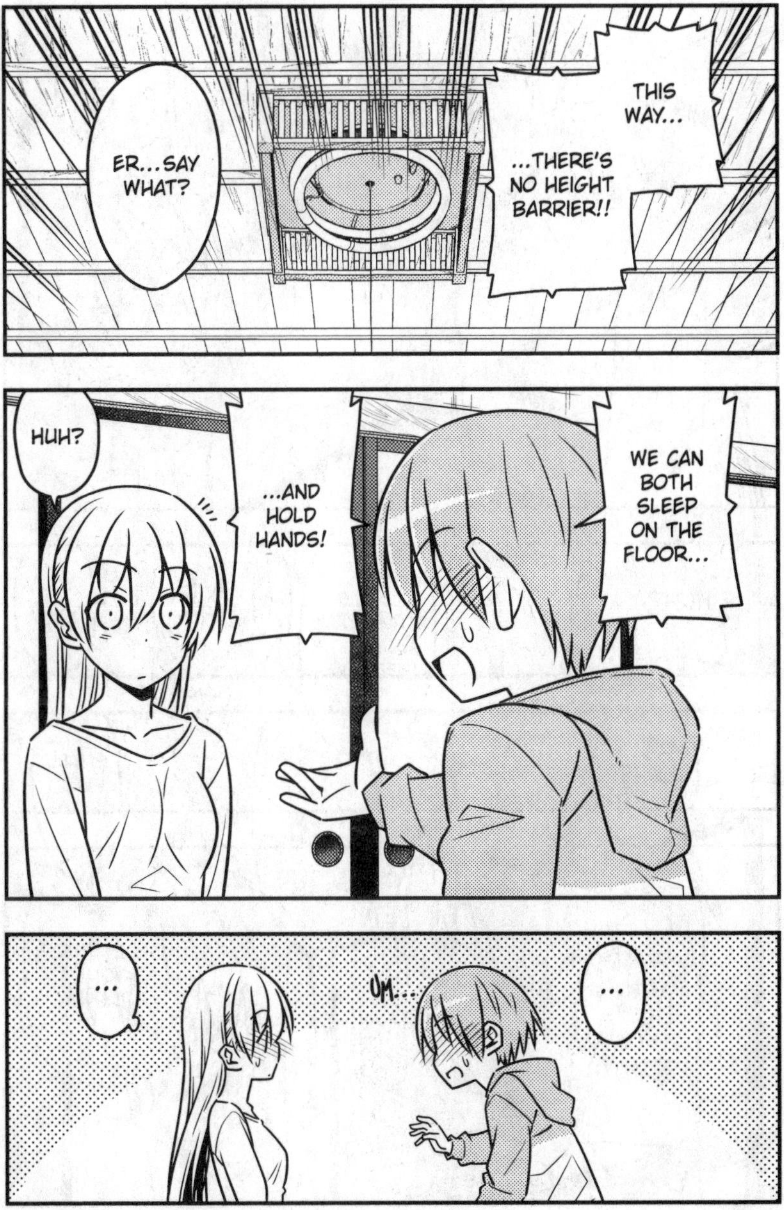
THIS WAY...
...THERE'S NO HEIGHT BARRIER!!
ER...SAY WHAT?
WE CAN BOTH SLEEP ON THE FLOOR...
...AND HOLD HANDS!
HUH?
...
UM...
...

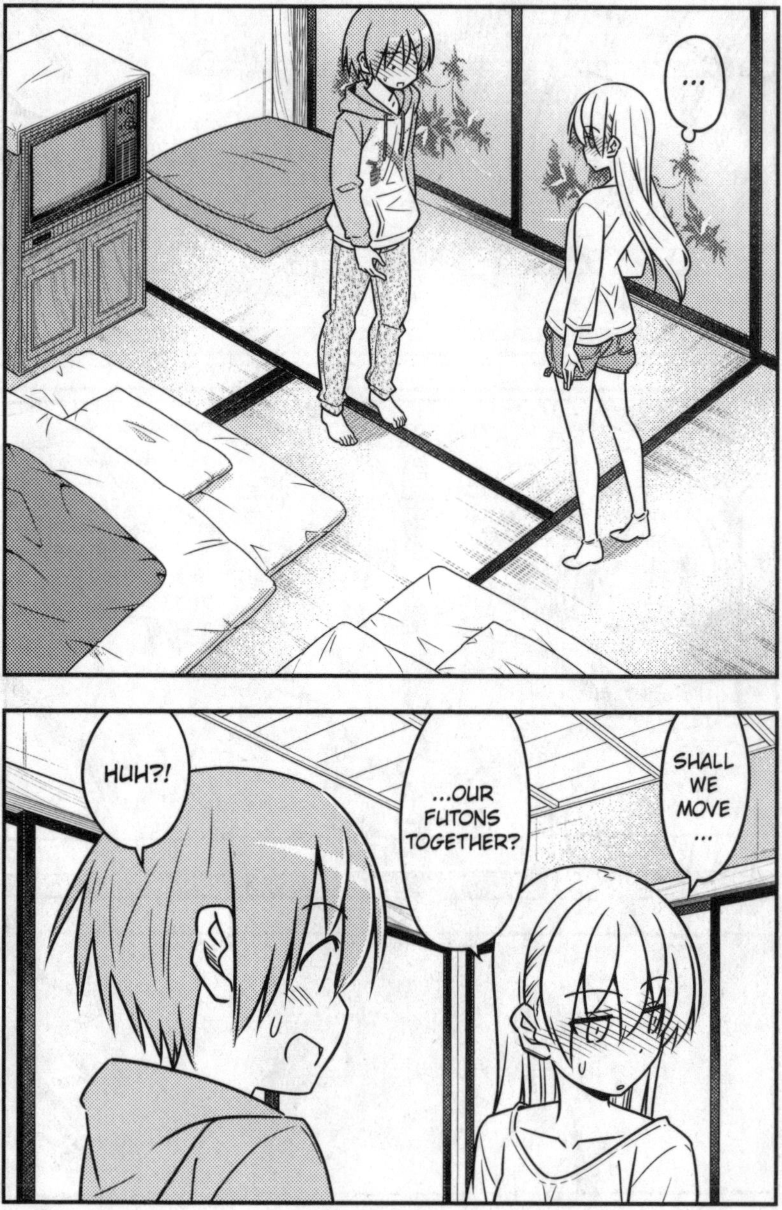
...
SHALL WE MOVE ...
...OUR FUTONS TOGETHER?
HUH?!

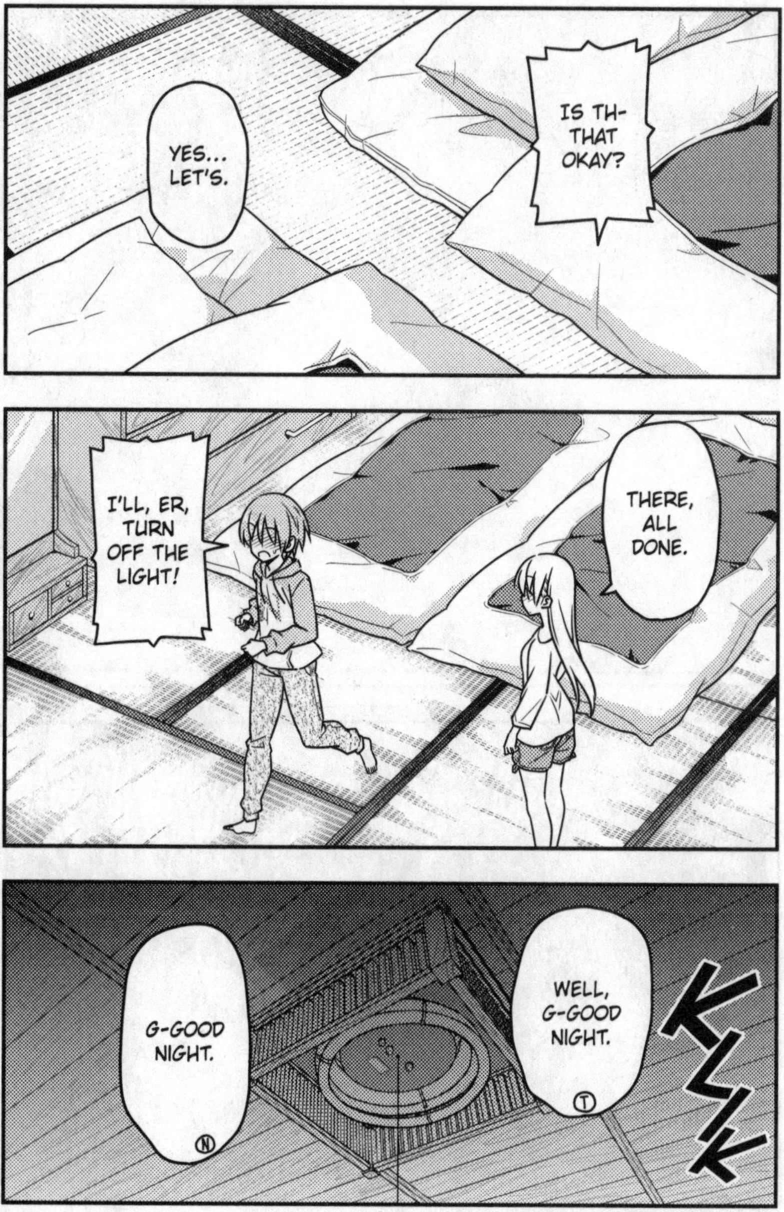
IS TH- THAT OKAY?
YES... LET'S.
THERE, ALL DONE.
I'LL, ER, TURN OFF THE LIGHT!
KLIK
WELL, G-GOOD NIGHT.
G-GOOD NIGHT.

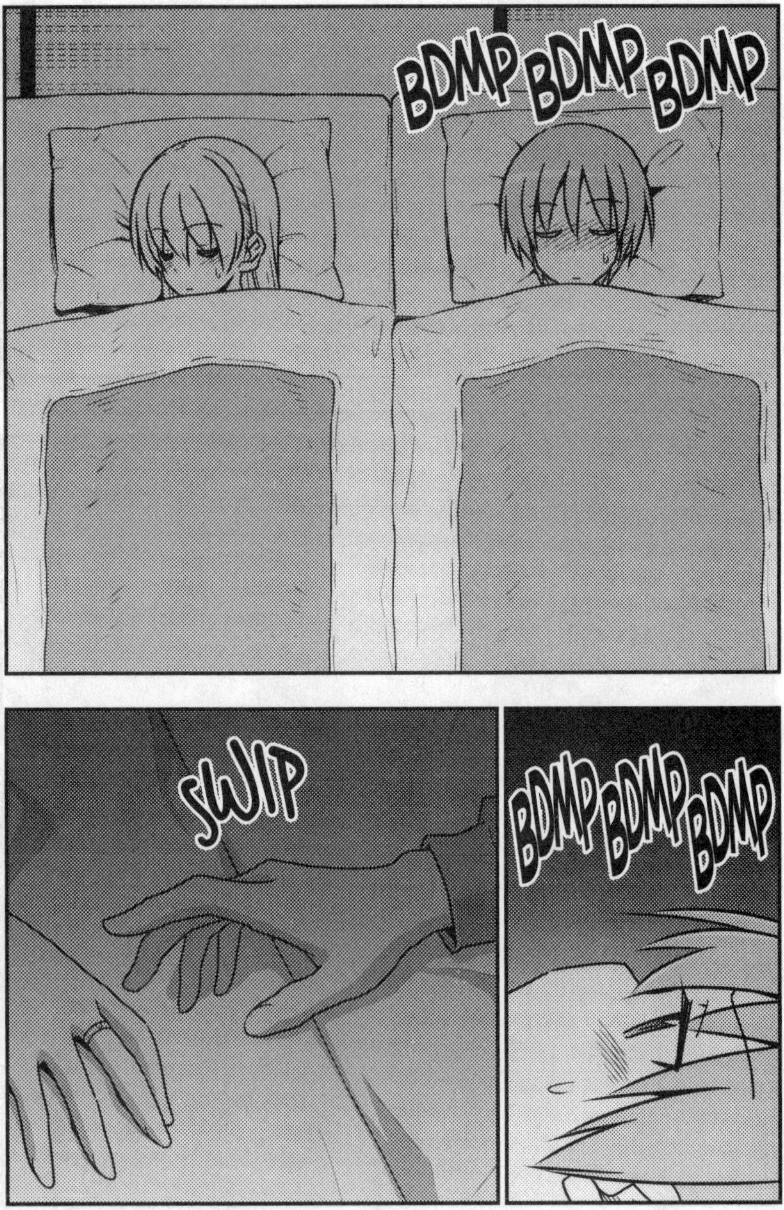
BDMP BDMP BDMP
BDMP BDMP BDMP
SWIP

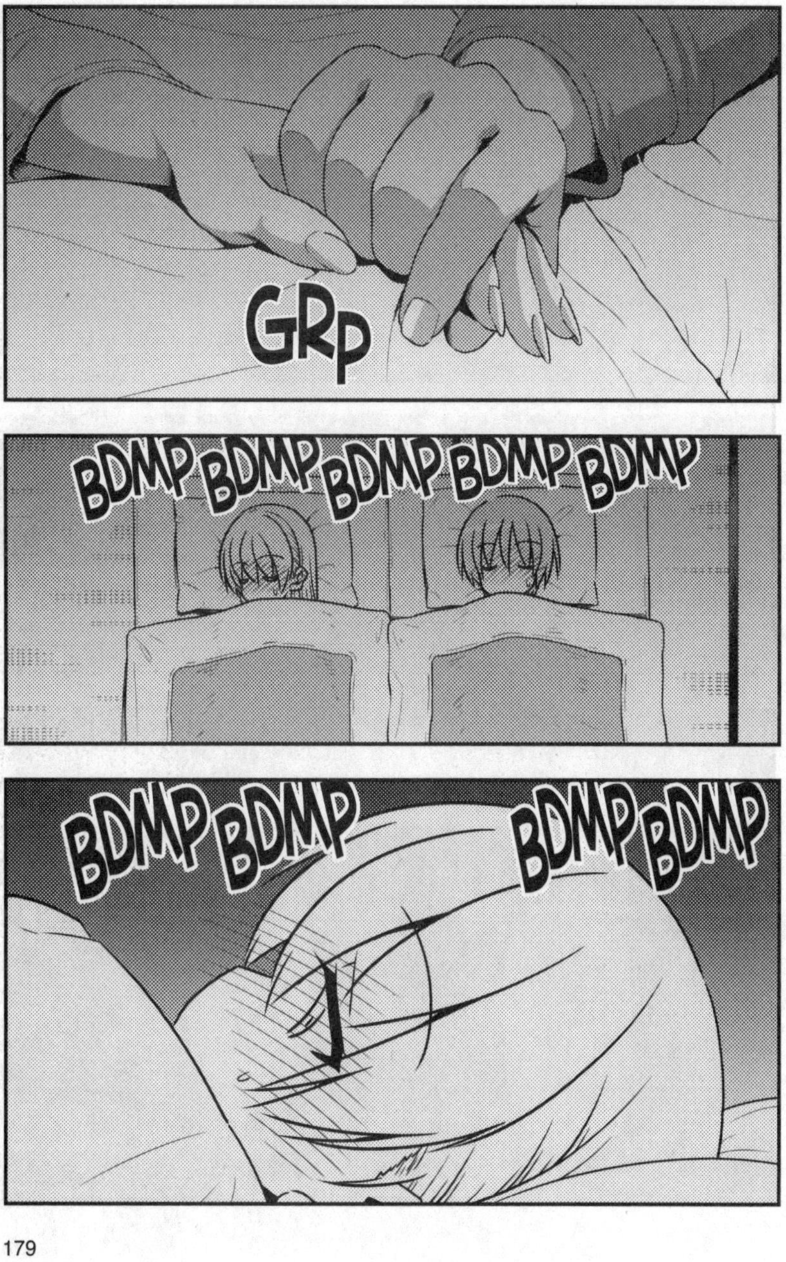
GRP
BDMP BDMP BDMP BDMP BDMP
BDMP BDMP
BDMP BDMP

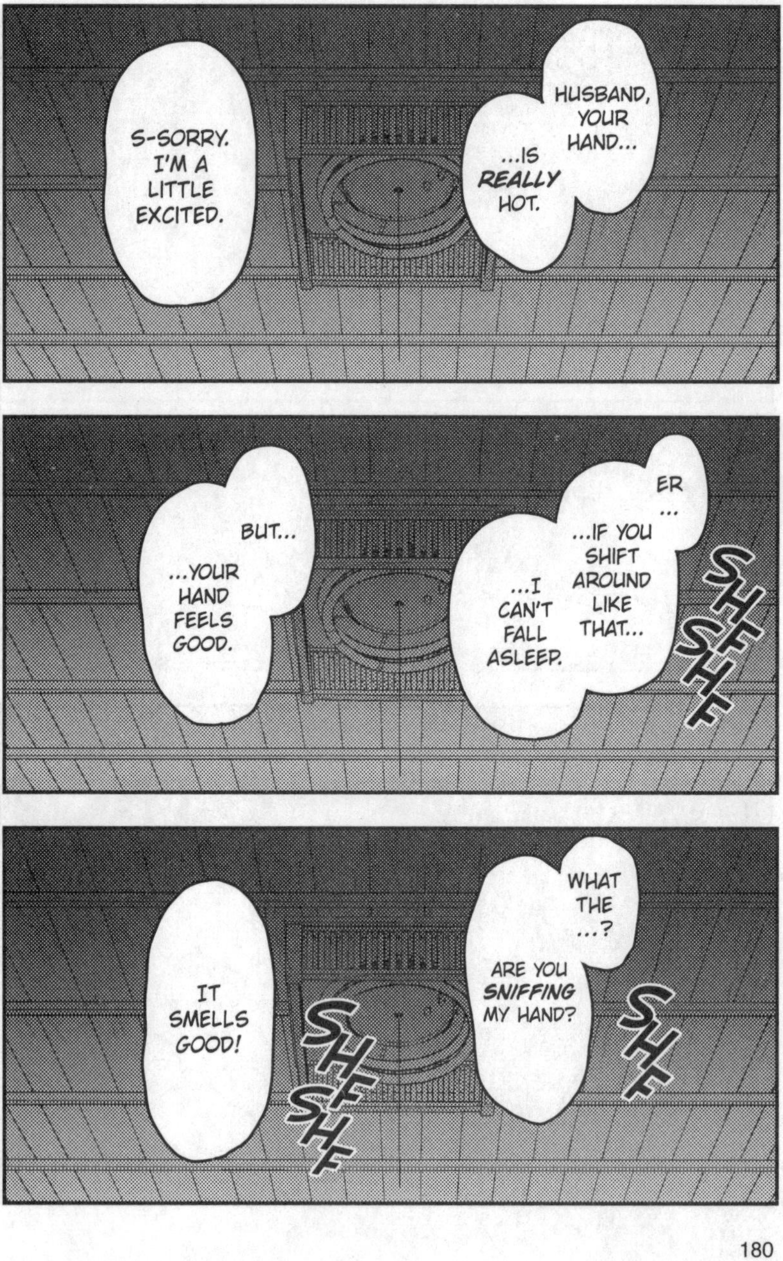
HUSBAND, YOUR HAND...
...IS REALLY HOT.
S-SORRY. I'M A LITTLE EXCITED.
ER ...
...IF YOU SHIFT AROUND LIKE THAT...
...I CAN'T FALL ASLEEP.
SHF SHF
BUT...
...YOUR HAND FEELS GOOD.
WHAT THE ...?
ARE YOU SNIFFING MY HAND?
SHF
SHF SHF
IT SMELLS GOOD!

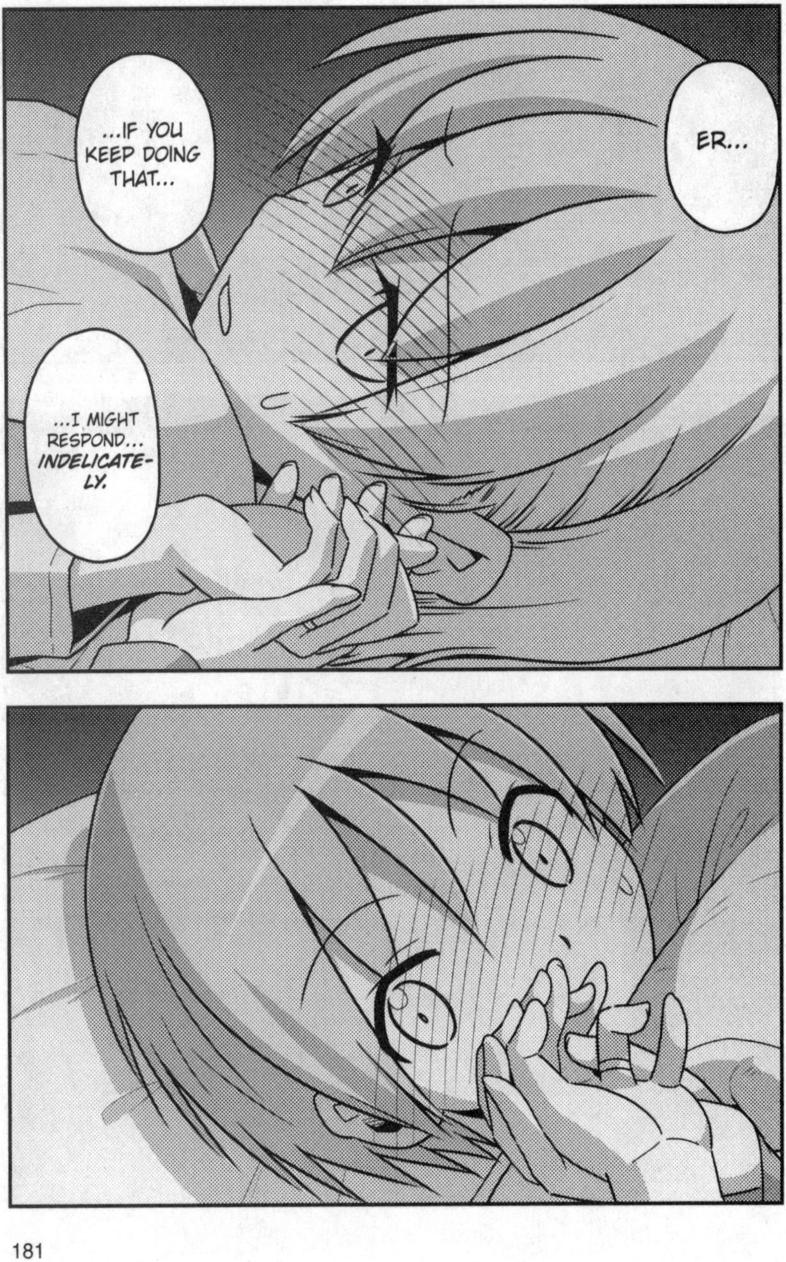
ER...
...IF YOU KEEP DOING THAT...
...I MIGHT RESPOND... *INDELICATE-LY.*

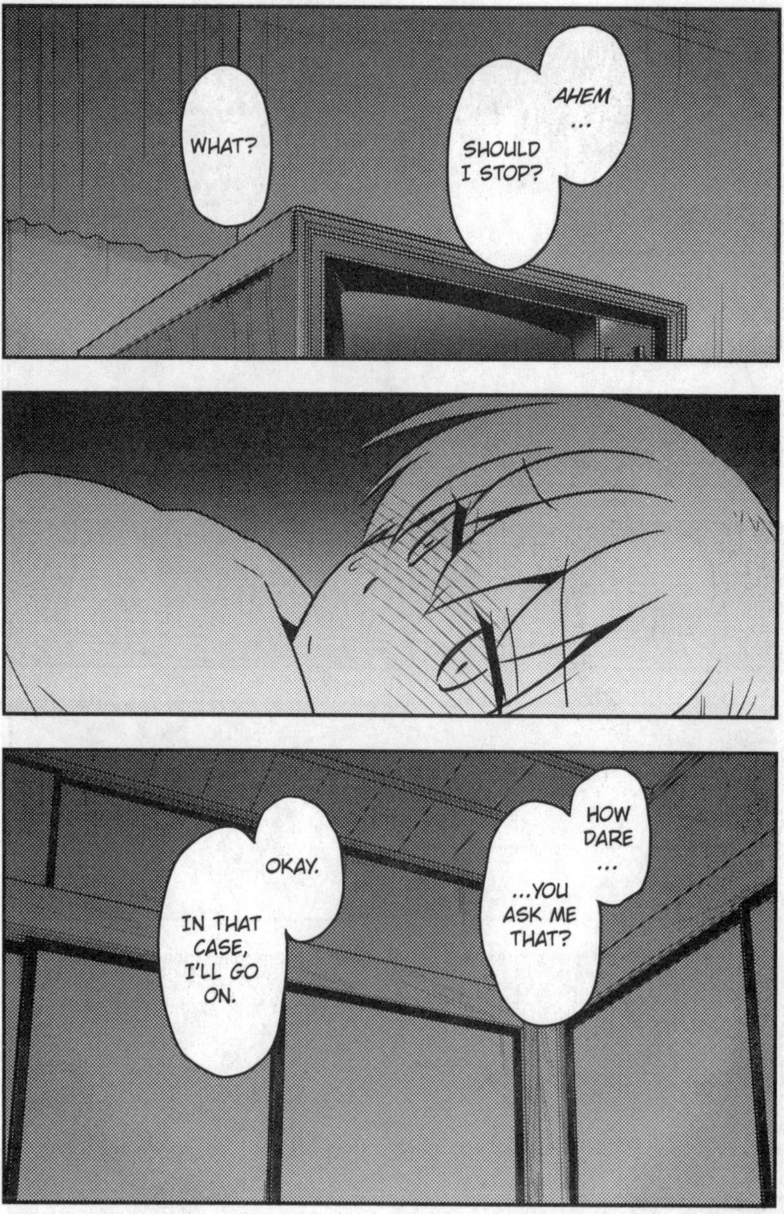
AHEM ... SHOULD I STOP?
WHAT?
HOW DARE ... ...YOU ASK ME THAT?
OKAY. IN THAT CASE, I'LL GO ON.

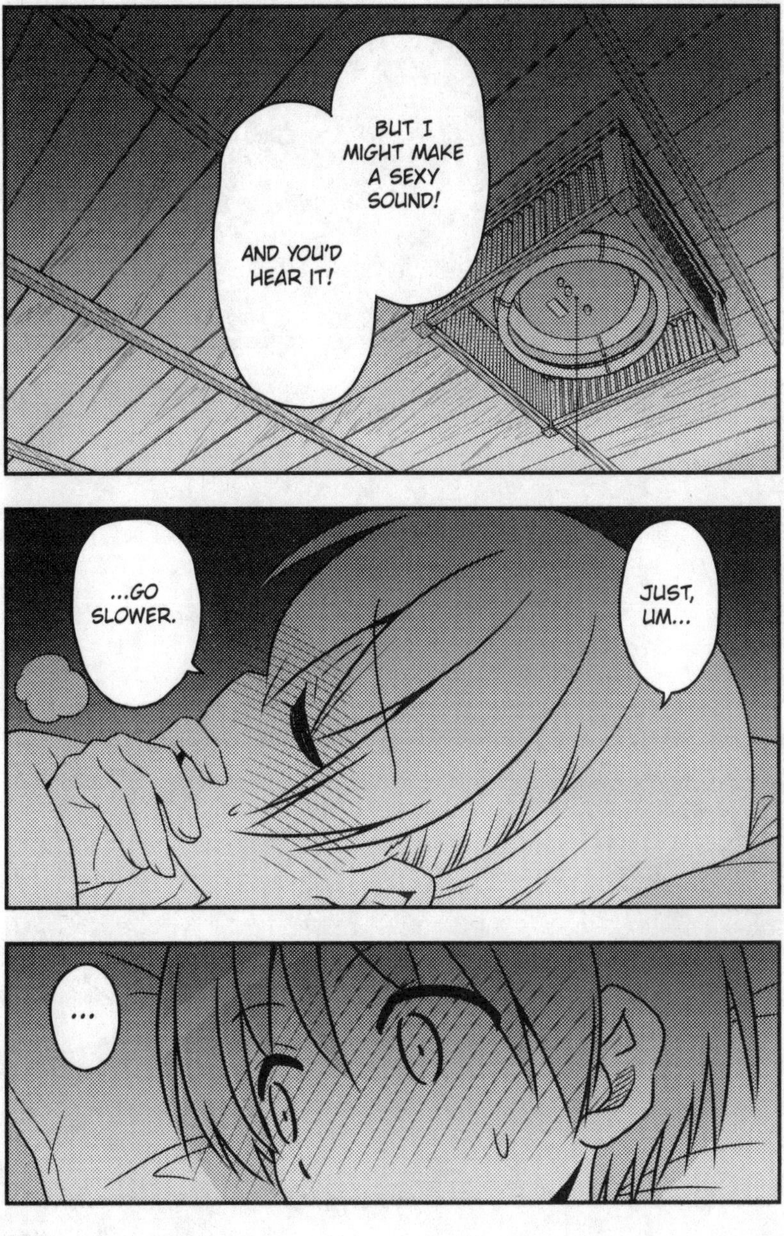
BUT I MIGHT MAKE A SEXY SOUND!
AND YOU'D HEAR IT!
JUST, UM...
...GO SLOWER.
...

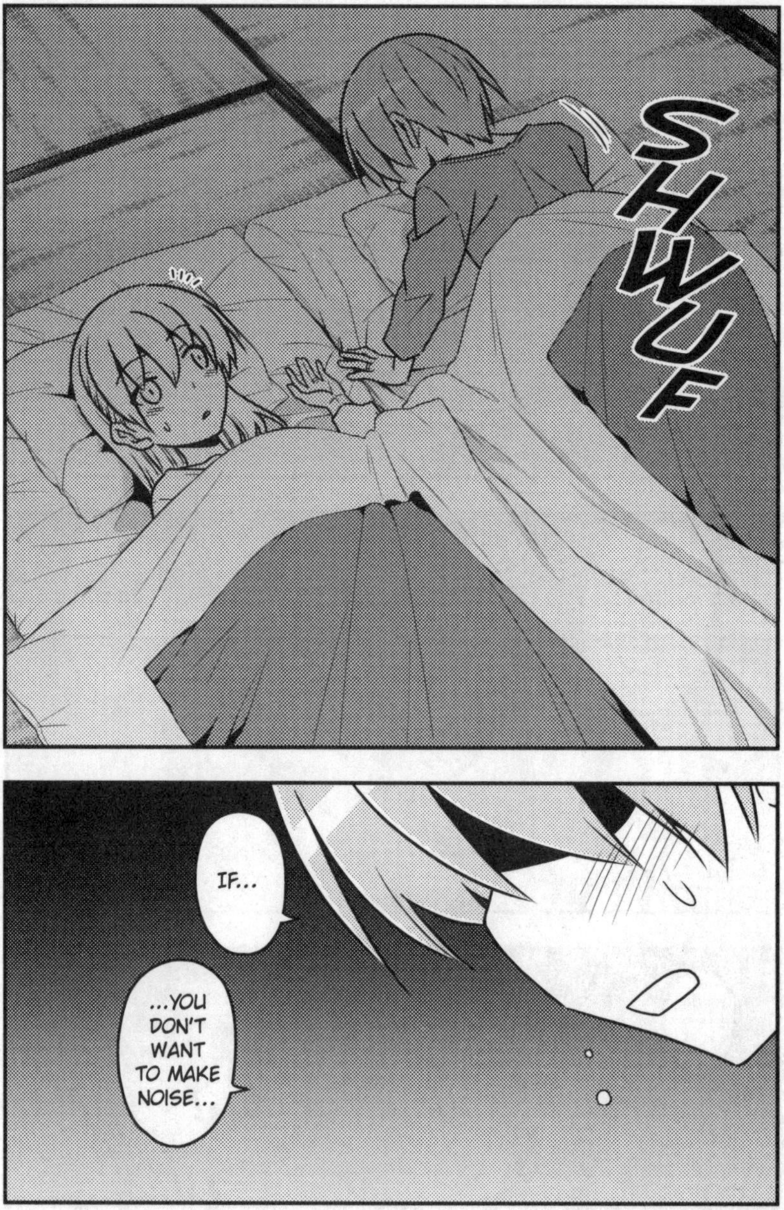
SHWUF
IF...
...YOU DON'T WANT TO MAKE NOISE...

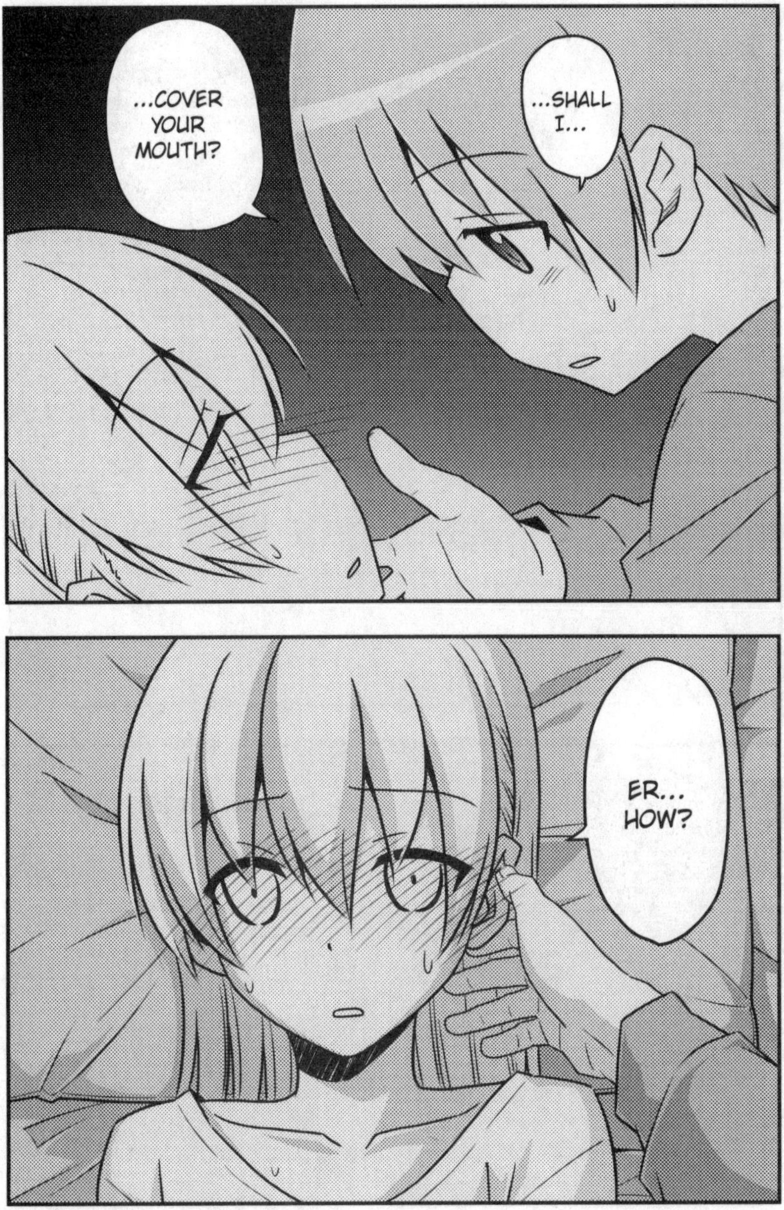
...SHALL I...
...COVER YOUR MOUTH?
ER... HOW?

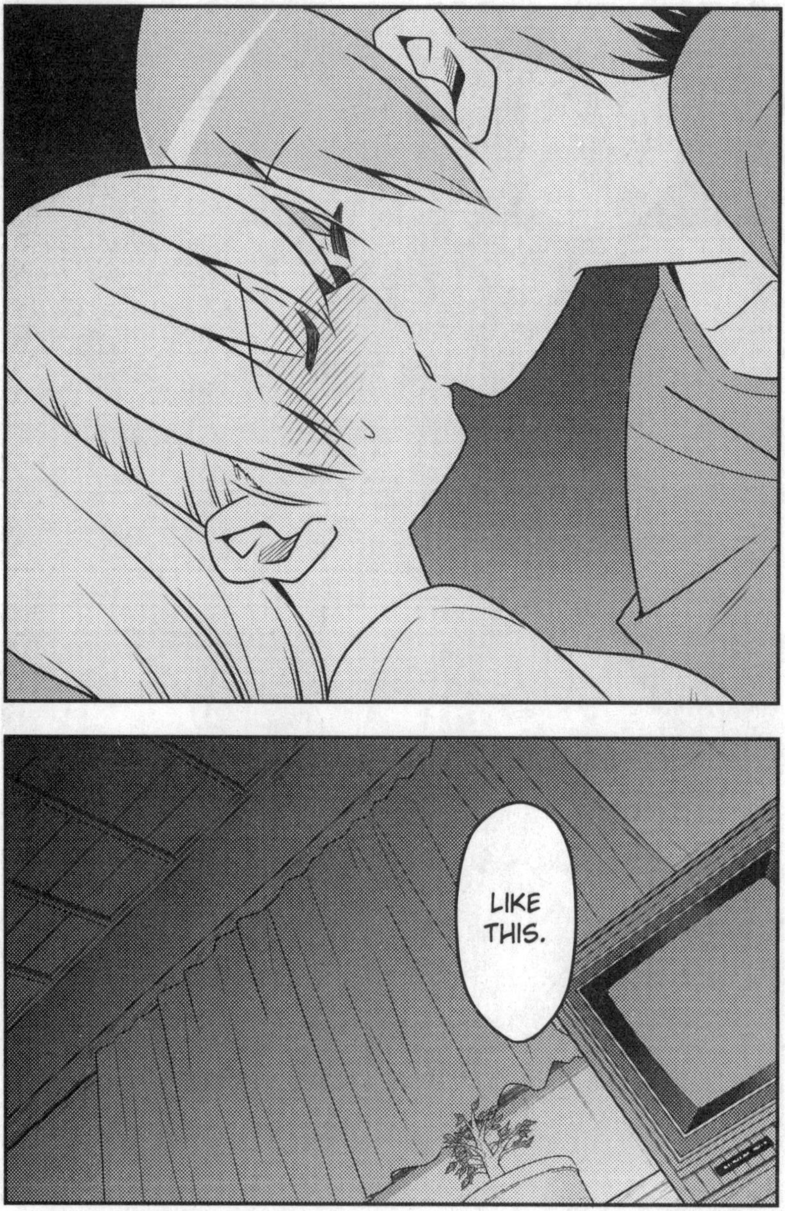
LIKE THIS.

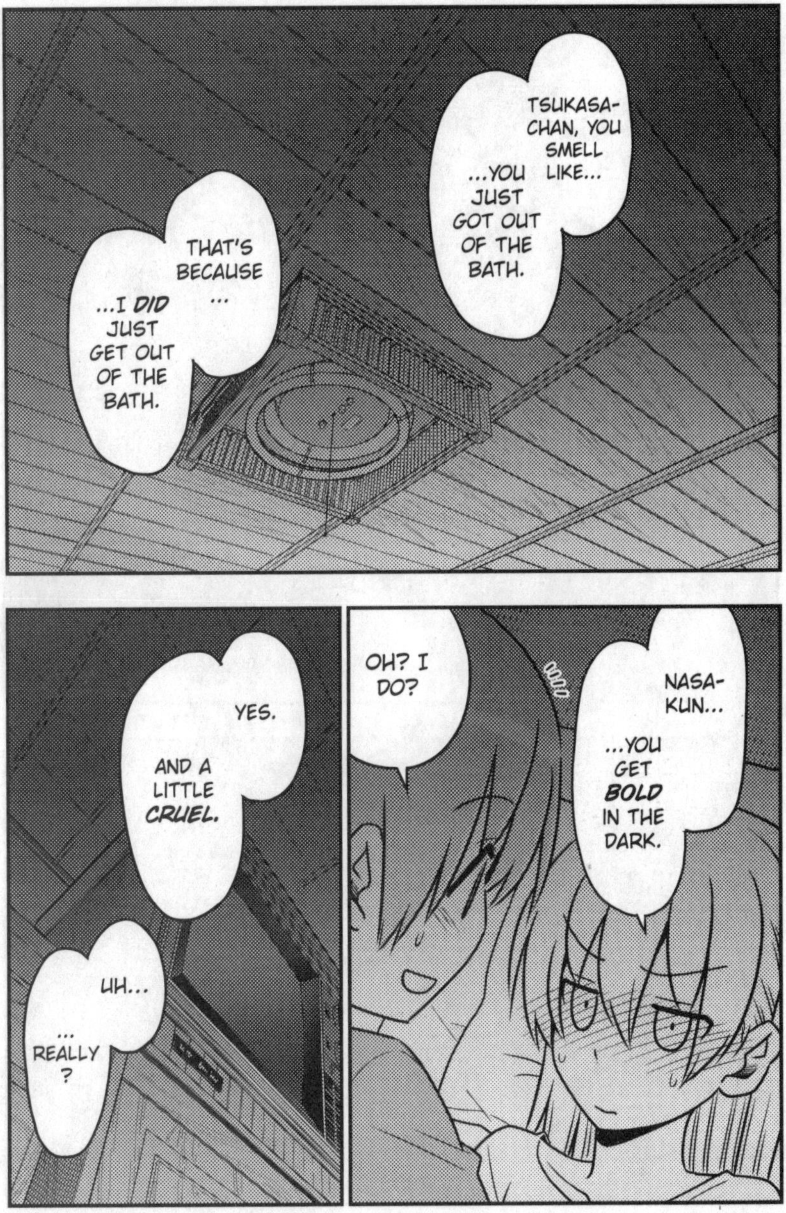
TSUKASA-CHAN, YOU SMELL LIKE... ...YOU JUST GOT OUT OF THE BATH.
THAT'S BECAUSE... ...I *DID* JUST GET OUT OF THE BATH.
NASA-KUN... ...YOU GET **BOLD** IN THE DARK.
OH? I DO?
YES. AND A LITTLE **CRUEL.**
UH... ...REALLY?

BUT WHEN YOU'RE EMBAR-RASSED ...
...YOU'RE JUST SO *CUTE.*
*SEE?*
THAT'S WHAT I'M TALKING ABOUT!
HUH?

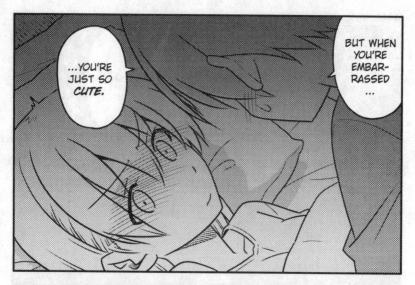

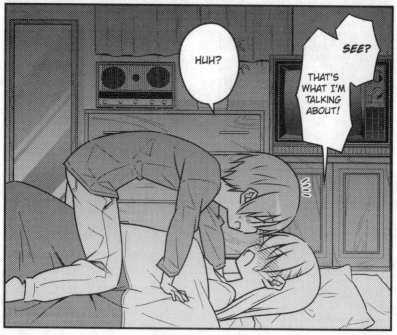

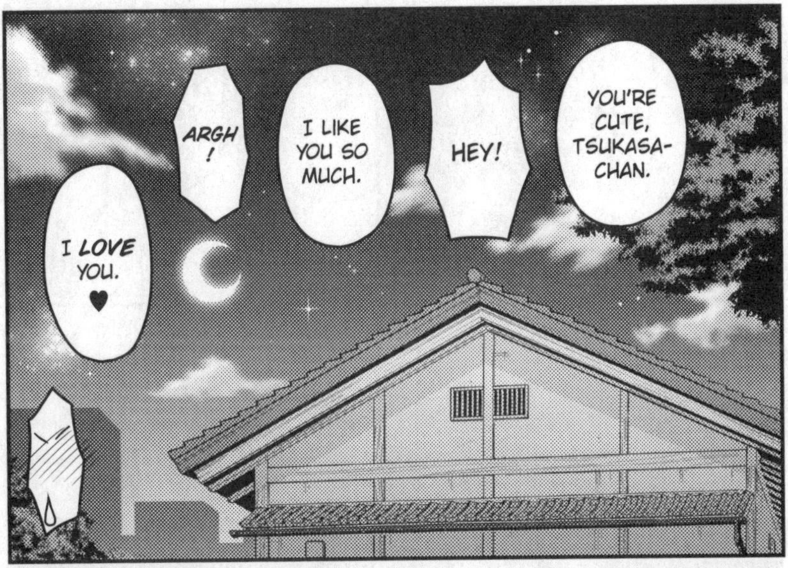
YOU'RE CUTE, TSUKASA-CHAN.
HEY!
I LIKE YOU SO MUCH.
ARGH!
I LOVE YOU. ♥
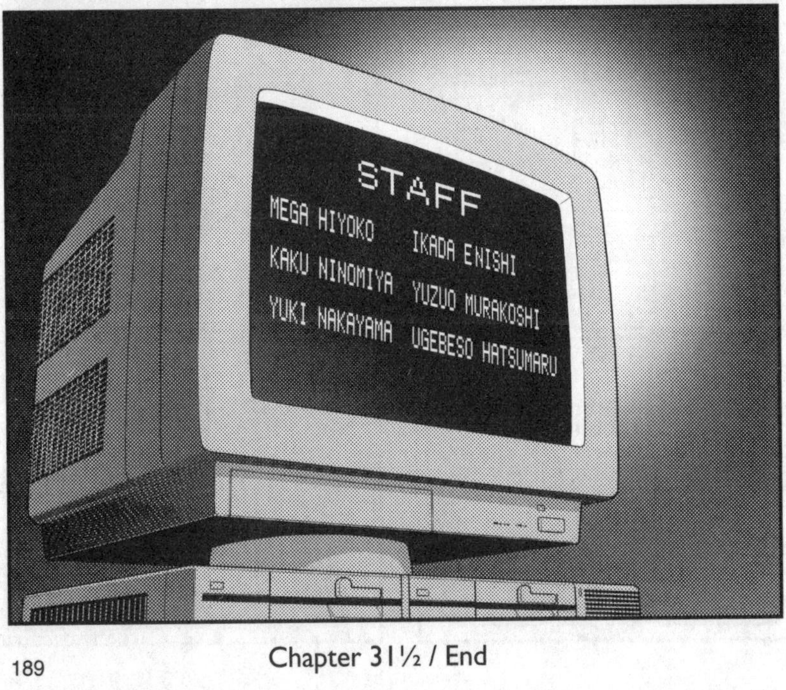
STAFF
MEGA HIYOKO
IKADA ENISHI
KAKU NINOMIYA
YUZUO MURAKOSHI
YUKI NAKAYAMA
UGEBESO HATSUMARU

Chapter 31½ / End

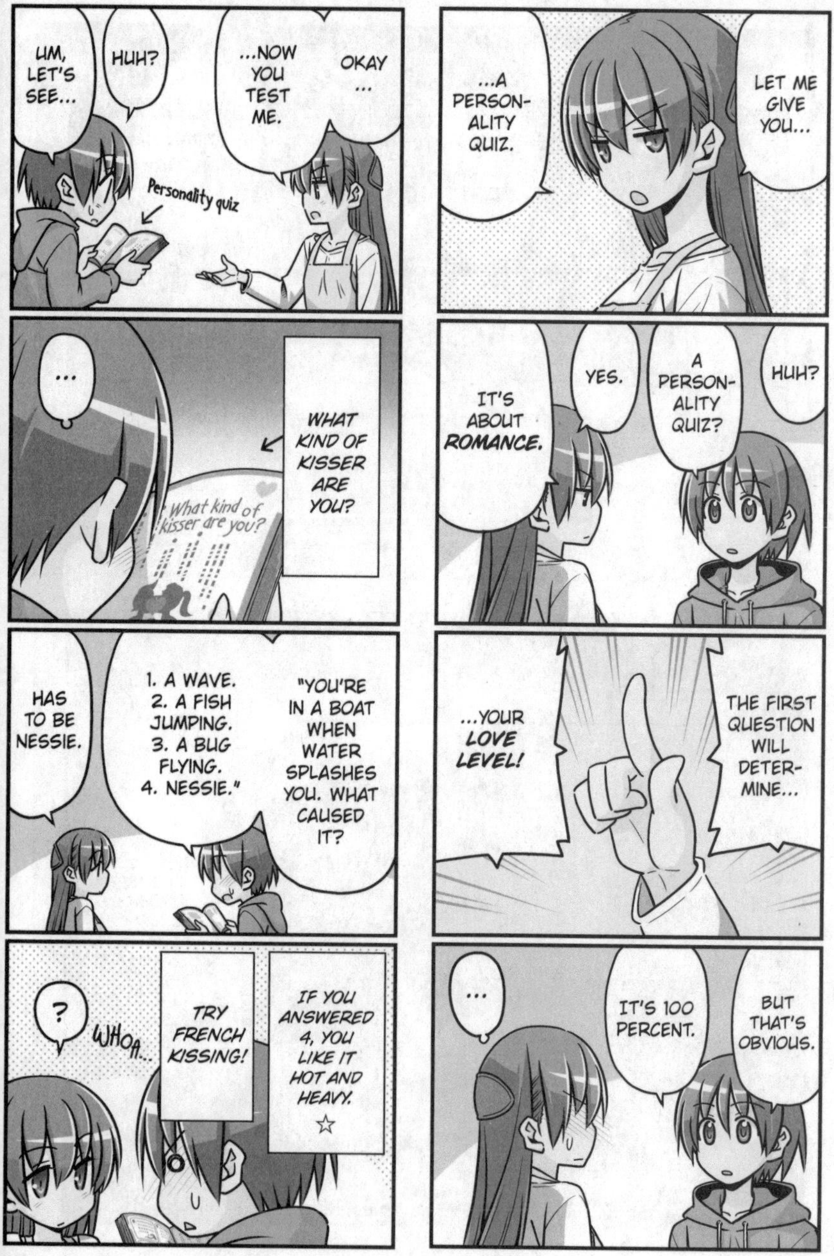
LET ME GIVE YOU...
...A PERSONALITY QUIZ.
HUH?
A PERSONALITY QUIZ?
YES.
IT'S ABOUT ROMANCE.
THE FIRST QUESTION WILL DETERMINE...
...YOUR LOVE LEVEL!
BUT THAT'S OBVIOUS.
IT'S 100 PERCENT.
...
OKAY...
...NOW YOU TEST ME.
HUH?
UM, LET'S SEE...
Personality quiz
WHAT KIND OF KISSER ARE YOU?
What kind of kisser are you?
...
"YOU'RE IN A BOAT WHEN WATER SPLASHES YOU. WHAT CAUSED IT?
1. A WAVE. 2. A FISH JUMPING. 3. A BUG FLYING. 4. NESSIE."
HAS TO BE NESSIE.
IF YOU ANSWERED 4, YOU LIKE IT HOT AND HEAVY. ☆
TRY FRENCH KISSING!
WHOA...
?

# Fly Me to the Moon

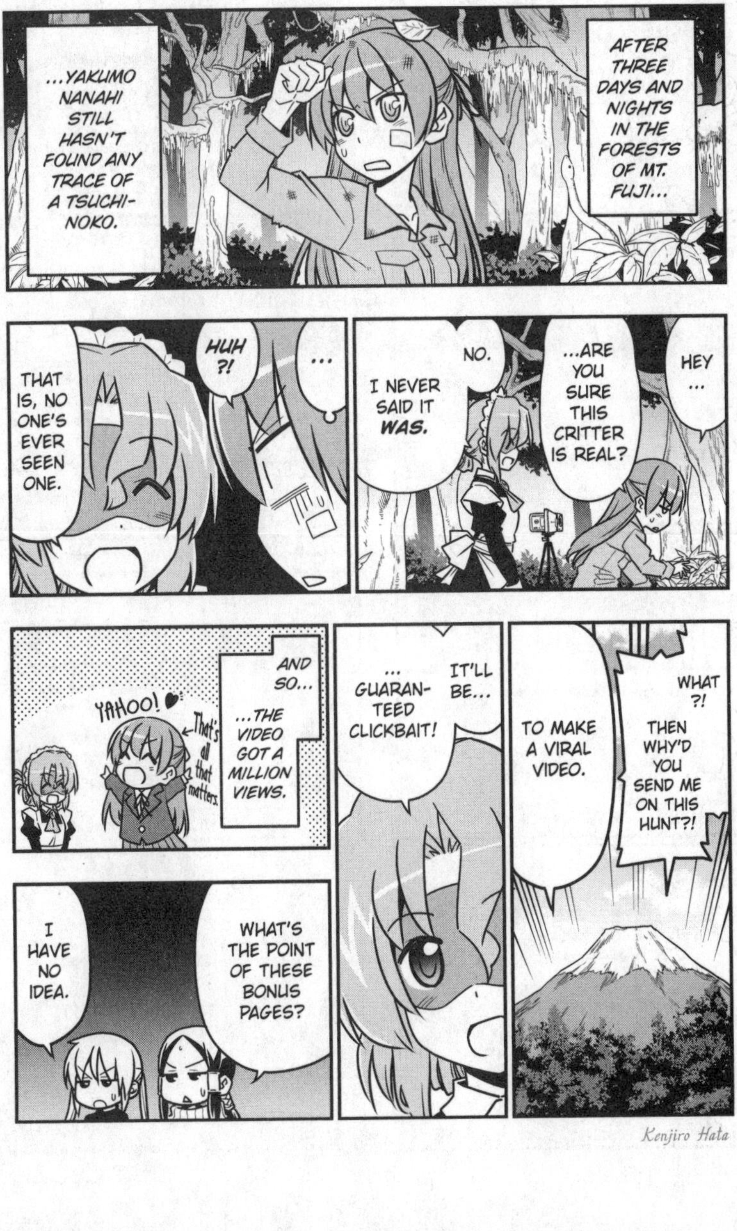
AFTER THREE DAYS AND NIGHTS IN THE FORESTS OF MT. FUJI...
...YAKUMO NANAHI STILL HASN'T FOUND ANY TRACE OF A TSUCHI-NOKO.
HEY ...
...ARE YOU SURE THIS CRITTER IS REAL?
NO.
I NEVER SAID IT WAS.
...
HUH ?!
THAT IS, NO ONE'S EVER SEEN ONE.
WHAT ?!
THEN WHY'D YOU SEND ME ON THIS HUNT?!
TO MAKE A VIRAL VIDEO.
IT'LL BE...
... GUARAN-TEED CLICKBAIT!
AND SO...
...THE VIDEO GOT A MILLION VIEWS.
YAHOO! ♥
That's all that matters.
WHAT'S THE POINT OF THESE BONUS PAGES?
I HAVE NO IDEA.

Kenjiro Hata

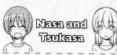

## Nasa and Tsukasa Respond to Reader Questions (Even Though They Were Directed to the Author)

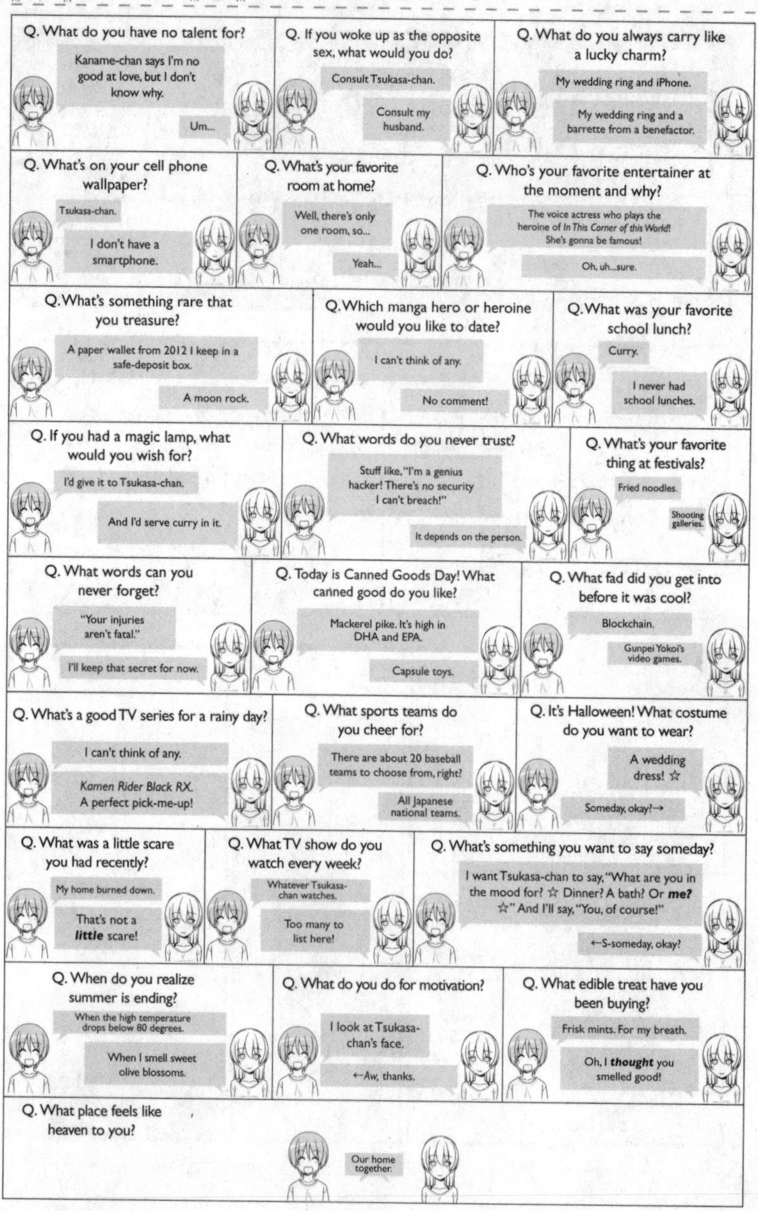
Q. What do you always carry like a lucky charm?
My wedding ring and iPhone.
My wedding ring and a barrette from a benefactor.
Q. If you woke up as the opposite sex, what would you do?
Consult Tsukasa-chan.
Consult my husband.
Q. What do you have no talent for?
Kaname-chan says I'm no good at love, but I don't know why.
Um...
Q. Who's your favorite entertainer at the moment and why?
The voice actress who plays the heroine of In This Corner of this World! She's gonna be famous!
Oh, uh...sure.
Q. What's your favorite room at home?
Well, there's only one room, so...
Yeah...
Q. What's on your cell phone wallpaper?
Tsukasa-chan.
I don't have a smartphone.
Q. What was your favorite school lunch?
Curry.
I never had school lunches.
Q. Which manga hero or heroine would you like to date?
I can't think of any.
No comment!
Q. What's something rare that you treasure?
A paper wallet from 2012 I keep in a safe-deposit box.
A moon rock.
Q. What's your favorite thing at festivals?
Fried noodles.
Shooting galleries.
Q. What words do you never trust?
Stuff like, "I'm a genius hacker! There's no security I can't breach!"
It depends on the person.
Q. If you had a magic lamp, what would you wish for?
I'd give it to Tsukasa-chan.
And I'd serve curry in it.
Q. What fad did you get into before it was cool?
Blockchain.
Gunpei Yokoi's video games.
Q. Today is Canned Goods Day! What canned good do you like?
Mackerel pike. It's high in DHA and EPA.
Capsule toys.
Q. What words can you never forget?
"Your injuries aren't fatal."
I'll keep that secret for now.
Q. It's Halloween! What costume do you want to wear?
A wedding dress! ☆
Someday, okay?→
Q. What sports teams do you cheer for?
There are about 20 baseball teams to choose from, right?
All Japanese national teams.
Q. What's a good TV series for a rainy day?
I can't think of any.
Kamen Rider Black RX. A perfect pick-me-up!
Q. What's something you want to say someday?
I want Tsukasa-chan to say, "What are you in the mood for? ☆ Dinner? A bath? Or me? ☆" And I'll say, "You, of course!"
←S-someday, okay?
Q. What TV show do you watch every week?
Whatever Tsukasa-chan watches.
Too many to list here!
Q. What was a little scare you had recently?
My home burned down.
That's not a little scare!
Q. What edible treat have you been buying?
Frisk mints. For my breath.
Oh, I thought you smelled good!
Q. What do you do for motivation?
I look at Tsukasa-chan's face.
←Aw, thanks.
Q. When do you realize summer is ending?
When the high temperature drops below 80 degrees.
When I smell sweet olive blossoms.
Q. What place feels like heaven to you?
Our home together.

## ABOUT THE AUTHOR

Without ever receiving any kind of manga award, Kenjiro Hata's first series, *Umi no Yuusha Lifesavers,* was published in *Shonen Sunday Super*. He followed that up with his smash hit *Hayate the Combat Butler.* *Fly Me to the Moon* began serialization in 2018 in *Weekly Shonen Sunday*.

# FLY ME TO THE MOON

VOL. 4

Story and Art by **KENJIRO HATA**

SHONEN SUNDAY EDITION

TONIKAKUKAWAII Vol. 4
by Kenjiro HATA

Original Japanese edition published by SHOGAKUKAN.
English translation rights in the United States of America, Canada, the United Kingdom, Ireland, Australia and New Zealand arranged with SHOGAKUKAN.

Original Cover Design: Emi Nakano (BANANA GROVE STUDIO)

Translation
**John Werry**

Touch-Up Art & Lettering
**Evan Waldinger**

Design
**Jimmy Presler**

Editor
**Shaenon K. Garrity**

The stories, characters and incidents mentioned in this publication are entirely fictional.



Printed in Canada

Published by VIZ Media, LLC
P.O. Box 77010
San Francisco, CA 94107

10 9 8 7 6 5 4 3 2 1
First printing, March 2021

ratings.viz.com
RATED T+ OLDER TEEN

**PARENTAL ADVISORY**
FLY ME TO THE MOON is rated T+ for Older Teen and is recommended for ages 16 and up. This volume contains sexual situations.

VIZ MEDIA
viz.com

MANGA STARTS ON SUNDAY SHONEN SUNDAY
shonensunday.com

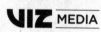

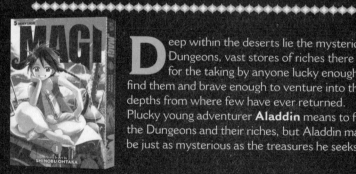